Goin' Up
And
Lookin' Down

Goin' Up
And
Lookin' Down

❖

THE BOOK ABOUT FLYING, AIRPLANES, PILOTS, AIRPORTS, PLANE PEOPLE, AND PLANE STUFF…

LYNN R. (BUTCH) PINSON

iUniverse, Inc.
New York Lincoln Shanghai

Goin' Up And Lookin' Down
THE BOOK ABOUT FLYING, AIRPLANES, PILOTS, AIRPORTS, PLANE PEOPLE, AND PLANE STUFF...

iUniverse books may be ordered through booksellers or by contacting:

iUniverse
2021 Pine Lake Road, Suite 100
Lincoln, NE 68512
www.iuniverse.com
1-800-Authors (1-800-288-4677)

Because of the dynamic nature of the Internet, any Web addresses or links contained in this book may have changed since publication and may no longer be valid.

The views expressed in this work are solely those of the author and do not necessarily reflect the views of the publisher, and the publisher hereby disclaims any responsibility for them.

ISBN: 978-0-595-47685-5 (pbk)
ISBN: 978-0-595-91949-9 (ebk)

Printed in the United States of America

Contents

INTRODUCTION

I heard another one. I got up off my knees as fast as I could and ran out from under the cool shade of the old mulberry tree where I was playing into the bright summer sun. Squinting upward I finally found it, a small dot way up in the sky, an airplane. In awe, I wondered once again how in the world does anyone ever get to fly in a real airplane?

That was in the summer of 1947, maybe 1948, and the love of airplanes had already infected this nine year old boy like a disease. Every airplane that went over our back yard I had to go take a look at it. Once I even saw one of the huge B-36 bombers fly over, the airplane that had propellers and jets on it and made a very strange droning sound.

Daddy often wondered why the ends of his cotton choppin' hoe handles were sawed off, never suspecting that I had discovered I could make toy airplanes from them. Making engine noises with my mouth as only a boy can do and holding those crudely manufactured toys in my hands, I imagined myself in the cockpit. I flew hundreds of missions all over the cotton field, the sudan patch and the barn yard, always returning to the dirt runway under the mulberry tree.

I not only made the little airplanes from hoe handles, but scraps of wood, tin cans, and baling wire. Sometimes I even got to buy a real wood or plastic kit from the local variety store and put it together. I even made some big enough to get into from old pieces of cotton gin pipe that Daddy would bring home for me from the cotton gin. I hung onto the impossible dream that maybe someday, somehow, sometime, maybe in a million years I might be able to fly an airplane myself.

It didn't take a million years, but it did take a bunch of them to finally realize my dream. It finally came true. I flew an airplane myself 27 years later! To any kid who might be dreaming the same dream, when you hear a small airplane pass over low, or see a jet thousands of feet high, or see a space shuttle on television, don't give up. Your dream can come true too.

I like to think that maybe one of those airplanes I saw flying over our farm home back yard as a small boy was the same one I once owned myself. Maybe my 1947 Cessna 120, N1605V, was on its way from the factory in Wichita, Kansas to its first owner and I saw it go over my house that hot summer day in southwest Oklahoma. "Well, it's possible!"

IN THE BEGINNING

In 1951 a new preacher came to the First Baptist Church of Tipton and it wasn't long before everybody found out that he could fly an airplane. I mean, he really knew how to fly a real airplane! Most folks in town said he was nuts, especially the little old ladies in the church, but there were a couple of local farmers and the Line Superintendent at the local Rural Electrical Coop that had been flying a Piper J-3 and a PA-12 for some time and they welcomed the new flying preacher into their group. His ability to fly impressed me much more than his call to preach and it wasn't long before I began pleading with Daddy to ask Brother Luther Cox if he would take me flying.

Late one November afternoon it happened. Daddy said OK if I wouldn't tell Mother, and he asked the preacher and my first airplane ride became a reality! Brother Cox put me in the back seat of that PA-12 and immediately headed for our house which he buzzed low enough that it left no doubt to anyone inside that an airplane had passed over. Of course, when Daddy and I got home the first thing I did was I tell Mother, who had no idea that such a thing was taking place but, she strongly suspected I was in that thing anyhow. She wouldn't speak to Daddy for weeks afterward and the only time she said anything to me was to issue the usual "Mother-type" instructions such as "Go to bed" and "Take out the trash".

But, oh my, my, it was worth it. I finally got to fly in an airplane, something that I had only been able to dream about from the ground as they flew over the farm. That first ride lit the spark of a fire that maybe someday I could do that myself. And one day I did.

A neighbor and friend, Lawrence Richards, told me many years later that Brother Cox also took him up for the first time. Lawrence said Preacher Cox climbed up above some clouds, chopped the throttle and spiraled down through the clouds in little-bitty circles until the ground was in sight and then asked Lawrence if that bothered him. Lawrence made the mistake of telling him "No", so Preacher Cox did the same thing again. The second time down through the clouds in little-bitty circles and Lawrence still had his stomach intact. The preacher then gave up and went back to the hayfield where the episode began. Preacher Cox tried several times after that to make Lawrence sick, but never got the job done.

SUPER CUB DRIVER

Earl Huffer served in the Army Air Corps in World War II but was assigned as an instructor for a bunch of Canadian pilots in the early part of the war. He was a local boy, had family living in Tipton, and after the war moved back and started making a living as a spray pilot, or "duster" as they were known in those days. For some reason though, he lived in Wichita Falls, Texas, a city about 60 miles away and drove to Tipton during the spraying seasons to conduct his spray business. Early in 1963, after I had returned to Tipton from a four year stint in college and a short time in the Army, I became acquainted with Earl and we became good friends.

One winter day we both were sitting at the local cotton gin office drinking coffee, got to talking, and of course I mentioned my desire to fly. That desire had been sort of rearranged and reprioritized due to school, college, Army, and girls, but never the less, it was still there. A couple of days later Earl called me and asked if I would like to ride to Tulsa with him in his Piper PA-18/150 Super Cub for the purpose of replacing it with a brand new one. The belly tank and wing booms would be transferred from the old airplane to the new one and Earl assured me we would be home by dark the same day.

Now, this was nearly 45 years ago and the spray planes of that day were not like the fancy whizzenzoomers of today such as the Ag Cats, Ag Trucks, Turbine Air Tractors, and Dromediers. Spray pilots back then usually used Cubs with fiberglas tanks attached to their bellies and spray booms attached to the wings. They could carry a whopping 90 gallons of water and chemical which contributed to the forces of gravity to make every effort to cause the Cub to fall out of the sky in a turn if you weren't very careful.

Some spray pilots were fortunate enough and had enough money to have one of the new Piper PA25/150 Pawnees that were actually designed by Fred Weick to be a spray plane. Weick was the genius who designed the Ercoupe, a weird little airplane which we'll talk about later.

Anyway, Earl's Super Cub cost $9,000 new in 1963. The same airplane today, if you can find one, will cost in excess of $75,000. The Pawnee cost a lot more than the Cub, so Earl had a Cub.

Well, we made that trip to Tulsa and back to Tipton at an altitude of no more than 150 feet above the ground and waved at everybody between here and there and back, grinning all the way. We waved at kids and dogs and a Momma hanging clothes on a clothes line.

Earl hired me to flag for him when he sprayed cotton, alfalfa, and wheat fields and I worked for him for four years. I made some good money, got 10 cents an acre, but the best deal was that I got to fly that Super Cub from the back seat on occasion. One day, Earl called me on the CB radio and told me to meet him in the middle of the airport where the grass runways crossed. I thought something was wrong with the airplane, but when I got there he was climbing in the back seat with the engine still running. He hollered at me and said, "Git in the front seat and see if you can get this thing off the ground!". I was "dee-lighted". It scared me silly, but the opportunity was too great, the challenge too big, and with Earl's help from the back seat I flew that Cub. Anyone who has ever flown a Cub should remember how the windows and fabric buzz when you go to full throttle. And oh, how great the smell of those wood, fabric, and glue airplanes is. "Smells like an airplane oughta smell!"

Our routine began much the same each morning. I would meet Earl at the airport before sunup, help mix the first load of chemicals, load it, and then tear out for the first field to be sprayed and "flag it". That meant I would either put myself on foot armed with a checkered flag or park my pickup directly in front of the Super Cub on the other end of the field so Earl could aim at me with the airplane. Just before he would get to me, I would (hopefully) move out his way. Sometimes things got exciting because with the Cub moving 90 mph and three feet off the ground I couldn't always get out of the way as quickly as I needed to and often got covered up with the spray as he flew over. Many times I had to go home and take a bath so I could quit itching.

Earl was the first man to ever trust me with the controls of an airplane and by doing so set off another spark to join the one Preacher Cox lit a dozen years previously. He retired from spraying back in the late 70's and was a kid at heart until the end. He drove a 1934 Chevy pickup with a souped up 327 Chevy V-8 engine in it until he started running into things with it. He was one of the best friends I ever had.

I was never able to figure out why he did it unless he thought he could collect the insurance on a wrecked airplane, but in early winter of each year we would steam clean the Cub to get all the goop and chemicals off of it and then stick it in the hangar until the next spring when the spraying season would begin again. Earl told me one day, "Why don'cha get that plane out about once a week, start it up, and taxi it around on the grass for a few minutes to warm the engine up and keep the battery charged up?" "OH", he said, "And just be sure to keep the stick all the way back and for heaven's sakes, don't get it going too fast!" I never did get airborne, but only by the grace of God. I drove that Super Cub all over Tipton airport many times, but fortunately never got the tail up or let it get away from me.

On those pretty summer mornings at first light when we would be fueling the Cub, mixing and loading chemical, another crusty, cranky, old spray pilot would be conducting his spray business about 200 feet away. Vernon Foster had more money than Earl and owned one of the pretty new Piper Pawnee 150's. It was really nice. We heard he would run it wide open all the time, never touching the throttle after takeoff until he got ready to land.

Earl and Vernon were competitive enough that they each wanted the other's business. That made for lots of good conversations and they would start talking out loud so the other could hear, then would start hollering at each other accusing the other of stealing the other's chemicals during the night. Of course that never happened, but it really did get loud out there.

Nobody ever had a real fight, just a whole lot of yellin' and cussin' going on, sometimes loud enough to be heard in town, three miles away. By noon, tempers and egos had subsided and we all would go to the cotton gin office and have a cup of coffee together.

Vernon, like Earl, was an instructor in the war (WWII) and did some instructing in Cessna 140s after the war. When I bought my 140 in 1976 I picked his brain a lot because the airplane was spooking me. I will always remember him telling me "Hell, it ain't gunna turn over! Git it out there in the middle of the airport and taxi it around until you can make it go straight!" It was good advice. I did and it didn't.

Pilots like Vernon and Earl were definitely from the old school. They could tell if an airplane engine was running right by just listening to it and could tell if the airplane was flying right by the way their butt felt. They're both dead now, but neither died from an airplane crash. Vernon died from cancer back in the 70's and Earl died in 2005.

BILL DUNN

When Nancy and I were married in 1965 we moved to our farm home a couple of miles south of Tipton and a half mile east off the highway. Our neighbors, Bill and Peggy Dunn lived on the highway. Bill was a pilot as well as a farmer and had been flying for a number of years.

Bill had flown several types of airplanes, was a good pilot, and had accumulated many hours in all kinds of weather. He was instrument rated and loved to talk about his flying experiences ... often for hours at a time to anyone who would stand still long enough for him to talk to. Quite often he would tell his stories whether you listened or not and you would have to sometimes walk off and leave him talking, but we loved him anyhow. Bill was a good man and a very good friend.

Bill had been flying airplanes a whole lot longer than I had and had many more hours in the air than I did by far, yet very little time in a taildragger. In fact, he really didn't like taildraggers at all. He would call me on the telephone at night and we would talk airplanes for hours and hours. I learned a lot from him both on the telephone and on those occasions I would go flying with him because he was always in the teaching mode. The only time I ever questioned Bill's ability was when he pulled the yoke so far back on take off on a little Cessna 150 the tail skid drug on the runway. I still enjoyed flying with him, however at that time as much as I loved flying and wanted desperately to learn how, I thought spending $15.00 an hour to rent an airplane was awfully extravagant for any kind of pleasure especially if you couldn't bring it home in a sack. I really had about decided I would never learn to fly because it cost so much. After all, I had just got married and Nancy and I planned to have kids, which are long term expenses.

Years later when things got a little bit better financially, I bought half of a 1946 Cessna 140. Good friend Bill approached me one day and asked me in all seriousness, "Oh uh, why in the world did you hafta go and buy one of those silly little thangs for? Why didn't you just get a 150 (Cessna) or just <u>anythang</u> with a nose wheel on it?"

After flying several hours in it I began to feel pretty confident in the little 140 so one day I asked Bill to take a ride with me. I knew he was nervous because I

5

still didn't have that many flying hours accumulated total time and he was in an airplane he didn't know much about and really didn't like too much to begin with. In fact, he had already told me, "All you can do with one of them little thangs is look at it, walk around it, and kick its tires."

It made me feel awfully good, even somewhat conceited, to know something that Bill didn't, at least for that day, so I enjoyed rubbing it in a little. Bill kept his hands in his lap and his feet on the floor while I took off and began to fly around a bit. He relaxed a bit and took the controls while we were in the air, but when we headed back to the airport for the dreaded, inevitable landing he said, "You better take this thing". I said, "Go ahead and land it", but he refused. Thank goodness I made a good landing. He would have never let me live it down had I bounced even just a bit. I don't think he took a breath though until I got the airplane stopped.

I understood his feelings about taildraggers a little better when he fessed up and told me about the time his first instructor "Woody" put him in a 140 several years before and how it went everywhere he didn't want it to and humbled him to the point he wondered if he would ever be able to fly anything at all again.

THE FIRST LESSON

In January of 1975 a little ad appeared in the classified section of the Frederick newspaper which simply stated, "New Improved Aviation Ground School. Open to general public. Only $2.00 per night for a three hour session. Class begins Thursday, January 30, 7:30 p.m. to 10:00 p.m. Call 335-2421, Frederick Airport."

Good friend Junior Jennings walked in the cotton gin office that cold morning where all the local guys went to drink a free cup of coffee, shoved that little ad in my face, and announced that he was going to make his wife Margaret go, and me and Nancy needed to go too, and we could ride with them. They would pick us up about 6:45. That's all there was to it!

When I walked in the house and rattled off in one breath to wife Nancy, "They're gonna start an aviation ground school over at Frederick next Monday and Junior and Margaret are gonna go and they want us to go with them and it might be a whole lotta fun and no, I'm not really gunna take flying lessons right now but just want to take the class". She just batted her eyes and said, "OK".

We went to the ground school twice a week for nine weeks. Nancy learned as much as I did, but she didn't want to take the tests and certainly didn't want to learn to fly. Junior decided two weeks before the classes ended that Margaret and I knew enough to pass the FAA exam, so he took Margaret and me to Oklahoma City in their Cessna 182 Skylane, Nancy went along for moral support, we all had a good time, but neither Margaret or I thought we passed the test. Two weeks later when I got the notice that I made a 78 Nancy hugged and kissed me and did the same thing a couple of months later when I flew home from Chickasha with that brand new Private Pilot's license in my pocket. But that's another story.

I had received some shade tree flight instruction from several people such as Earl Huffer, Junior Jennings, Ott Everson, and Bill Dunn, but George Stapp was my first real live, legal, flight instructor. George also taught that ground school that we were going to. The honorable intentions I had related to Nancy not to take flying lessons quickly dissolved after I saw my friend Chuck Ball take off one day in a Cessna 172 all by himself. I really, really, did not intend to do anything except go to the ground school until then. I took my first flying lesson two weeks after the ground school started.

George was 35 years old, weighed about 130 pounds, was somewhat skinny, and had flown helicopters in Vietnam. Most importantly, he could teach me how to fly and sign the hours off in a log book and it counted for real.

He somehow managed to cram into me most everything a person needed to know to pass the FAA written examination, but the biggest thrill of all was when he introduced me to N373KV, a little red and white 1964 Cessna 150 and taught me how to make it go up, stay up, and then come back down when I wanted it to and not before.

He taught me that an airplane would not drop like a rock if the engine quit. In fact, since then I have had engine problems on five different occasions and arrived perfectly safe back on earth without damaging either me or the airplane. I won't go so far as to say that it was not an anxious several moments, or even a little spooky, or that the hair didn't stand up on the back of my neck, but never the less, I did get me and it down safely.

Most of the time an airplane will not die dead all at once anyhow unless the pilot gets stupid and lets it run out of gas which is not the airplane's fault. They will usually spit or sputter or have a partial loss of power like my Cessna 140 did one nice pretty day, but then you still can make a safe landing somewhere. Sure, your face will get hot, you neck will get tight, and your hair will sweat, but if you do as George said to do everything will turn out just fine.

After 7.3 hours of pointing, showing, shoving, and yelling, George had the nerve to get out of that 150 one February morning, shut the door, pat it on the tail and leave. Told me to go do it myself he said. Not once, but three times I took off and landed that little red and white airplane with that very empty right seat. I could hear George's voice talking to me even though he wasn't there and I actually did it! I flew that airplane all by myself on February 21, 1975! I soloed!

Outside of getting married and having kids, there was no greater thrill that morning I soloed. George asked the Air Force to send their T-37's upstairs out of the pattern for a few minutes while I flew. The Air Force Captains in the "Box" (RSU) told me I did good, George told me I did good, and Nancy told me I did good. I did good! "Mainly because I didn't tear up the airplane."

A few days later I was out flying solo and I slipped up and landed that Cessna 150 sideways. George was gone for the day, but had given me signed permission to do some solo work. I had been flying for about an hour doing some air work, but then it came time to land. What I did not know was that a cross wind had come up. When I touched down, the airplane lurched and jumped, the tires squawled, and I thought I had ripped all three wheels off the airplane. After a very busy time of turning, pushing, and pulling everything I could find, I was extremely relieved to find that I was still right side up. I even stopped, opened the door, looked out, and made sure the tires were still on it. I decided it was time to quit for the day and as I taxied to the terminal building I felt really awful for letting that crosswind sneak up on me, even worse for making such a horrible landing and really giving serious thought to taking up motorcycling or boating instead of flying.

Michael John Hynes, the son of the airport manager was an instructor and when I confessed what I had just done and he saw my face he knew I was about ready to hang it all up. Michael John said "Let's go see what you're doing wrong." Well, I knew what I did wrong, I landed the stoopid airplane sideways, almost ripped the landing gear off, and the wind was blowing higher, and I really wanted to go home. Michael John was persistent though and talked me into going back out and flying again. He made me fly section lines every direction until I could hold that 150 straight in a hurricane. My flying career had been salvaged.

A couple of months later after the air work, the slow flight, the stalls, the spins, the emergency landings, the cross countries, and the take-offs and landings, George announced that I was about ready to go for my check ride. But … not before "Hell Week". That was the last week of training that George picked at me and criticized everything I did so much because it wasn't perfect that I wanted desperately to open the right door of the 150, throw George out, and watch gleefully as he fell to earth.

The day I filed a flight plan to Chickasha to go see the FAA designee George Hector for the private pilot check ride there was no doubt I was ready. Confidence and knowledge overcame fear and that forty minute ride with Mr. Hector was a picnic compared the previous weeks with George Stapp. George Hector confirmed what George Stapp had been telling me for weeks as he showed me for sure that an airplane, especially a Cessna, would not immediately fall out of the sky if the engine quit. He also made sure I realized that I was only going to get a license to continue learning.

Mr. Hector was gruff and didn't smile very much, but the oral exam was not bad since he only asked the questions I had missed on the written test. He also told me a few "Quotations from The Book of George" such as, "Always maintain your airspeed lest the ground rise up and smite thee". When we went out to fly though, things got a little tense. When I finished pre-flighting the airplane, Mr. Hector asked if we were ready and I said, "Yes, but you will have to get in through the left door because the right one is wired shut." He said "What for?" I said, "Because the door latch on the right one broke yesterday." He muttered something unintelligible and climbed in and I breathed a nervous sigh of relief.

After the forty minute check flight and we were getting out of the airplane, I asked him if he wanted to see the airplane log books. Without cracking a smile he said, "Hell no, if I look at the log books I'll condemn the sonofabitch."

When I pushed the throttle forward on that almost condemned Cessna 172 and took off from Chickasha with that new private pilot certificate in my pocket there were not enough words in the English language to describe the feeling. I was soaring with eagles and in the words of John Gillespie McGee, I could now "Slip the surly bonds of earth and dance the skies on laughter-silvered wings" and even take somebody with me. "Hoo-Boy!"

The door of the wonderful world of flight was now wide open. I owe a great deal to all those guys who encouraged me and especially to George, my instructor. They turned me loose in a whole brand new world and I am eternally grateful.

I was saddened and shocked to learn that George Stapp died of a heart attack three years later. He had moved from Frederick to Houston and was flying helicopters to off shore drilling rigs in the Gulf of Mexico, but he died in his car on a freeway in Houston. I can still hear his voice talking me out of flying messes as I fly today. He was an extremely good instructor and a very good friend to boot.

George Hector retired a few years later, but for years he remembered me as the only student he ever passed in spite of a wired shut airplane door and a condemned airplane.

MY FIRST AIRPLANE

Every pilot has at one time in their life wanted to own their own airplane. I was no exception. When I was taking lessons I would hear people talking about how much it cost to buy an airplane and how much it cost to overhaul an engine and all the other expenses involved so I told myself and others that I would never, ever be able to do that. But ... after getting my private license and renting several 150's, 172's, Cherokees and a Piper TriPacer, the thoughts of ownership became more persistent in my mind. I began to think, "Maybe" and started reading the airplanes for sale section of all the newspapers still knowing that in reality I probably would never be able to actually buy one, but I always cut out the possibilities just in case the good Lord decided to hand me one on a platter someday. The one that really caught my eye appeared one day in the Daily Oklahoman and was for a 1946 Cessna 140. Even though I wasn't sure what a Cessna 140 was or all the implications that go with one, the price was reasonable so I cut out the ad and carried it in my pocket.

Otto Everson was a local electrical contractor who lived in Tipton and had an office downtown. Ott had been flying a long, long, time and owned a 1973 Bellanca Super Viking. I wandered into Ott's office one morning just to talk airplanes. It so happened that it was my and Nancy's eleventh wedding anniversary and Nancy had gone out of town to a wedding shower for a friend and I was just killing time until she returned so we could go out for an anniversary dinner. The subject of buying an airplane came up and Ott asked if I knew of any good'un's for sale so I showed him the clipping of the 140. He wanted to know what I thought about it and I cautiously mumbled that maybe I could stretch things and come up with half the $4000 asking price.

Well, without batting an eye and with no hesitation at all Ott picked up the telephone and called the number in the ad just to see where the airplane was. It happened to be in Shawnee, Oklahoma and in less than five minutes of half serious haggling he leaned over to me with his hand over the mouthpiece and said, "We can get it for $3900, waddaya think?" I gasped and Ott told the guy "OK" and bought the airplane. He said we could be partners but he wouldn't fly it very much and I could probably buy him out someday but for now he would pay half, besides all that he got a hundred dollars knocked off the asking price.

I got very nervous very quick. Wife Nancy was out of town and she didn't even know I was an airplane clipping carrier and she wouldn't be back home until sometime that afternoon and here she was going to come home expecting to be taken out for our anniversary dinner and was going to find out her husband just bought half of an airplane!

The excitement of what Ott and I had just done though overcame the fear of Nancy's wrath and the conversation that followed started to revolve around just how we were going to go retrieve our new possession. That was really a concern because at that time I did not know how to fly a taildragger. Despite the fact that Ott said it was a piece of cake and that I HAD had some time in the Earl's Super Cub many years before, I begged out of the trip. Truthfully, the main reason I did so was to give me time to think up what in the world I was going to tell Nancy when she got home.

Ott said he bet Junior and Margaret would fly him to Shawnee in their Skylane. Sure enough, they were tickled to death when Ott called and told them what he and I had done. Within the hour, Ott, Junior, and Margaret were winging their way northeast to Shawnee. After they took off I realized I had a lot of time to think about what I had just done. Nancy still did not know.

The next several hours were filled with extreme anxiety. I went to the airport way too early and stared at the eastern sky for what seemed an eternity. Finally, I saw Junior and Margaret's Skylane appear on the horizon, enter the pattern and land. They were both grinning from ear to ear and told me that Ott was not far behind. Finally, a speck appeared, got closer, and a tiny, shiny, Cessna 140 airplane flew over, waggled its wings, descended, and landed ever so softly. There it was! My half of an airplane!

The landing Ott made that day in the 140 was one of the best any taildragger pilot could ever hope for. Not even a bounce. Then he taxied up in front of us and shut it off. My goodness, I was so proud. That little airplane was so bright and shiny it would knock your eyes out. It was polished aluminum, had metalized wings, and was trimmed in Cessna green just like the factory painted it. It also had a nearly new interior.

After the close up looking, the bragging, and the tire kicking, Ott said, "OK, let's you go try it out!" I again craw-fished and persuaded Ott to again perform piloting duties because it was slowing dawning on me that I had just bought something that I did not know how to fly. I couldn't just get in it and go fly it like I had been doing those 150's and 172's. At least not now.

Ott had been flying for a long time and had flown taildraggers a lot, but in recent years he had been flying his Bellanca Super Viking, 300 horsepower with all the whistles and bells that would cruise about 200 mph and get him where he was going with the latest in Navigational aids. The Cessna 140 had an 85 horse-power engine and top speed was 107 mph. A bit different.

Until that day, Ott had not flown a Cessna 140 in about 20 years. I climbed in the right seat and Ott made a good take off. We flew around a few minutes and then came back in for Ott's number two landing of the day. He did good again, airplane and earth touched about the same time, and we were rolling out but we got to talking instead of looking and paying attention.

Suddenly, we both looked out at the same time and to our surprise, instead of still being on the runway we were back in the air about 50 feet high with no power, no airspeed, and very few ideas. The earth started coming up rapidly and we hit it firmly enough to justify the term "Whang-bounce". Dirt flew as we barely missed the drainage culvert going under the taxiway and we immediately found ourselves back up at the 50 foot altitude again. As the 140 started its descent back to earth for another bounce, Ott rammed the throttle as far as it would go and for what seemed an eternity the little airplane tried to recover itself from what it had been subjected to.

As we staggered out across a cotton field, the little Cessna shuttered and shook as we gradually gained altitude and airspeed. Just at that same moment I took a quick look at the crowd that had now gathered to see the new airplane in town, just in time to see Nancy drive up. She had come back into town, stopped to get some bread, and someone at the local grocery store told her that her husband had lost his mind and bought an airplane while she was gone and she'd better get to the airport fast if she ever wanted to see him again cause he probably was gunna kill himself.

The little Cessna forgave Ott and I and started flying again and we flew around the pattern again. Both of us were still holding our breaths as Ott landed it again. Neither of us said a word until we got stopped, the engine was cut off, and the wheels solidly chocked. Junior came us to us laughing and declaring that was one of the best air show routines he had ever seen.

Nancy was actually smiling. I started to say "Happy Anniversary" or "Ott made me do it", but nothing seemed to fit the occasion. I don't have the same air-plane anymore, but thank goodness I do still have the same wife.

TACKLING THE TAILDRAGGER

Folks who don't know the difference between a tricycle geared airplane and a taildraggin' airplane probably won't appreciate what I'm about to tell, but my very dear friend Lloyd Howard earned himself an extra room in his Heavenly mansion as a result of his volunteering to teach me how to fly my newly acquired Cessna 140. The three or four hours he spent with me in the cockpit of that airplane were far beyond the call of any duty.

To explain. A taildragging airplane like the Cessna 140 has what is called a "conventional gear". It is an airplane with a little bitty wheel on the rear end instead of like most airplanes you see today that have a bigger wheel under the nose, thus, the name tricycle. I now call that a training wheel since I learned how to deal with it, but that statement will probably put a wrinkle in all those pilot's noses who can't fly one.

Airplane drivers who don't like taildraggers will more than likely squint their eyes when the word "taildragger" is mentioned and will usually ask, "What did you hafta bring those things up for?" Some folks who have tried them and lost will probably tell you a horror story of how evil they are. Others will tell you how versatile and agile they can be. But, any hangar flying story about "conventional" gear airplanes will be for sure interesting and entertaining.

Lloyd was a very good friend and also a very special person because of the patience he demonstrated when he finally gathered up enough nerve to teach me how to fly that little Cessna 140. At least he stayed in the airplane as long as he could stand it before he announced that surely I would be able to get it in the air and back on the ground without tearing it all to pieces. The heck of it was, all this new learning process took place after I thought I already knew how to fly an airplane. After all, I had the new license, had accumulated about 150 hours in Cessna 150's, 172 Skyhawks, and Piper Cherokees, and become fairly comfortable in whatever I flew as long as it had tricycle gear.

I found out many years later that Lloyd really didn't want to do it, but out of pure friendship did it anyhow. I really think he just didn't want to see that little Cessna or me get bent or broken.

The first couple of hours with me in the left seat and Lloyd in the right seat were spooky to say the least, especially that first hour. The left brake didn't want to work at all and if we didn't watch out and be real careful, the airplane would go in little, bitty circles on the ground. Lloyd however, knew how to put a quick fix on that and with enough left brake to stay sort of straight Lloyd was able to direct things.

After a very squiggly trip from the parking apron to the end of the runway, I did the customary runup, wiggled the controls, and announced that I was ready to go. With the airplane more or less straight with the centerline of the runway I cautiously eased the throttle forward until it wouldn't go any further and things began to happen real fast. The 140 un-straightened itself and zigged to the right. I applied left rudder and it zagged to the left. I then stomped the right rudder hard, zigged back to the right, only worse. Then I stomped the left rudder as hard as I could along with a very generous helping of left brake and then found that all three of us, the airplane, Lloyd, and me, were headed to a cotton field about 50 feet off the runway.

In a panic, I then pulled back on the wheel a little, left the runway, straddled a runway light, but had just enough speed that it was trying to fly so then we began seeing all kinds of green and white stuff (cotton plants) passing under the airplane. By that time we were airborne, just barely, and I thought if I stomped right rudder enough it would bring us back onto the runway which it did. By that time the propeller was throwing the cotton over the airplane. We bounced back onto the runway and I pulled back on the wheel hard trying desperately to get the airplane to stay in the air.

Lloyd was yelling things in what sounded like a foreign language or an unknown tongue as we catapulted into the sky with just enough flying speed to be airborne. The 140 was staggering and shaking as much as Lloyd and I were, but in a few seconds we gained enough airspeed we were really flying instead of staggering. Lloyd was white as a sheet and I couldn't say words yet.

That was my first takeoff in a Cessna 140. Lloyd suggested that we climb up and fly straight and level for a few minutes to let the sweat dry, let the nerves calm down, and talk about the upcoming landing. Once you get a taildragger in the air they behave pretty close to any other airplane except maybe a little more sensitive on the controls so it wasn't a big deal to just fly it. But, we had to get that thing back on the ground without tearing it up and killing both of us. I was pretty sure

Lloyd could get it back on the ground even if I failed, but could he grab it quick enough to salvage anything awful I might do? Besides, right then I didn't know if he could quit shaking long enough to land it or not.

I wanted to put the landing moment off as long as I could because I was convinced now that Bill Dunn was right as he could be when he said that all a taildragger was fit for was to walk around and kick the tires. But, a landing was inevitable so I entered downwind and began to set up for the landing.

A Cessna 140 is equipped with a spring steel landing gear which is a very strong gear, but spring steel means just that, "SPRING"! If you touch the ground a little too hard you can be sprung back into the air only to return to the ground with a little harder hit resulting in a much stronger sprong and of course being sprang much higher. If this process is repeated over two times, the ground gets further and further away with each bounce. These thoughts were going through my mind as well as thinking about the smooth surface under the nose where I was accustomed to having a wheel. There was no such thing on a 140, the wheel was on the rear end.

I did fine on downwind, base leg, and final approach. The airplane flew just like the familiar 150s and 172s, but once the wheels touched the runway, things began to happen. Every thing went to hell in the proverbial hand basket. The spring steel gear did just that, it sprang. Everything I've just talked about did indeed happen and it did it very good. Coupled with my feet madly working the rudder which made the tail wiggle, things got busy in a hurry. After the second "Sprong", I was again headed for the cotton field mentioned earlier. Lloyd was yelling again, insisting that I give it full throttle, go around, do it again, and do it NOW! The thoughts of having to do it all over again paralyzed me, but there was nothing else to do. I gave it full throttle and took off again, flew the pattern, and on the second attempt I got my hands and feets and Lloyd's hands and feets all working together and between the two of us we were successful in getting the 140 stuck to the runway and stopped without tearing anything up or off. That was once.

That was several hundred hours and 31 years ago. I am happy to say now that I can now take off and land a taildragger with the greatest of ease most of the time, but I never, never, never take one of the little beasties for granted. I still have a love for the Cessna 120s and 140s in spite of the fact they will sometimes bite you if taken for granted. There are not too many of the little Cessnas around anymore and even fewer pilots willing to strap one on. The memories of those first hours will never go away. My heartfelt thanks to Lloyd Howard for opening the door of taildragger flying for me.

YOU CAN LAND THAT ANYWHERE!

After I became a bit more experienced in the 140 and felt reasonably comfortable when I opened the hangar door to let it out, Junior Jennings began suggesting all sorts of things I could do with it. His reasoning was that since it was a taildragger I could just go plop it down anywhere I wanted to. If I saw something on the ground I wanted to look at, well heck, just land and go look at it. In the fall and winter in southwest Oklahoma wheat fields were abundant so a wheat field landing was first on the list.

Remember, Junior was the guy responsible for the push and shove that got me started flying in the first place so this was not an unusual next step. He gave me the want-to so bad and made me realize that the long wished for goal was both attainable and affordable. After I soloed, Junior and Margaret would quite often see me flying around and hurry to the airport just to watch me land. They called that entertainment. More than once I couldn't get the 140 stuck the first time, so I landed, and landed and landed, all on the same approach. He always insisted that I could only count one landing though. So, I trusted Junior and believed that if he said I could land in a wheat field, well, I should just go do it.

So, one day I picked out one of my own wheat fields and drove over it in my pickup to make sure it would be firm enough to hold me and the airplane up without sinking in the dirt. I then went to the airport, got the 140 out, came back and circled the field, lined the little Cessna up, dropped in over some power lines, and set it down with the greatest of ease into about three inches of green wheat … and soft dirt.

I did just fine until the tail wheel came down and started sinking in the dirt. When that happened it was kinda like throwing a concrete block out on a rope. The tailwheel started digging in pretty good so rather than come to a full stop I decided I better just keep moving and get the heck out of there. There wasn't enough wheat field left to take off so I made a great big circle back to about the spot I set down, pointed the 140 back into the wind, slowly gained speed and took off again.

I breathed a big sigh of relief when I finally broke ground and the airplane started flying again. Dirt was flying everywhere when I looked back over my shoulder. It looked like a west Texas sandstorm.

I didn't know it at the time, but a neighbor, Eugene Young, was on a tractor plowing about a mile away, had been watching me circle around, saw me go down, saw the sandstorm, and assumed that I had crashed. He got off the tractor, ran to his pickup, and started driving to where he thought I was, but aborted his rescue mission when he saw the 140 slowing rising back into the sky above the tree line. He was not a happy man and let me know about it a couple of days later. It was nice to know that he was concerned about me though.

Junior, bless his heart, never let me forget that landing. He found out about it even before I got back to the airport and he and Margaret were there to talk to me about it when I landed. I could see him grinning and laughing and pointing at my landing gear wanting to know what all the green stuff was hanging on it.

WHEN THE ENGINE QUITS, LAND!

I have said before that if a problem occurs with an airplane engine the airplane will not immediately drop out of the sky like a greased brick and spatter all over everything. It will in fact, unless it should explode which is very unlikely, glide quite a distance with the engine developing no power at all. Even that doesn't happen very often. Usually there will be partial power available and you can make a safe landing.

One of the many days I was out boring holes in the sky with my Cessna 140, I had such a problem for the first time. It was a beautiful day and I was just up there looking down. I had flown over a nearby lake and had just turned around to wander back toward home when I got the feeling that something was not right. The engine sounded a little louder for some reason and my toes began to wiggle on the rudder pedals. Toes and rudder pedals are not supposed to wiggle. The hair on the back of my neck started twitching so I decided to quit gawking and fly directly home. Something just wasn't right.

Then, not only my toes but my feet were wiggling and there was no mistake about it, a distinct vibration was coming through the rudder pedals and the whole airplane seemed to be jiggling right along with my feet and toes.

I found out that if I reduced power the shaking would let up just a bit. The problem with that though, when I reduced power the airplane started going down. When I applied power the airplane shook worse.

I had always been reluctant to land at Coyt and Wilma Johnston's Pleasant Valley Airport because it had power lines across the south end and other power lines running down the east side of the runway. No hint of reluctance that day. I looked over, saw Coyt's grass strip about a mile away and power lines or not, I headed for it like a lost duck, giving the 140 short bursts of power to maintain altitude, but not enough to shake it to death.

When I had the runway under my nose, I chopped the power to land. Knowing that I had only one shot to make a decent landing, I glided in over a Cessna 150 that was getting ready to take off. Thank goodness that pilot didn't start his takeoff roll because I swooped in right over the top and plopped the 140 down right in front of him. The 140 stuck and a good landing was made in spite of the 150, the power lines, the sweat and the shakes. (Mine and the airplane's)

The engine idled just fine so I wondered if all that shaking had been my imagination, but I shut the engine down, climbed out of the airplane, raised the cowling and looked. I didn't see anything unusual so I climbed back in and re-started the engine. When I gave it power, it shook, bad. There was a problem.

That was the first time I had to call wife Nancy and tell her, "Oh uh, I'm O.K., but.…"

It turned out that three of the cylinder head bolts on one cylinder had worked themselves loose and the whole jug was trying its best to separate itself from the rest of the engine and throw itself off. As the piston moved, so did the jug. A quick diagnosis by Lloyd Howard and a couple hours work a few days later got the little engine back where it ran like it should and I cautiously took off from Coyt's strip and flew home, but feeling for wiggles all the way.

◆   ◆   ◆

Another time it became necessary to come down was when a small piece of metal broke off from somewhere, got sucked up the intake tube, and lodged under one of the valves. Same airplane. N89092. I was up one day just flying and looking around when "Wham", all of a sudden the engine sounded like I had pulled the throttle only I had not. I was able to maintain an altitude of about 800 feet but couldn't get over 1750 rpm. I was about eight miles away from the Tipton airport, so I headed for it like a sick duck. I knew I had only one shot to get the airplane down, no way to make a go around if I screwed up, so I aimed for the east/west grass runway, slud over some telephone lines, and made pretty a good landing. Hair stood up on the back of my neck again though.

◆   ◆   ◆

Number three happened one day when Lloyd and I were going to fly a couple of guys to Ada. Lloyd had this slick ole Cessna 182 and he graciously agreed to let me fly it from the left seat, but he wanted to go too. The two passengers were in the back and Lloyd was in right seat.

Lloyd taxied up in front of the terminal building, came in and said, "Let's go". Our two passengers got in, Lloyd got in, and I started to make a quick pre-flight, but Lloyd assured me he had already looked things over, so since it was Lloyd's airplane and he said everything was OK, well, it was OK.

I did the run-up, taxied onto runway 17 end at Frederick, and hollered, "Reddy-go?" There being no objections, I eased the throttle in and the take off roll began. Just after lift off and about 100 ft in the air, oil began streaming up the wind screen. I said, but not loud enough, "I'M ABORTING TAKE OFF.... GOT OIL!" and pulled the throttle back to set the big Cessna back down on the remaining runway, since I had probably 4000 ft left.

Lloyd didn't hear me or see the oil, and he thought I had pulled the wrong knob back, so he rammed the throttle back in and away we went ... back up again. Then he saw the oil.

He said, "I GOT IT!" He took the controls, and we made a 180 (sort of) and landed on runway 30. By that time oil had covered the wind screen and we couldn't see outside much at all. Sure did make a mess of the outside of that airplane. Lloyd told me later he was sorry he took the airplane away from me. But it turned out OK. Oh, Lloyd forgot to put the oil filler cap back on....

The two guys in the back wouldn't ride with us again though.

◆   ◆   ◆

The incident that actually put me out of the airplane business occurred in March of 2003. That was the one that probably spooked me the most.

I had taken off from Pinson's Cottonpatch one evening in my 1947 Cessna 120 to fly to Frederick to get some gas, but decided to fly around Tipton for awhile before heading over to the airport. After about 30 minutes of just flyin', I headed to Frederick. About 5 miles northwest of the airport, with no warning whatsoever, the 85 Continental suddenly went nuts. I had a sudden loss of power and loud clanking and banging noises filled the cockpit. I pulled carb heat but nothing happened. I started losing altitude and the engine began to run rougher.

With my heart in my throat and hair standing straight up, I knew I was in big trouble this time. I picked out a wheat field to put the little Cessna down in and started to make a descent, but then the engine revved up again and I saw the big 75 acre parking apron at Frederick Municipal in front of me. I had hope.

I crossed a highway about two miles away from the airport and then the engine died. I was down to about 600 feet now and picked out another wheat field ... then the engine picked up and ran again, very rough, still rattling and banging.

I started down about four times total, picked out emergency landing fields that many or more before I could see that I had the concrete apron made. I began a normal approach to the apron from the north and when I knew with no doubt I could glide the rest of the way, I came back on the throttle and the engine died for the last time.

As my instructor George Stapp had taught me how to do so many times, I made a power off, full stall, dead stick, three point landing and coasted to a stop about 200 feet from the Frederick Airport terminal building. That was the longest cross country I ever made.

I got out of the 120 and thanked God for delivering me to safety. We got the airplane down without tearing it or me up.

I called good friend Donnie Coleman, told him what had happened, and he was at the airport in less than three minutes. We pushed the Cessna into the big hangar and then I called Nancy and asked her to come get me. She said, "What's the matter?" I said, "The airplane won't start." She said, "OK, I'll be right over."

When she got to Frederick and I got in the car and told her what really happened, I think my life was more in danger than it had been the hour before.

The Continental 85 had swallowed a valve to cause its distress. The valve broke off about a half inch up the stem and had beat itself to death on top of the piston, finally driving itself into the top of the piston sideways. Later when the engine was torn down, the top of the piston and the inside of the cylinder looked like crumpled up tin foil. The piston is now a paperweight on my desk.

◆   ◆   ◆

The last incident so far, was one really pretty October day in 2005. My grandson Jake had been wanting his first ride with me so I figured this was the day to do it. I got brother Keith's Ercoupe out of the hangar, cleaned it up a bit, and took off from Pinson's Cottonpatch airport for about 30 minutes that morning. Landed, left the airplane out in the open, then went back later in the afternoon and flew another 30 minutes or so. Then about 5:30, the whole family arrived, complete with cameras, and Jake got in the right seat and we fired the Ercoupe up and took off. A perfect evening to fly. No wind was blowing at all.

Jake and I flew around a bit, made a couple of low passes down the runway so everybody could take pictures of us, and then I gave the controls to Jake. We were about a half mile away from the south end of Keith's runway. Jake had no sooner taken the yoke when all of a sudden, smoke began pouring out from under the instrument panel. Jake said, "WHAT'S THAT?" I said, "I'VE GOT

THE AIRPLANE!" We were flying the coupe with the canopy top open so the smoke could get out, but it kept coming in too. I headed directly to the south end of the runway telling Jake all the way, "When we get down and quit rolling, you get out as fast as you can and run to the rear of the airplane!!! Got That?????

Well, we made a good landing, rolled to a stop, and Jake was 100 feet behind the airplane before I even looked to see if he was still sitting in the seat beside me. The smoke had quit because I had killed the mags right at touchdown, so at least the airplane wasn't on fire. (But I didn't know that while it was doing it.)

Jake and I both smelled like burnt rubber. All the family had run down the runway to see about us. When we all decided we were alright, more pictures were taken and the day turned out alright after all except grandson Jakes' first airplane ride was a bit shorter than expected. His only comment was, "Poppa, that was cool!"

YOU CAN'T AFFORD THE DIVORCE

Considering my experiences in my early days of hanging around Earl Huffer, Vernon Foster and later my friendship with Lloyd Howard, all of whom were crop dusters, it seemed only natural that the desire to fly low, sometimes very low, would rub off on me too. Earl never got over 200 feet in the air and Vernon didn't get that high. Lloyd would fly cross country a little higher, but never, never over 1000 feet above ground level. Crop dusters just don't see any use in flying any higher than necessary and none of them like to talk on the radio. In fact, they didn't even have radios unless they put a CB in the airplane.

Lloyd was always buying and hauling in wrecked airplanes and rebuilding them, so he was always looking for a bargain. He once located a little 1961 PA25-150 Pawnee Spray plane in the back of a hangar not far from home and told me it was cheap and I ought to buy it to play around with. Someone had borrowed the tailwheel and the rear end of the airplane was propped up on a bucket, but after looking at it I decided it was a bargain. I then talked big brother Keith into buying half of it. The deal was done and Keith and I owned a spray plane! We got it for $4000.00.

I told wife Nancy that I really wasn't going to go in the spray business, I just wanted to fly one of the things for the experience and thought I could make some money when we got ready to sell it. She said that was just fine just as long as I just flew it and did not squirt anything out of it because I would not be able to afford the divorce if I even got an idea to dodge highline wires, fence posts, and cows. That sort of deflated me because I had already got the idea that I could at least spray my own hay field and maybe kill mosquitoes around the house and barn with it. But, I reluctantly promised that I would behave myself considering the cost of becoming unmarried.

Lloyd loaned me a tailwheel to put on it and then flew the airplane home for me. I cleaned it up, got a lot of the smell out of it, neutralized the chemical hopper, and with the help of Lloyd's junk pile cleaned up some old nozzles and fixed it back where it could really spray stuff if it wanted to. Ag planes are "Oneholers", meaning that there is only one seat for the pilot and no one else, so when you fly one of the things it is just you and the Lord and you hope that He knows what to do just in case you don't.

I was pretty nervous the first time I flew it, but really did just fine. The most un-nerving thing about the Pawnee was it was about eleven feet from the cockpit to the prop spinner and when the airplane sat three point on the ground the cowling top was parallel with the ground. On takeoff when the tail came up, the nose went down, and it looked like the prop was going to dig a trench in the run-way because it sloped down so much.

I flew several hours in that Pawnee and wouldn't take anything for the experi-ence. I would put thirty or forty gallons of water in it, go up, and watch it come out the nozzles as I flew merrily over the country side. The water looked like a sil-very ribbon trailing behind me. It wasn't long that I began to feel like I was flying a fighter plane because I could fly very low and nobody would think anything about it because that is where Ag spray planes are supposed to be. Try that in a Cessna Skyhawk and everyone sees you and says, "Boy, look how low that idiot is flying" and you get in a heap of trouble for violating some law, but it's no big deal in a spray plane.

Early one summer morning I took off and immediately spotted one of my neighbors plowing cotton in a field nearby. I could not resist the temptation so I leveled the Pawnee about fifty feet off the ground, dropped in on his cotton field at eye level like a professional and aimed directly for the cab on his tractor. He saw me coming and got so excited he plowed up six rows of cotton for about a quarter mile. He even had the tractor cab door open getting ready to jump out when I pulled up out of the way. He was shaking his fist at me as I went by.

I thought about stripping the Pawnee of all the spray booms, painting it Navy Blue and putting white markings on it like a WWII Corsair fighter plane, but I found out I could sell it for a pretty good profit after playing with it for a couple of years. A fellow from Colorado wanted it worse than we did so Keith and I went out of the spray plane business. The only bugs we killed were the ones that the airplane hit, but we both had an awfully good time with it. We also found out that it really got hot in the cockpit in the summer time because there weren't enough of those little bitty vent holes to let the air blow in.

GRAVEL BOMBS, BALLOONS, AND BURGERS

Airplane pilots are always thinking up different things to do to amuse and entertain themselves with an airplane, some of them goofy, some downright idiotic, but for the most part still safe fun.

When 80 octane Av Gas was selling for 60 cents a gallon and it didn't cost much to fly, a whole bunch of us either owned airplanes or knew where we could get one to fly without too much trouble. We were always hanging out at the airplane patch anyhow, so one day we decided to have one of those "play days" that we had heard folks in other towns talk about. We decided to do it up real good, invite the wives and kids to watch us do silly things, and then cook charcoal broiled hamburgers on an outdoor grill for everyone after the games were over.

One thing we had heard about, but didn't know exactly how to do it, was the fine art of balloon bustin'. We understood that it involved the release of a helium filled party balloon from mid-field just as an airplane would leave the runway and then the pilot would chase the balloon all over the sky until he either lost it or would bust it with the propeller. Most of us had never done anything like that before so most all of the balloons escaped injury and floated off into orbit somewhere. We had a good time trying though. Larry Abernathy refused to give up on his and chased a balloon all the way into the next county with his Ag Truck before he lost it.

Another fun thing was flour sack bombing. We heard that you could fill a plastic baggy with flour, drop it out of an airplane, and hit a target with it. It was supposed to go "poof" when it hit the target and make like smoke. We soon found out that was a gross exaggeration of skill. Whoever said it was easy to hit a 50 gallon barrel or even a swimming pool for that matter with a baggy full of flour from 200 feet or higher in the air was nuts. We scattered flour sack bombs all over the western half of Tillman county.

Brother Keith was our official flour sack bomb tester and a few days before the play day he tested some by throwing them out of his Ercoupe. He reported they were not heavy enough and suggested we add some rocks to make them fall faster. The problem was, though if they hit anybody or anything they became somewhat destructive. He did it anyhow and loaded about a half a cup of chat screenings to each baggy to mix with the Gold Medal flour.

The day of the official games arrived and while the hamburger coals were heating the balloon bustin' and flour sack bombing began. We had a great time, got a lot of flying in, but didn't bust hardly any balloons. Ronald Haynie almost bored a hole in the wing of Junior and Margaret's Cessna Skylane with one of the rock filled baggies and we then decided it was time to quit fooling around and eat the hamburgers.

It was still daylight though when the hamburgers were gone and someone remembered that good friend Jerry Bryan was hosting what was called a "Ham Radio Field Day" at his farm near Otter Creek about ten miles from the airport. A bunch of ham radio operators were out there in his back yard communicating with other hams throughout the world. They were practicing response time for a simulated emergency situation should one ever occur.

We decided to provide them with a real emergency and bomb them. Five airplanes loaded with rock/flour bombs complete with bombardiers took off on the mission. We flew in trail at low level to the target and our surprise attack was an outstanding success. Man, it was great! Tora, Tora, Tora! We did surprise the heck out of them, but the downside was that we didn't hit anything with our bombs. All we did was make a bunch of noise flying over because all the bombs missed Jerry's back yard by at least a quarter mile. The Ham radio operators came much closer to hitting us with the rocks and clods they threw back at us as we flew over.

I mentioned earlier that brother Keith had tested the rock/flour baggy bombs. The bombs he dropped from the Ercoupe were left on and near the runway. No need to pick them up because it was just flour (and gravel) anyhow and we figured they would dissolve and go away eventually. That night though, about 3:00 a.m., the City Police and a County Sheriff's Deputy called Joe Grubbs and asked if he would come to the airport. They said that they had found a bunch of plastic bags full of suspicious white powdery stuff scattered over the airport and since Joe was chairman of the airport commission he needed to know about it and maybe even do some explaining. Joe had a heck of a time convincing them that there was no need to analyze the stuff because it was only Gold Medal flour.

ANOTHER FLYING
PREACHER

In 1968 we were once again blessed with a pastor of the Baptist Church who had a love for airplanes and flying. Rev. Cal Hunter, "Doc" as I called him, had his pilot's license, flew a lot at one time, but family, finances, and other interests such as photography, amateur radio, pawn shops, and of course the ministry had overshadowed his flying interests. So, when he moved to Tipton he had not flown in several years.

It wasn't long though that he renewed my interest in Ham Radio and I got him interested in flying again. In addition to being my pastor, he became my best friend. It was an innocent enough re-start.... Doc had to be in McAlester, Oklahoma at 1:30 p.m. one day to preach a funeral and then back in Tipton to perform a wedding at 6:30. It was impossible to do except with an airplane. I had not had my license very long and was willing to fly anyone anywhere, so I rented a good ole' 1964 Cessna 172 and volunteered to fly Doc to McAlester and back and promised he would make the wedding if he did not preach very long at the funeral. After the funeral when he arrived back at the McAlester airport I had the Skyhawk preflighted and ready to start. We made it just fine, landed at Frederick at 5:30, drove to Tipton, and he walked in the wedding just in time to say "Dearly Beloved". It wasn't but just a few weeks later he got a new medical and started looking for an airplane to buy.

He found a Piper Tri-Pacer and made a deal for it, but didn't have quite enough cash to pay for all of it. I bought 30 hours flying time in advance for a bargain $10.00 an hour to help him raise the money. The Tri-Pacer was a neat little airplane except it didn't have near enough wing on it. In fact, it was short and stubby. Good neighbor Bill Dunn heard I was flying a Tripacer and came over one day with real concern on his face and said, "Oh Uh, Do you know those Tri-Pacers can fall out of the sky and KILL you?"

I flew the Tri-Pacer those 30 hours plus some more and never did fall out of the sky. True to rumor and fact, it did hit and roll like a sewer lid when it was landed, and true, it would not stall clean, but simply mush straight down at 1200 feet per minute. I will admit it felt funny when I made a steep turn from base leg to final. There was a definite "slud" feeling. Kind of like falling down with your hands in your pockets. Just plain weird.

When Doc began fooling with airplanes again, another good friend Ed Fox wanted to too, but he let a little thing like running off the runway into a mud hole give him the shakes and he never did quite recover his composure and nerve after that. Ed never got hooked up with a real live flight instructor, just sort of flew whenever he could with whoever he could and kept saying he had to work for a living or something like that. Problem was though, he had an itch and couldn't get it scratched.

Doc found a 7EC Champ one day and bought it. To relieve Ed's distress he volunteered to teach Ed a few things about flying … the economy course, so to speak. He and Ed had a bang-up good time for awhile taking off and landing and going up and down, the usual sort of fun things except Ed had an awful time keeping the Champ going straight down the runway, landing and taking off. Nothing unusual for a beginning taildragger pilot though. Well, Doc suggested that they just stay on the runway and taxi back and forth with Ed stomping rudder and brake to practice keeping the tail behind him. Ed was doing just great until the mechanical brake cable snapped on the left side and the Champ suddenly lurched to the left because the cable wrapped itself around the wheel almost locking it and Ed took his first cross-country right into a mud hole about 100 feet off the runway yelling "WHOAA" all the way.

There were no witnesses to this event, but somehow the back side window of the Champ got broken out. The story was told that as the airplane was leaving the runway, Doc's cap blew off and he stuck his hand through the window trying to grab it. Doc didn't admit it though and Ed's eyes were closed.

After the Champ was retrieved from the mud hole with the aid of a pickup and rope and they got the mud cleaned off, Ed said, "That's it … no more…. I've had it!" As much as we tried to talk him back into the cockpit he just wouldn't do it. Such a shame too, because Ed might have eventually made a good pilot. Many times after the incident Doc would say, "You still thinkin' about that mud hole Ed?"

I WANT ONE OF THEM!

There is an eight years age difference in my brother Keith and me, he being the older. We have always gotten along very good with each other, seemed to have a lot of the same interests, and have enjoyed working and playing together. We farmed together, bought and sold guns together, and he even picked up the Ham radio hobby when I did, but when I began taking flying lessons, he was not the least bit interested. In fact, he told me he didn't mind me talking about my flying lessons and what I was doing, but "Just don't Bill Dunn him", meaning don't overdo it and talk too much.

In 1976 I was asked to fly to Tulsa to pick up Lloyd Howard and Joe Grubbs. Lloyd had sold a Citabria to a guy there and had agreed to deliver it. Joe just went along with him for the ride. Since I was flying a Cessna Skyhawk and there would be plenty of room I invited brother Keith to ride along with me. Even though he had not been infected with the flying bug, he trusted my ability as a pilot enough to get in an airplane with me.

We had a very enjoyable flight to Tulsa and sneaked into Harvey Young Airport, a small, but busy airport just a couple of miles south of Tulsa International and crammed into the congestion of eastside Tulsa between 11th and 21st streets. We flew to Bixby, a small town south of Tulsa, then dropped down to pattern altitude of about 800 foot, turned north at the stoplight and flew straight up Memorial Street to Harvey Young. The city had virtually surrounded the airport, but folks could still go there on weekends and watch the Cubs, T-Carts, bitty Cessnas, and other flying machines do touch and goes as long as they could stand it.

I had entered the pattern, turned final, and just as I was about to land, in fact I was flaring the Hawk just ready to set it down, brother Keith yelled out "WHATTZAT!" That yell scared me to death because I thought we were about to have a mid-air collision with another airplane, bird, or car. Barbed wire fences were also all around us so the possibility of hitting something wasn't that far fetched. But, brother Keith had simply spotted a funny looking little airplane parked in a mess of other planes and was just asking what the heck kind of airplane that was that was parked in amongst all the others. Since he wasn't driving the Cessna, he had the time to gawk around and see such things as trees, houses, airplanes, shopping centers, and more airplanes.

After we landed, Keith and I walked over to see what it was he had seen. It turned out to be a low winged, single engine, tricycle gear, silver airplane with two tails. Keith circled it once and announced that he wanted one of those. That surprised the heck out of me because he sure hadn't expressed an interest in flying himself, much less he didn't even know how to fly anything yet period! He had not even had the want-to to fly and as far as I knew had just had been listening politely as I had been relating all my flying adventures so far. But that day, he had fallen in love at first sight with an Ercoupe, an airplane that looked sort of like a midget B-25 bomber only much, much, smaller. And it had only one engine instead of two. And no guns.

By that time, Lloyd and Joe landed and Keith took them to see the Ercoupe as well, but Lloyd wanted to leave town as quickly as possible, a wise thing to do just after you have just sold an airplane, so the four of us loaded up in the Skyhawk and took off for Oklahoma City to get a hamburger at Expressway Airpark, a small airport on the northeast side of the City.

Keith could not forget that Ercoupe. He talked about it while we ate the hamburger, talked about it on the way home, and was still talking about it a couple of days later. He wouldn't admit it, but I knew unofficially the search was on for one of the little split tailed airplanes.

After we got home, just for fun I started looking around for a "Coup" that might be for sale. The thoughts of ever really finding one of the funny little airplanes never occurred to me. I had seen only one once before and my first thought at the time was that it was a little military plane of some sort. I was looking mainly for the fun of having something to look for because by then Keith had sort of cooled off a little. The word got out that I was looking though and it wasn't but a few weeks later that lo and behold we heard there was one at Eldorado, Oklahoma, only 40 miles from home. I called the owner and yes, he would sell it, yes we could come look at it, and yes, it was priced reasonable. I asked Lloyd Howard if we could take his Skylane to go look at it. Lloyd wanted to see it too, so he, Keith, and I loaded up and flew over to look at the Coupe.

It was a good thing Lloyd went because in a couple of hours Keith was the proud owner of a 1946 415-C Ercoupe. Paid the whoppin' price of $3500 for it. But since he didn't know how to fly it, Lloyd agreed to fly it home, even though he had never flown one himself.

We watched Lloyd take off and Keith and I followed in the Skylane. All the way home Keith kept muttering to himself, "What have I done?" What he had done was commit himself to learn to fly. There was no choice now, no backing out now since he now owned an airplane he could not fly and he couldn't just drive it around on the ground forever.

We found out later that there were a couple of guys who were also interested in buying the airplane and were standing in the shade of a tree about a half block away watching all the haggling and tire kicking and were going to buy the Coupe if Keith didn't.

An Ercoupe is a two control airplane, different from all other airplanes which are three controlled. You make an Ercoupe go where you want it to on the ground by steering it like a car. Just turn the steering wheel. There are no rudder pedals because the rudders are interconnected with everything else. You just turn the wheel side to side or pull it back and push it in. While flying in the air you do the same to go left or right and just pull back to go up and reduce power to go down. That's it. Since there are no rudder pedals to wiggle with your feet and no individual brakes to mash, just one brake pedal for both brakes, you stomp hell out of the floor. Airplane drivers who are accustomed to flying the other type aircraft with the 3 control system (like me) go nuts stomping the floor trying to make the airplane turn with their feet, but since there are no peddles to stomp all you can do is squish the carpet and make the aluminum floor pop. I have heard that some folks will glue sponges to the floor so there will be something to put their feet on and mash.

The first few days after Keith bought it, Lloyd taught him how to get the thing up and down and sort of gave him back yard instructions, but before Keith got too comfortable flying around with just a drivers license we told him he better go get the proper papers. He finally did and it wasn't long before he too earned his private pilots license and got some flying time and a check out in a Cessna 150 as well. He had to rent the 150 for some lessons and also his check ride because he would have only received a limited license had he got it in the Ercoupe.

Ercoupes are funny little airplanes. They were designed to be stall proof and spin proof, are very safe airplanes, and were actually sold in Macy's Department Store in New York City when they first came on the market. They were also sold at department stores in Denver.

Keith still has his Coupe. It and a lot of the airplanes I owned over the years were hangar mates at Pinson's Cottonpatch Airport in Tipton. Anything anyone might ever want to know about an Ercoupe Keith knows it because he has become a "Coupespert" after owning his for over 30 years. He even met Fred Weick one time, the man who designed the airplane. He knows the ancestry of the Coupe all the way back to the beginning and every variation that was ever done to them including a one-time made twin engine Ercoupe. They even tried one out with a jet engine attached to it.

N3539H is not for sale and will probably be in the family forever unless Keith decides to be buried in it, but if not, his great grand kids will get to figure out what to do with that funny looking little aluminum airplane. He and I flew it to Oshkosh in 2000 and even after getting lost over Wisconsin a few times, it still got us there and back to Oklahoma.

Soon after Keith bought the Coupe he decided he wanted to be able to look out the back window of his house while he sat in his Lazy Boy recliner and look at it instead of having to drive to the airport to see it. But, to do so he had to fix a way to get it into his back yard through a cotton field. I really thought he was kidding, but when I saw a road grader pushing perfectly good cotton plants to the side one day I realized he was dead serious. It wasn't long before "Pinson's Cottonpatch Airport", a half mile grass strip, was born parallel to the highway one mile south of Tipton, Oklahoma. Even became 6OK3 on the charts.

Keith invited me to fly in anytime I wanted and even invited me to squat there if I would help build a pole hangar big enough to cover his Coupe and the 1948 Cessna 170 I owned then. I anted up some money, even offered to build some sides to the building, and now Pinson's Cottonpatch is the reliever airport for Altus, Frederick and Tipton.

There were not too many accommodations at Pinson's Cottonpatch, in fact it was covered with blow dirt for a long time, but there is a water well full of cold sweet water and 2500 feet of smooth grass now to glide in on. In an emergency, I can walk about 50 feet, go in the back door of the house to cool off or warm up and sometimes even get a free coke or sandwich.

It's nice to sit in a lawn chair under the wing of the Cessna and feel the breeze on a pretty spring day. Sometimes other folks land there too. It sure surprised Keith the first time a strange airplane set down and taxied up in his back yard. Turned out a fellow from Hollis, Oklahoma flew over to visit some family in a Cessna 180, saw the strip, and just put it down. A stiff legged Mooney landed there one day too. We never did figure out who it belonged to.

Keith started giving away window stickers to folks who landed there after awhile that said "I landed At Pinson's Cottonpatch Airport", mainly because of their bravery. When he first built the strip, final approach for 17 took you over the peak of a 50 foot tall hay barn. If you landed the other way on RW35 you were staring at a big, square, black, gaping hole where the barn door was supposed to be. Keith figured if anyone had the guts to land over the barn they deserved something besides a drink of well water. Unfortunately (or fortunately) the barn was destroyed by a wind storm and the obstruction is gone, but he has been thinking about setting a highline pole with a light on it in the middle of the runway to renew the challenge.

A dream of Keith's was realized one October a few years ago when he and his Ercoupe made a trip to Central Arkansas to participate in the annual "Chicken Ranch Ercoupe Family Fly-In and Picnic". This gathering of Ercoupe flyers had been a happening for almost 20 years and had drawn an average of about 50 of the little split-tailed airplanes and many more of their dedicated owners each year for three days of tire kicking, mutual admiration of each others airplanes, and just plane fun.

Keith had wanted to go for at least 16 years, maybe longer, but something always came up to put a stop to his plans, but that year he finally decided to see if his Coupe could get to this less than desirable landing strip situated somewhere in the area of Dardinelle, Arkansas.

The Chicken Ranch grass strip was about 2200 feet long with one end butted up against a mountain. The other end was about 12 feet wide and went between two catfish ponds. That was reason enough in my opinion to think twice about going there. You landed pointed toward that mountain and when you take off you point away from the mountain regardless of which way or how fast the wind is blowing. Keith let it slip that several gutless folks drove in instead of flew in, thus the difference in number of airplanes verses the number of folks. But Brother Keith flew!

Everybody there ate their meals in a chicken house and some of the folks slept on bales of straw in the same chicken house, however Keith's idea of roughing it was not quite that severe, so he bought a Best Western Motel room in nearby Dardinelle. He reported that he ate a lot of no-fat, healthy heart, Arkansas breakfasts and suppers served by the hosts of the event.

WE AIN'T GUNNA MAKE IT!

It was mentioned earlier about the trip to Tulsa Harvey Young Airport when Keith saw his first Ercoupe. Lloyd, Joe, Keith and I took off from Tulsa that morning about 10:30 a.m. and by the time we got to Oklahoma City the temperature was getting close to 95 degrees and the winds had picked up a bit, close to 20 mph or so. Joe had been talking all morning about how good the hamburgers were at "Expressway Airport", or "Crosswinds" as I found out later some folks liked to call it.

Expressway lay in a hole just to the right of and below Interstate 35 on the northeast corner of Oklahoma City. If you looked close as you drove up the northbound lane of I-35 you could look down about sixty feet and see airplanes parked along side the runway. A city street, Northeast 63rd, ran east and west about twelve feet off the end of runway 02 on the south end. On the south side of 63rd street was a Braum's Ice Cream factory right in the glide path. You had to skim over the top of the ice cream factory and dump in over the street just before touchdown if there were no cars or trucks passing by. If there were, you had to stay high to avoid hitting a car.

After informing Oklahoma City approach that I was descending into their city for a landing at Expressway, I dodged the half dozen television towers and set up for a landing on runway 02. When I crossed over the ice cream factory and 63rd Street, a bunch of hot air rising from the concrete rose up to meet us and the Cessna began to float in the hot summer air.

I said, "We're floating", as the Skyhawk skimmed along down the runway about four feet off the ground. Lloyd said, "Well, land the airplane." I said, "It won't go down". Lloyd said, "You better land the airplane". I said, "We ain't gunna make it!". Lloyd said, "We will if you'll land the stupid airplane!".

We floated about half the length of the runway on that cushion of hot air and Lloyd yelled, "Are you gunna land or what? There's the end of the runway!!!" Sure enough, as we breezed past the center taxiway, still floating three to four feet off the ground I could see the north end of the runway. I finally upset the hot air cushion with a burst of power, pulled back on the yoke, ballooned a bit, and the

Skyhawk whumped in. Lloyd muttered, "It's about time!" as he reached for a cigarette.

Joe and Keith weakly agreed from the back seat. They had been speechless during the whole landing process. Sweat flowed freely from all of us. Expressway Crosswinds Airpark had always had a reputation for being a bad place to land anything, but after the hamburgers and a cold coke we all felt better. It remained a hellava place to grease one on though up until it was closed in the late 1990's.

BURIAL AT SKY

I received a telephone call from Larry Abernathy one day asking if he might possibly use my Cessna 120 for a short, but necessary trip. I didn't loan out the 120 to just anybody, but I knew Larry could fly it with little or no difficulty so there was really no concern. I was curious though why he wanted the little Cessna because he owned a Twin Baron and a Cessna Ag Truck. After he told me what he was up to though, I quickly agreed to let him use the 120 before he decided to make me fly his mission instead of doing it himself.

It seems as though Larry had reluctantly agreed to distribute the final remains of a dearly departed person in the form of ashes over the departed's hometown of Manitou, Oklahoma. The Baron and Ag Truck flew too fast and he needed an airplane that would be slow enough so he could open the window and pour the fellow out. Larry told me he did not know exactly when the burial was to take place, but probably in a day or two. I told him to take the 120 whenever he needed it and then sort of forgot about the whole deal. The airplane was hangared at Cottonpatch Airport in brother Keith's back yard and would be no problem for Larry to get to it.

I forgot to mention the conversation with Larry to brother Keith though. A couple of days later on a hot, windy, summer day Keith was mowing his yard when a stranger drove up in Keith's front driveway and strolled around the corner of the house carrying a small box. He said "Hello" and then asked Keith if he was ready. "Ready for what?" Keith replied. "Ready to scatter these", the stranger said. Keith said "What's that?" The stranger said, "Well this is …," and he told Keith the guy's name.

By then Keith had decided he needed to find out just who this nut was and what in the world he was talking about. Keith parked his lawnmower and started for the telephone to call just anybody, but the stranger saw his concern and stopped him and said, "Aren't you the pilot and isn't that your airplane out there?" Keith said, "Yes, but …!"

About that time Keith looked out and saw Larry's pickup drive up near the hangar where my 120 and Keith's Ercoupe were parked. Larry got out, walked up, everybody greeted everybody and shook hands with everybody except the fellow in the box, and in spite of some uneasy laughter, things relaxed a bit. After Keith had been fully informed as to what was about to take place Larry took possession of the box and its contents. The stranger left scratching his head at what had just transpired, but had some degree of confidence that the mission would be accomplished.

As Larry was pre-flighting the 120, he asked Brother Keith if he would like to go along for the services, but most of all just for the ride. After all, the flight was only a 20 mile round trip and even though it was gusty and hot, it wouldn't take very long. Keith was still covered with dirt and grass clippings and Larry had been spraying all day and wasn't much cleaner and both of them smelled about the same so they climbed in the 120, fired it up, took off, box and all.

When I talked to Larry a couple of days later he told me the trip was a success of sorts, but as he was thanking me for the loan of the 120, he grinned and told me that if I ever heard voices coming from the tail end of the 120 to not get too upset. I asked why, and he said that when he opened the window of the airplane and opened the box to pour the ashes out…. well, like Paul Harvey says, "You're ahead of me aren't you?" Sure enough, the fellow in the box did get scattered somewhere over southwestern Oklahoma, not necessarily over Manitou though, but probably in a lake about 15 miles away since it was so windy, and Larry said a whole bunch of the ashes blew right back in his face and into the back end of my airplane.

Nope, no voices yet.

JOE GRUBBS

Joe Grubbs is probably the most unselfish man I have ever known. Not once has Joe ever refused to quit what he was doing and help me or someone else when he was needed. He gave me encouragement when I needed it the worst, helped me fix things on airplanes that to most people would have been unfixable, and often talked me into doing things that I probably knew I could have done but was afraid to. Not only that, every time I would try to pay him for his trouble he would grin and tear the check up into little bitty pieces as I watched or cram the cash back in my pocket saying, "I'll quit working for you if you're gunna try to do that!"

I asked Joe to go with me to look at a 1948 Cessna 170 I was thinking about trading my 140 for. After having two emergency landings with the 140 I was a little uneasy with it, besides that I had convinced myself I needed a 4 place airplane. Bud Sutton from Newcastle, the 170 owner, and I had agreed to meet in Duncan, a town about 90 miles away and I wanted Joe to see the airplane because I needed his expert airplane opinion to tell me if it was any good. As usual, he arranged his schedule to help me out of another mess I had gotten myself in and agreed to go.

Joe and I gave the 170 a going over, flew in it, and after receiving Joe's expert opinion, I traded for the airplane. We took off from Duncan having only previously flown one of the things for about 45 minutes some years before. I was being extra careful not to do anything drastic with it just yet so it was straight and level flying for me. I just wanted to get it home so I could really take a good look at it. About half way home I asked Joe if he would like to fly it, and he did, but as soon as he took the controls, he immediately pulled back on the yoke as far as it would go, the airplane shot up almost into a stall, then he pushed the yoke forward and we went into a steep high speed dive. He then turned abruptly to the left, then to the right, and almost put the airplane on its back.

After I got my breath, I yelled at Joe, "What in the world are you doing?" He grinned that silly grin of his and said, "Well, just thought I would see if the wings would fall off.... better to know now than when you don't expect it." Thanks to Joe the wings never did fall off that airplane.

◆   ◆   ◆

Joe decided to build an airplane one time. I thought he had lost his mind, but to Joe the word "can't" is just not in his vocabulary so when he made up his mind to build an airplane, by dang, he was going to build an airplane and there was no stopping him.

He bought a partially build EAA Biplane, but after he got it home he decided what was already built wasn't built good enough so he tore it apart and started the project all over from scratch. It took 22 months of hard work, a little blood, a whole lotta sweat, some tears, and his wife Barbara nearly ran him off, but he did it … he built that little airplane and it was a beauty.

All the time he was working on it, (which was all the time with the exception of when he had to go to work at the local Rural Electric Coop and about three hours of sleep each night), he said there were only four people who were going to get to fly it when he finished it and yep, for some reason I was one of the four. Why he included me I don't know. I told him he was nuts because I was not about to take even the remotest chance of dinging that little airplane after all the hard work he put into it.

Joe flew it. Lloyd Howard flew it. Larry Abernathy flew it. All of them came down with silly grins on their faces and glowing reports of how great it felt. Joe kept on saying to me, "Your turn". I said, "No way, but I would like to just sit in it, but that's all."

I sat in it once, then twice, and I sat in it several times more, and finally one day Joe convinced me to just start it up and go taxi it a little, "Just to get the feel of the controls". "Better take the brain-bucket (crash helmet)", he said, "And also, by the way, give it enough power to raise the tail so's you can feel it real good". Uh huh, I knew what would happen if I gave that thing too much throttle. It did too. That day I just couldn't resist the temptation. I taxied down to the west end of the grass runway, did a mag. check, took a deep breath, and pushed the throttle all the way forward. That little one-holer, open cockpit, two winged airplane with 135 Lycoming horses up front took me for a ride I will never forget. It flew just like a sports car would drive. It responded instantly at the touch of the stick and landed so easily and tracked so straight it was unbelievable. I didn't tear it up either. Talk about fun.… Hoo Boy!

◆   ◆   ◆

One of those really cold winter mornings, the kind that makes you wonder if the world would shatter into a million pieces if someone dropped so much as a shoe, Joe and I decided to go look at a 7AC Champ that we heard was for sale. The sky was clear blue, the temperature was about 18 degrees, there was no wind, and an icy frost covered the ground. Everything else, trees, bushes, houses, cars, everything, was also covered with a thin coat of ice. It was so pretty it was eerie. The trees sparkled like they were loaded with diamonds as the sunlight reflected off the ice. It was just one beautiful, crisp, winter morning.

I met Joe at the local coffee shop and he asked if I thought the Cessna 140 would start. I thought it might with a little nudging, but what for did Joe want it to start for? That kind of morning you are supposed to just drink hot cups of coffee and sit in front of a fire instead of trying to start airplanes. Wrong.

It seems as though Joe had seen this advertisement in the paper about the Champ that was supposed to be parked on the ramp at Lindsey, Oklahoma, a small town about 90 miles away. Joe figured this was as good a morning as any to go look at it. After a while the logic of that seemed to soak in so we went to the airport, rolled out the 140, and sure enough, after priming it and pulling the starter, it just grunted. Joe then proceeded to prop it. After several pulls, it finally started and ran rather reluctantly, but it did keep on running so Joe climbed in on the right side.

However, when he shut his door, my door popped open. I shut mine again and Joe's door popped open. We had on so many clothes and the cabin was so narrow we were about 6 inches wider than the cabin. We finally had to scrooch up and hold our breaths so both doors would stay shut at the same time.

Airplane nuts do silly things sometimes and some folks might call what we were doing totally irrational and I suppose a golfer or a fisherman might say Joe and I were downright crazy, yet they wouldn't hesitate to go shoot a golf or try to catch a fish on a day like that. Joe and I and the little Cessna waddled out to the end of the runway and when the 140 was warm enough to take full throttle without dying, we took off and headed toward Lindsey, being careful not to breath too deeply so the doors would stay shut.

After we had flown facing the sun for about seven miles, Joe said, "Can you see where you're going?" I said, "No, I thought you could." Turned out that neither one of us could see any direction because of so much frozen moisture in the air. We quickly discussed the situation and decided that probably the wisest thing we could do would be to return to the airport and go see that Champ in the Chevy Pickup. It was a good idea because both doors popped open again when we landed.

We were able to get back at Joe once in return for his friendship, generosity, and goodness. At that time we had local EAA Chapter 652 and all the members nominated him for the Experimental Aircraft Association's Major Achievement Award one year and he won it. Only ten such awards are given each year and Joe got one. He didn't even know what we had done until he received a letter from EAA President Paul Poberezny asking him if he could come to the annual EAA Convention and Fly-In that year to accept his plaque. Joe couldn't go to Wisconsin so they mailed him his plaque. We were all very proud of him.

SPACIALLY DISORIENTED IN KANSAS

There really should be a law requiring airports to paint their name somewhere in a conspicuous place on a runway, a hangar, or post it inside the terminal building because sometime in a pilot's flying life he or she will land at an airport and think they are somewhere other than where they really are. Even worse, they may not have the foggiest idea where they are except somewhere on planet earth. If anyone ever tells you different, they lie!

About 6 months after I got my license, I loaded wife Nancy and our two small daughters, Kari and Jo, into a Cherokee 140 and flew to Olathe, Kansas, a suburb of Kansas City, to visit my cousin Sandra and her and family. It was a beautiful October day. We weighed all our stuff, packed it in the airplane, and took off headed northeast with Stillwater, Oklahoma as our first intended stop. We landed there, went to the potty, ate some peanut butter crackers, reloaded, and took off again for Kansas City. We crossed over into Kansas and Nancy was studying the sectional chart since I had designated her as chief navigator so she wouldn't dwell on the purpose of the Sic-Sac hanging nearby. The kids were fine. The smooth air and drone of the engine had put them to sleep right after take off.

A few miles into Kansas, the coke I drank at Stillwater became active. There was nothing I could do except cover my lap with my jacket and use the "Human Element Range Extender". Nancy assumed the duties of holding the yoke and keeping the nose of the Cherokee pointed where it was supposed to be pointed. That necessity taken care of, I took control of the airplane back from Nancy and resumed flying.

As we neared our destination I saw a nice smooth concrete runway over the nose of the Cherokee, so I called Johnson County tower at Olathe. They answered right back and advised me that a Cessna 150 was on downwind, the winds were light from the north, and I was cleared for a straight in approach to land on runway 35, number two behind the Cessna. I had the runway and the 150 in sight so after it turned final I followed it in and made a really nice landing.

There seemed to be slight problem though. The airport was not nearly as large as I though it should be and was not nearly as busy as I thought it would be, but I taxied in, parked, unloaded the family and we went into the terminal building. I began to get a funny feeling because something just was not right. I said "Howdy" to a couple of fellows sitting there drinking coffee and talking, all the while trying to find anything anywhere that would say where we were. Nothing … not even a newspaper was laying around. The gnawing feeling got worse.

I finally swallowed my pride and asked the two coffee drinkers the awful, embarrassing question, "This IS Johnson County Airport isn't it?" Grinning, one fellow said, "Naw, this here is Ottawa Airport. Johnson County's about 20 miles northeast of here up the turnpike!"

Now the truth was known. I had landed at the wrong airport. The only excuse was that while I was occupied with the "Range Extender", Nancy had veered off course about five degrees and I didn't notice it.

I turned several shades of red, gathered up my little family, thanked the grinning coffee drinkers, and quickly reloaded the Cherokee. We took off and I again called Johnson County tower, trying to decide how to tell them where we were, where we had been, and why we had not landed at their airport yet. When they asked me where in the world I was and where I had been, I just told them that one of the kids got awful bad sick to their stomach and we had to land quick and quick was at Ottawa. The Johnson County Tower folks just grunted.

As I flew that 20 miles up the Kansas Turnpike I couldn't help but wonder about the coincidence of a Cessna 150 landing at both airports at the same time. When we landed at Johnson County it looked like I expected it to be, lots of concrete, lots of runways, and a big building with the name of the airport painted in big letters all over the front.

About twenty years after that incident in Kansas, when I was manager of the airport at Frederick, Oklahoma, a young man landed one day, tied down his airplane, walked in the terminal building very calmly and confidently, and remarked that "North Texas sure was pretty!" I told him yes it probably was, but he wasn't in it, he was in Frederick, Oklahoma. He literally fell to the floor on his knees and cried out, "FREDERICK! FREDERICK! I'm supposed to be in Wichita Falls, TEXAS! My instructor will kill me!"

After an embarrassing telephone call to his instructor in Mineral Wells, Texas, he got his instructions on how to go directly home and quickly departed. I don't even think he went to the bathroom.

I just grinned, just like those two coffee drinkers did in Kansas that embarrassing day. I learned later that that same young man landed again a few minutes later in Vernon, Texas about 20 miles away. He was lost again. After that phone call his instructor told him to not take off again under any circumstances. He was coming after him to take him home.

HOW DO YA' GET
ANYWHERE FROM HERE?

Pilots are often asked the question, "When you're up there in an airplane, how do you get from one place to another and know where you are since there are no roads or turnpikes up there?" That is a very good question considering the story about the trip to Kansas.

Really, there are several methods that work good unless you get distracted by having to pee in a bottle or something like that. Radio navigation, flying the VOR's, ADF's, Lorans, and GPS's are used primarily. All kinds of new gadgets are now available to keep pilots from wandering out into space if they have the money to pay for them. Some do. Most don't.

Since I didn't at the time, my favorite system of flying myself from one point to another quite often caused many hard nosed instrument pilots to squirm uncontrollably, but you see, my Cessna 120 didn't have all those whistles and bells on it so if it's not severe clear or almost so, I just didn't fly. Granted, I didn't get to fly lots of days, but at least I got another day down the line to do it in and didn't get myself smashed like a bug on one of those rocks in the sky.

I like to fly by "Dead Reckoning" and "Pilotage". Some say that means if you reckon wrong you get dead lost, but I don't think I get as lost as a died in the wool instrument pilot would if he lost his electrical system and all the instruments go belly up and blank and he can't remember how to fly by looking outside the airplane. Some of those guys don't even carry a chart, just a set of approach plates. Most of us VFR (If we can see, we go) pilots can't find our butt with both hands with a set of those.

I've had some passengers stare at me in disbelief when I take off and say, "Well, lessee, Pauls Valley is (or wherever) thataway, so we'll go east and skim Lawton, go by the sewer lagoons, then point towards the three little lakes north of Duncan. Pauls Valley is just the other side of Interstate 35." Or if I'm going to Oklahoma City I point more north than east at the sewer lagoons and go until I hit the turnpike, follow it to Chickasha and then you can see Oklahoma City pretty good from there. If I happen to wind up over something I'm not familiar with, it's nice to see some different country anyway.

Yes, I use a sectional chart, sometimes a road map, sometimes even find out what town I'm over by reading the water tower, grain elevator, or even a road sign, but I do get where I'm going the first try most of the time and have a ball doing it.

I had a friend tell me one day about a trip he and his wife made to a place down deep in Texas. They were flying along relying on their newly acquired LORAN, an expensive, hi-tech, piece of navigation gear at that time that told him where to go and how to get there until his wife noticed a red light flashing on the thing. That meant only one thing, that it was not working properly and all of a sudden he realized he did not know where they were. Worse, he didn't know where anybody else was. He did do the smart thing though, even though embarrassing, he landed at the first airport they saw and asked the question, "Oh Uh, Do you know where this is and where I am?"

No exception, anybody who has ever flown an airplane anywhere has found themselves at one time or the other temporally spatially disoriented which means "lost". If they tell you different, they lie. A pilot will not, I repeat, will not, admit to flying somewhere only to find when he got there he was not where he thought he was if he can help it. Especially if his wife is with him.

I always prided myself on the ability to find my way across country with nothing except a chart and a line drawn on it. After all, that's the way George taught me, but I too have found myself "spatially disoriented", spatially being somewhere within a two state area. I always was able to find everyone else eventually.

Whenever you do get disoriented and don't know at the moment where you are, it's tough to find out unless you know a few tricks. Some airports do have the decency to paint their name on the parking ramp or on top of a building in large letters readable from a half mile up, but many airports don't do that, as we've already talked about. Some airports don't even keep a local newspaper laying around so a pilot can slip in and take a peek to see where he is without having to ask. Telephone books are becoming useless because they now list every town within a 50 mile radius.

One time I flew a fellow to Springlake, Texas. Now, I had never heard of Springlake, Texas, much less know where it was supposed to be, but come to find out, it was one of those many little places in West Texas that all look alike, a little bitty community surrounded by a whole bunch of dirt. First thing I did was check the chart to see how big the airport was. Sure enough, no airport was listed. "Thass alright", sed the fellow, "There's a nice little landing strip right behind this guy's house, lined with cedar trees, and real easy to see, and even paved." The guy used to be Speaker of the House of Representatives for the State of Texas, so it's a good'un. "You sure?" "Oh yeah, no problem!" Uh-huh.

We had a real nice flight from Altus, Oklahoma to Plainview, talking, eating Fig Newton cookies and drinking Diet Dr. Pepper. I then took the highway going northwest of Plainview following the waving arms and pointing finger of my passenger as he directed us to our destination. The only problem was though when we got where he was pointing, Springlake wasn't. Another place was and it didn't have an airport.

Well, if we were not where we thought we were, where were we? It is always the pilot's responsibility to know such things, but in this case my passenger had been so sure I let him navigate and I didn't know a whole lot more than he did. I dropped down to circle where we were for some clue and was tickled to death to see that someone had painted the word "DIMMIT" in large letters on the grain elevator … both sides in fact. Salvation was near. According to the chart, Spring-lake was about 15 miles due south. After a short flight thataway, I found it and the little asphalt strip was indeed there along side the cedar trees. A Frito Lay corn processing plant and a half dozen houses was all there was of Springlake, Texas. I plopped the big Cessna down, my friend did his business, and then I found our way back home. I made my friend keep his hands in his lap.

I not only read grain elevators, but water towers, billboards, and road signs. As a last resort I would land at the nearest airport and ask, but only in an emergency. Having to face the folks that would always tell you, but do so with a silly grin on their faces is just too much.

I had often poked fun at the inability of some pilots to fly without the aid of the high-tech stuff and to be perfectly honest I put off buying one of those new gadgets called a GPS as long as I could stand it because I thought it would ruin my skills as a grassroots pilot. Up to that time I also thought all I could afford was a $7.35 Sectional Chart and only bought one of those every couple of years or so or until it fell apart, whichever came first.

When the day came though that I finally yielded to the temptation of elec-tronic wizardry and wonder and purchased one of those little gadgets I found out that I liked it. The only reason I gave up was a couple of days before I left for Oshkosh, Wisconsin in 1994, Brother Keith loaned me one of the very first man-ufactured GPS's made by Magellan just in case I got disoriented. It was not all that reliable since there were not that many satellites then and even though it didn't work all that great on the trip and was big as a shoebox, I saw the possibilities and got the fever for one of the new models that came on the market a year or so later.

I paid big dollars and bought a Garmin 90 GPS (Global Positioning System), a neat little package no bigger than the smallest cellular telephone (at that time) that was so smart it could tell me not only where I was, but how to get where I was going, how fast I was going, and what time I would get there. It would also tell me how to get somewhere else if I decided I didn't want to go where I thought I wanted to go in the first place. And it would do it while I was flying!

It also had a little bitty map with a little bitty airplane that moved as I did on a 2" x 3" screen, and all the time it gathered its smart stuff from three to eight satellites circling the earth.

Since I really drove more than I flew, I often tried to take it with me in the car, but it drove wife Nancy nuts when I would tell her we were off course. It also began to beep to warn me that we were in a special area like Class C airspace and I couldn't hear it, but Nancy could. I didn't get to take it too much when she was with me.

AIRPORT MANAGER

The summer of 1984, Lloyd Howard bought an Aerial Spraying business in Frederick, Oklahoma and moved his business there from Tipton. I then had to travel to Frederick for my free cup of coffee. It was on one of those visits that Lloyd told me I should apply for the weekend attendant's job at the airport. That was in August, my cotton crop was "laid by", and all I had to do on the farm was sow wheat sometime in October and look after the cattle so getting paid for hanging out at an airport didn't seem like a bad idea.

I talked to Beverly Akin, the Frederick Airport Superintendent, and she said all I would have to do was be there all day on Saturdays and then Sunday afternoons from 1:00 till 4:00. I would get paid for actually doing nothing since there was very little aviation traffic and only a couple hundred gallons of fuel sold each month. "But", she said, "You need to go talk to City Manager Charles Martin for final approval". I went by City Hall on the way home, Charles hired me on the spot, and I became an instant airport employee!

It was a neat job. I could fly to work when the weather was nice and when the weather was bad I would watch television, drink coffee, and walk down the ramp a couple of blocks and talk to Lloyd. I worked weekends and holidays for several months, and really was having a good time. That winter Beverly decided we needed to paint the inside walls of the terminal building so I had to help do that in addition to sweeping the floor and other airport stuff, but soon we were back to the routine of not doing much.

In March of 1985 Beverly told me she was getting a divorce from her husband, was going to quit as manager, and was going to move back to Durant and that I should apply for her job as airport superintendent.

That was kind of a scary thought, but the farming business wasn't all that profitable, so after a lot of talking, evaluating, and praying, I asked Charles about the job. He said there were other applications but I would be considered. I guess I won because on May 1, 1985 I was hired as Superintendent of the airport. I had no idea at that time how long I would be there nor what opportunities would open as a result of that decision. It turned out to be a life altering decision.

The airport at Frederick was and still is a unique place. It was built soon after the beginning of the big war (WWII) in 1942 and covers 1442 acres, 150 acres of that paved in concrete. It was a multi-engine training base from 1942 until early 1945 and young Army Air Corps cadets were sent there for the sole purpose of learning how to fly an airplane with more than one engine attached to it. The Cessna UC-78, or "Bobcat" as it was sometimes called, was used mostly, however there was a class or two where the B-25 bomber was utilized. One B-29 Superfortress was known to have landed there as well but not for training.

The airport was built with five active runways. The main runway was 6000 feet long by 150 feet wide. Two other crosswind runways were 6000 feet by 150 feet, a third was 3180 feet by 60 feet and the fourth one was 4500 feet by 150 feet. Today, only the 6000 feet by 150 feet and two cross winds are active. Those are still useful when the winds exceed what is called the crosswind component of an airplane (or the gut level of a pilot) and a pilot can land safely into the wind rather than have to set the airplane down sideways. Many a grateful pilot has come into Frederick and landed on one of those runways when they could not land anywhere else.

Over 7000 pilots trained there during the war including a popular comedian of the 50's and 60's, George Gobel. Story is that George used to sit on the street curb in front of the local Cresent Drug Store and tell stories to anyone who would listen to him. He and his stories eventually wound up on television and occasionally were told on the old Johnny Carson Tonight Show. He said Frederick, Oklahoma was never bombed by the Japanese because he was there.

When the war was over the U. S. Government sent everybody home, closed the base almost immediately, and deeded the whole place to the City of Frederick. All the buildings, the 150 acres of concrete ramp and runways, including all the growing grass and weeds. Frederick Army Air Field had served its purpose.

The local pilots cautiously brought their little Cessna 140's, Champs, Taylorcrafts, and Cubs out there, hangared them all in one big hangar, and didn't even use the runways to take off and land because the apron was a 70 acre slab of concrete. They just opened the hangar door, fired their airplane up, and took off in whatever direction the wind was from on the apron. The city and county folks began holding the county fair out there too. It became a popular place and from about 1950 to 1970, the county fair, the local pilots, and a couple of spray pilots were the only folks there. In the early 60's, N. O. Brantly designed and began manufacturing the first Brantly Helicopters in one of the large hangars. Other than that, it was a pretty quiet place.

When I took over as airport manager, all but a few of the original buildings had been given away, sold, or torn down, but the concrete and weeds were still intact. A couple of large hangars were still there as well as tons and tons of concrete foundations, concrete chunks, and piers scattered all over the place. Some of my duties were to keep the grass and weeds from growing in all those cracks in the concrete and keep the other 1200 acres or so presentable. It was a heckava job even with about half of the 1242 acres being farmed in wheat and cotton.

I pumped airplane gas, swept hangars, made coffee, and fed the cat. When word got out that there was a new airport manager in town, folks from surrounding towns started flying in to see what I looked like and see if I was a friendly sort or one of the cranky ones. Most all the people who flew in were "just plane folks". They were folks who loved airplanes, men and women alike, who loved to fly for the sake of flying, loved the way an airplane looked, smelled, felt, and like to go up just to be able to look down. One old pilot in his 80's told me it was as though someone had shot a whole bunch of little tiny airplanes in his bloodstream one time and it was like a disease.

I tried to make everyone feel welcome and provide them a friendly place to fly to. Most folks liked what they saw and our business grew. A whole gaggle of flyers from across the border in Texas began coming over on weekends, especially when they found out I sold gas cheaper than anyone else around. Another group of flyers from Lawton, about 50 miles away, started coming over to visit, drink a coke, eat some Snickers, popcorn, peanut butter and crackers, and of course buy the cheap gas. If they were really hungry I would loan them the airport van and send them into town for some barbeque or a hamburger. The local Chamber of Commerce even adopted the slogan "The way is up and the sky's the limit". I always liked to think it was for our benefit.

One time the front page of "The Daily Oklahoman" reported that jillions of pounds of explosives, munitions, and weapons left over from World War II might be buried in over 200 ex-army installations in the United States, one of which was Frederick Army Air Field (Frederick Municipal Airport).

The news startled a bunch of local folks and got a whole lot of people excited, including me, especially when I started receiving telephone calls from folks wanting to know what I was going to do about it. I got a call from a very nice young lady from a radio station far, far, away telling me since I was sitting on a powder keg and I should start doing something, just anything, like go into a panic or something, and dig all those bombs up.

Of course, I denied any knowledge of such a thing since that is the accepted thing to do when you have no idea of what is being talked about or what you are being accused of and I explained that in my opinion it was very unlikely anything presenting any danger was buried at the base since it was only an advanced multi-engine training base and not a launching pad for bombing runs. After all, if anything was there it has been there for forty five years already and nothing had been blown up yet.

Things quietened down a bit after a few days, nothing got blown up, the newspapers forgot about it, and I was assured by our local Emergency Management Director that he would come pick me up and scatter my ashes if my world did come to an end. He wouldn't agree to dig up the concrete foundations though.

I later wished I had said "Yes", that there was indeed something evil lurking under each one of the abandoned concrete foundations and maybe someone would have come out, dug all of them up and hauled off that concrete.

◆   ◆   ◆

We did some fun things at Frederick Municipal during the years I was Manager. In addition to the annual Frederick Army Airfield Reunions and Fly-In's, we had things like we used to do at Tipton like trying to drop a flour sack in a barrel and the familiar balloon bustin' contests. Even had the hamburger cook outs and a pancake breakfast or two. KSWO-TV from Lawton even came over and gave us video coverage on the 10:00 p.m. news.

Nine airplanes and their pilots left Lawton Airport one Saturday morning bound for Altus where they did a spot landing, then flew to Frederick for a precision landing, then on to Walters for a short field landing, then back to Lawton. It was a contest cooked up as part of the Lawton Airport Appreciation Day activities. The pilots had to figure their fuel burn for the trip, estimate their time in route, and make their landings as good as possible to make points. The more points they got was worth the effort since the prize was $1000. Not bad for a couple hours of fun.

I judged the landings at Frederick and everyone did a fine job except one Bonanza pilot got so involved in flying the pattern just right, making his approach just right, managing his power, attitude and altitude to perfection, that he forgot to lower his landing gear. I had a handheld radio and had to tell him to "Check gear down NOW" just before he embarrassed himself completely. He almost got his picture in the Sunday newspaper. He owes me a steak dinner too. He also lost the race.

The crosswind runways at Frederick, even though not considered as very important by the FAA folks at Ft. Worth, were often used when the wind got up above 25 mph straight out of the east or west. Charles Shelton, a local spray pilot used one of those runways one morning when the winds did just that. The 25 mph with gusts to 37 mph came and were straight out of the east. Charles was out spraying alfalfa fields, got through, and tried to land his Pawnee at his private strip which is a 17/35 (south/north to you ground-bounders), ran out of rudder and aileron, and the Pawnee was still sideways to the runway. You can't (or not supposed to) land an airplane that way.

Charles remembered all that concrete at Frederick and was tickled to death to have a place to land into the wind. He came in after landing, got a cup of airport coffee, and took a rest on the ugly soft couch. After seeing that the wind was not going to lay for awhile, he left and came back later in the day and flew the Pawnee back home when the winds had died down a bit. If those "unnecessary" runways had not been there, Charles would have been in a heck of a mess.

One day a cute little lady identifying herself as "Carole" from the Army Corps of Engineers arrived at the airport and said she was there to seek out and list for possible destruction all hazardous things that may have been left at Frederick after World War II was over. I figured this probably was a spin off from the buried bomb scare and agreed to help her find whatever it was she was looking for.

Since Frederick Municipal Airport used to be Frederick Army Air Field and was definitely a military base during the war we qualified and Carole and I began looking around. All the old underground gasoline tanks had already been removed so the only things we could find that might be a hazard were the old WWII water tower and two concrete water valve pits that were over eight feet deep and had water standing in them. I said, "Very good, when do you start?" She said, "Well, we don't have any money right now, we're just making the list (and checking it twice), and maybe someday we'll get the money to do something with this stuff."

Sure, big deal, some day get money from the Government. Fat chance. Carole drove off in her government car and I forgot all about the deal, but then about six months later cute Carole showed up again and said, "We got money!" Then she left again and didn't come back again for a long time.

I forgot about the whole thing again and then about a year and a half later here cute Carole showed up again and said for sure they were going to come to Frederick and blow the water tower all up (or down) and bury the water pits the next March. March came … no blow. April came, lots of telephone call promises, but still no dynamite. A telephone call did come that said May was positively sure. May came. Not even a pop.

Then a bunch of guys came and after several weeks of looking, measuring, digging, and doing, they got their act together. From all the planning you would have thought they were going to blow up the Empire State Building.

Finally on June 18, a crew arrived and started digging around the base of the water tower. They bored holes in the base for the dynamite and put up a red and white plastic fence several hundred yards around the tower. Two days later on June 20 at 3:11 p.m. guards were posted all along the fence and someone yelled over a megaphone, "Fire in the hole!" The expected "Whoom" didn't happen. Instead a couple of muffled pops and the old water tower fell lazily over on a stake. "All poop and no blow." All it did was go "Whump!" and fell over. The people lined up against the barriers several hundred yards away from the tower just shrugged their shoulders. Cars from downtown lined the roads and the local citizens who thought they were going to see a major explosion with lots of dirt and concrete flying around just said, "Awwwww.... nuts" The only danger I could see happening was someone was going to get a sunburn waiting for them to blow up, or in, or down, or off. The whole ordeal took about six seconds. It reminded me of the time Geraldo Rivera had a hiped up TV special when he opened Al Capone's vault in the basement of some hotel in Chicago and there wasn't anything in it except a couple of beer bottles.

After the old water tower was gone a lot of local folks got upset then because it was gone. They asked why didn't we leave it for historical sake and posterity? Well, it was dangerous, had begun to lean a bit, and until the steel ladder leading to the top was cut off about 15 feet off the ground and the door was welded shut, it was an invitation to everyone who might want to explore it. I know that to be a fact. I tried it.

Back in the early 1950's when one of the Tillman County Fairs was being held at the airport, Cuzzin H. L. and I decided to climb that thing. H. L. was always more daring than me. He's been to Africa seven times since then stalking lions and flowers and has even been thrown out of two African countries and almost got shot by Edi Imin. H. L. climbed about half way up that tower, turned a little green, and came back down, saying "Wuddn' nothin' to see up there anyhow".

I climbed about ten foot off the ground, got scared, quickly descended, and said not "NO, but Heck No" and we both went back to the County Fair trying to figure out how to brag about what we did not do. No telling how many kids like us tried that tower on for size over years.

After it fell it laid out there for a week or so and looked like a beached whale until a track hoe that looked like a steel dinosaur looking thing started eating it and spitting out the re-bar.

The old tower's absence was very conspicuous. I couldn't help but look where it had been every morning when I came to work. It did change the landscape and skyline of the area, but after a week or so everyone forgot about it.

I was manager of Frederick Airport for almost 15 years. It was fun. But, in 1999 I was offered a job with the Oklahoma Aeronautics and Space Commission and it was time to move on to lots better stuff. I was getting tired of spraying the weeds in the cracks and mowing the grass. Now I could tell somebody else, "You uh, better get the grass outta those cracks!"

STUDENTS

One thing missing at Frederick Airport all the years I worked there was a certified flight instructor, so when an old, crotchety friend from Quanah, Texas came up with the idea of sending one of his CFI's (Certified Flight Instructor) he had imported from Tennessee to Frederick one day a week to give lessons to anyone who might be interested, I jumped at the opportunity and said "Yes"!

Len Miller was almost 80 years old at that time. He's over 90 now, still flying, still instructing, and still cussing. He has mellowed somewhat over the years, but he used to be one of the most foul-mouthed individuals I think I ever knew. He really is good at heart, just loud and crude.

Len had a contact with a flight school in Bolivar, Tennessee. The school was popular with foreign students because they could come over from Europe and get their ratings much cheaper than in their own country. Whenever the school would graduate a brand new, young, low time, instructor Len would hire them to come instruct for him. He let them build time so they could go on to bigger and better things, folks got flight instruction and it helped Len out as well.

Over a period of time Len sent about four different young men to Frederick in either a Piper Warrior or a Cessna Skyhawk every Thursday and it wasn't too long that we had a half dozen folks taking lessons. It was fun to see the grins, excitement, and the nervousness that Rexie Stalls, Fred Stevens, Jim Jon Carr, Gary Gray, Steve Hoover, Larry Cox, and Donnie Coleman generated each week as they explored a little deeper into the wonderful world of flying.

Rexie took the same lesson over and over again for months because he couldn't fly often enough to remember what he learned the last time, but when he did get it together enough to realize it was about time for him to solo, it scared him so much he quit again and didn't come back for a couple of months. When the day did come that Peter Bramer, a young instructor from England, told Rexie in that smart British accent to let him out of that Cessna 172 and go do it himself, Rexie almost wet his pants.

Rexie said he immediately broke into an intense sweat the moment Peter got out of the airplane. He then started praying as visions of his wife and children flashed before his eyes, but he knew there no return, no looking back now. He was committed, especially when he pushed the throttle forward and flew off into the sky.

He said that three minute trip around the airport ranked right up there with the feelings he got when he got married, when he saw his kids being born, and when the Lord saved his soul, but he made it. He took off and landed three times and every one was a squeaker. No bounce, no ripple, every landing was one to brag about. His shirt tail was displayed with pride because anyone who solos an airplane has their shirt tail cut off with anything handy such as scissors, pocket knife, or hatchet. It is properly labeled with the name of the pilot, the date of the levitation, the airplane "N" number, the instructor's name, and is nailed on the wall. That's just tradition and the way it's done.

It took nearly three years for Rexie to finally get his license. I honestly didn't know whether he was ever going to pull it off or not, but persistence paid off one Sunday afternoon in October when the examiner at Wichita Falls, Texas handed him his private ticket. He went through a grueling three hour check ride and when Rexie returned to Frederick he looked like he had been rode and put up wet, but the grin on his face told the story even before he said a word.

Gary Gray was a little more confident when he was learning. I saw the airplane land the day he soloed and a whole bunch of arm waving was going on inside the cockpit as it taxied to a stop. Peter got out and then Gary also joined that special group of folks who have flown an airplane all by themselves. He also made some beautiful landings in front of a whole bunch of spectators. I picked up Peter in the pickup after he got out of the airplane and we followed Gary back to the terminal building. His first words were, "Heck, this thing flies a whole lot better with HIM outta here", as he nodded at Peter. To this day, I don't think Gary has his license. He's flown a lot of hours and even recently bought a Piper Comanche, but just doesn't have the time to finish up.

Fred never would fly by himself. He and Peter just kept going in little circles around the airport trying to perfect his landings. He never did want to venture more than two miles away from the airport either. He just liked being up, but not too far away. He loved to ride with anybody who would let him in an airplane, but just lacked the confidence it took to do it himself.

Besides Peter from England, Per Pfingst (a real name) came over from Germany, Atle Severinsen was from Norway, Russell Janzen from New Jersey (almost a foreign country), and Thierry Moreau hailed from France. None of them stayed very long, just long enough for us to get to know them. They all did a pretty good job of teaching. Len would cuss them all out at one time or the other, especially Atle. Len let Atle fly a little Stinson taildragger back to Quanah one day and Atle ground-looped it and tore the landing gear off. Atle went back to Norway shortly after that, after he received the customary cussing. But, the real goal of all these young men was to become big-time jet pilots flying people or cargo and Quanah, Texas and Frederick, Oklahoma were just stepping stones to greater things. The last time we heard from Atle, he and his dad were sitting in a boat on the shore of the North Sea drinking beer.

Steve Hoover's instructor, Russell Janzen did the unheard of in aviation circles and actually ASKED Steve if he wanted to solo one day. Steve of course, being of sound mind and gripped suddenly with a great deal of fear naturally said "HELL NO". Nobody in their right mind is going to volunteer to do something like that, they've got to be volunteered. Kind of like being asked if you want to saw your leg off. Most students have to be pushed, shoved, intimidated, or whatever, you have to be made to do it. Occasionally someone will volunteer to solo, but they should never be given a choice. Russell should have said, "I don't wanna ride with you anymore today, you can do it, so go do three touch and goes and don't tear the airplane up". "By the way, good luck", and "Oh, what's your wife's telephone number just in case?"

They actually made an appointment for Steve to solo. Set it up for the next day at whatever o'clock. Well, it rained that night and the next two weeks it rained, there were 37 mph east winds, low clouds, 35 mph west winds, and 210 mph north or south winds. Steve had also been truckin' so the "scheduled" solo did not take place until one Sunday morning several weeks later. It was a miracle that Steve even came back to the airport. It probably never left his mind that he was going to have to guide 1500 pounds of machinery off the ground all by himself, hold it up in the air for awhile, and then get it back on the ground three times without bending it or himself.

Anyway, early that Sunday morning Russell got out of the Cherokee and Steve took to the skies all by himself like the proverbial homesick angel. When he got down his shirt was so wet with sweat the scissors would barely cut the shirt tail off. Another success story.

It was a lot of fun to see the enthusiasm of all the student guys as they tackled the task of learning to fly an airplane. Their statements of, "I do just fine until it comes time to land and then it all goes to pot" and, "I don't think I will ever catch on to it" sounded so familiar.

FLYING POT-PORRY

A west coast publication called "The Pacific Flyer" arrived at my office one day. On the cover was a color picture of a yellow Piper J-3 Cub and two boys. The story inside told of a couple of teenaged boys who had left Soma, California on a July 18 morning with twelve gallons of gas, a fist full of charts, two sleeping bags, cameras, two changes of clothes, and $24.00 in cash.

The boys and that J-3 Cub took an 8000 mile meandering trip that included circling the Statue of Liberty in New York Harbor. They flew 119 hours, stopped 85 times (which meant they had to hand prop that Cub at least 185 times), went to Oshkosh, Niagara Falls, into Canada, and arrived back at their home in California several weeks later with their heads so full of stories and adventures that they will never stop talking about the trip.

Those two boys, Chris Price, age 17 and Josh Brownell, age 18, had chosen Frederick Airport as one of their stops on that magnificent trip and we didn't know it. They stopped in for fuel and food in late August on their way back home. We greeted them, gave them the usual tour of our facilities and loaned them the van to go get a burger. We recognized that they were a couple of adventuresome kids, but little did we realize that we would be reading about them a couple of months later in a national publication. When we saw the pictures of the Cub and Chris and Josh, and read the article, we knew those boys had to be important, but most of all we knew without a doubt they loved to fly.

There were always folks hanging around the airport and finding an excuse to fly around for some reason or the other. Of course the local students, Rexie, Donnie, Gary, or some of the others were always out boring holes in the sky with the Piper Warrior and the T-37 Military jets from Sheppard Air Force Base were always screaming in the pattern.

◆　　◆　　◆

Occasionally a big ole' Douglas DC-3 freight hauler would stop over for fuel on its way from El Paso to Ohio. It usually came in at midnight, but when it did arrive during the day that thing created quite a sight and people would see it come over town and then drive out to take a look. The sound of those Pratt and Whitney R-1250 600's was music to the ears. That particular dusty old DC-3 had seen much better days as far as being cosmetically pretty though, in fact it was bare bones inside, completely gutted for cargo and had only the two seats way up front for the two fellows flying it. There were lots of air holes scattered throughout the aircraft, but it served its purpose of hauling cargo very well. That airplane was probably built somewhere in early 1934 according to the 4 digit serial number I saw on its well worn data plate.

Cecil Whatley from Lawton would drop in occasionally while airing out his vintage Cessna 190, another classic from five decades ago. The 300 horse power "Shakey-Jake" engine was equally as soothing a sound as the 1250's were on the DC-3.

In contrast, John Cassidy and his folks would come whizzing in with his two pilot controlled Cessna Citation Jet, an airplane a generation away from the DC-3 and C-190. It was always a pretty airplane to see land and take off since its engines sounded entirely different from the engines on the T-37's that we had grown so accustomed to hearing. The "Tweet's sounded like dog whistles. The Citation sounded like a real airplane.

◆   ◆   ◆

Dog lovers who fly think an airplane is sorta like a good dog ... you like to have them around, they are awfully good companions, you can scratch them, pat them on the head, talk to them, wash them, tell them you love them, and as long as you treat them nice they will do all sorts of nice things for you. But, if you forget to feed them or don't take them to be mended when they feel bad, or mistreat them, they might turn on you and bite you on the butt.

Then one day something happens and you suddenly are without one (dog or airplane). An awful emptiness fills up the pit of your stomach. When you open the hangar door (or back door) and it (airplane or dog) is not there it hurts. It (he or she) is not around to pat on the nose and love anymore.

I can't help but think of a mighty fine black lab named "Poncho" who once lived with Jerry and Barbara Hostick, or an awfully good birddog named "Jill" who took Donnie Coleman hunting, or a faithful German Shorthair named "Molly" who was a faithful companion of Joe Grubbs. Their hearts hurt so bad when they lost them. Just like when they sold their airplanes.

◆   ◆   ◆

Ever watch anybody roll in and out of an airplane? I sure don't mean to make fun of anyone because of age or handicap, but "John" was a backseat passenger in a Comanche that flew into Frederick one day. I was walking out to the airplane to see if they needed gas as everyone started getting out and "John" leaned forward from the back seat, twirled 90 degrees, stuck his rump out the door, sat down on the wing, laid back onto the wing on his back, stuck both legs straight up in the air, did another 90 degree turn while on his back, lowered his legs, sat up and slipped slowly off the leading edge of the wing and planted his feet on the ground.

Never saw anything like that before. When he got ready to get back in the airplane an hour later he simply reversed the procedure and "bingo", he was again sitting in the back seat of the Comanche.

Now, "John' could walk just fine, but he was at that time 83 ½ years old and his benders and jointers were a little rusty and didn't work like they used to. He was a pilot from way, way back and still loved to fly and didn't mind going to a little extra trouble to do so when he could, thus the unusual exit/entry procedure.

If I ever reach 83 ½ years old, I probably will have to be hauled around in an airplane in a box, so I had nothing but great admiration for "John".

While visiting with "John" that day, he told the story about the time he propped a Culver Cadet and the throttle was a little too far forward. The Culver started rolling, he caught the wing tip by a built-in slot and the airplane started going in circles and he was the pivot point. After lots and lots of hollering, arm waving, and advice from some friends with good intentions standing well out of the way, "John" and the Culver got stopped, but only after it tipped itself up on its nose and smelled the dirt. That day ended early for both of them.

After "John", his buddy Clarence, and Charlie the pilot left in the Comanche I couldn't help but have a lot of admiration for my new found friend. Thank God for 83 ½ year old folks who still have the want-to to keep doing what they love to do and to friends who have the patience to help them keep doing it.

PRE-FLIGHTS

Before each flight in an airplane there should be a pre-flight inspection by the pilot. The purpose being to make sure the wings are still on the airplane and that the oil hasn't fallen out of the engine. The pre-flight should begin in the mind of the pilot who should be the first to determine if he or she is fit to fly in the first place even before the airplane is in sight. Once that is determined the pre-flight moves to the airplane.

The pilot is supposed to check the airplane all over to determine if it is airworthy. Airworthy means, "Is it fit to fly?" The hinges, holes, cracks, flaps, ailerons, elevators, rudder, trim tab, fuel tanks, oil level, and tire pressure, should all be checked or looked at to see if they are still there from the last flight and also to see if everything is working properly because once the airplane leaves the ground and then something is discovered missing, broken, or wrong, the pilot and passengers could be in a heap of trouble.

One pilot I know jumped in his airplane one day, took off for a short trip, and when he landed he discovered he had made the flight with a home-made aileron locking device still firmly bolted in place. He said he thought the controls felt a little heavy, especially in a turn.

I also watched a very busy man in a great big hurry return to the airport from doing some business downtown, hurry to his airplane, untie it, put himself and his briefcase inside, and fasten his seat belt. Then I could see the thought occur to him about the pre-flight, or lack of it. He unbuckled his belt, climbed out onto the wing, stood up and looked over the nose to see if the propeller was still attached, then peered to the rear to see if the tail was still there. Apparently satisfied that all the parts were still attached, he crawled back into his airplane, fired it up, and left.

I saw another fellow who went out to his airplane, untied the wing tie-downs, got in it, fired it up, rolled about two feet, and quickly came to a sudden stop. The tail was still firmly attached to the concrete with a rope.

A "fly for hire" pilot flew in one time in a Comanche 250 with a very important passenger (VIP), or so I was told. The pilot was a very smart pilot because he told me so several times, however after his very important passenger did his business in town and returned they got ready to leave. The pilot got in the Comanche, then his passenger got in, and they were ready to go.... almost. Problem was, the three tie down ropes anchoring the Comanche to the concrete ramp were still in place and were still securing the airplane firmly to the ramp. A buddy of mine was watching all this with me out of the front window of the terminal building. He said, "Aren't you gunna tell him?" I said, "Nope, that guy told me he was a smart pilot and how good he was all afternoon and he'll find out the airplane won't move soon enough." We couldn't see just how red his face was from where we were in the terminal building, but the eastern sky glowed a little brighter as he climbed over his passenger in the right seat, exited the Comanche, untied it, and crawled back over his passenger to get back in the airplane.

I always told anyone who was going to fly with me to go take a leak or something if they were in such a big hurry. While they were gone or figgeting somewhere, I pushed, prodded, dipped, poked, wiggled, and looked everywhere there was to look on the airplane. Then I could holler "Clear" and start the engine with no regrets.

SERIOUS LOOKING

I was often asked if I would go look for things that got lost and could be found much easier from the air. I have looked for cows, stolen cars, minnows, horses, flooded roads, storm damage, and people. Most times the trips did not present too much of sense of urgency, but the trips that made my heart beat faster and the fear that I might find what I was looking for were the ones I remember the most and hurt the worst.

Some of the searches were not bad, like the time I flew over a massive flooded area to check on a family that had been stranded by the swollen waters of a creek. As I flew over the farm house, which was totally surrounded by water, the lady of the house came out waving her dish towel at me indicating that they were alright in spite of being isolated for a week by flood waters.

Once I was asked to look for a family of four that were missing somewhere on North Fork Red River. They had started what was to be a simple five hour raft trip down the river only to find that the river was many miles longer with all the crooks, curves, bends, and double-backs. When they didn't arrive at their intended destination by sundown, relatives and friends got worried. The next morning arrived with still no word and things got serious, so I was asked to fly the river to see if I could find them.

I located them about an hour later, exhausted after having spent a very scary night on the river, lost with only bugs and coyotes for company and no food or water. When I dropped the Cessna 170 I owned then down low to confirm that it really was them the lump in my throat grew bigger when I saw the smiles and tears as they waved back at me. A couple of days later I ran across the lady in the local grocery store and got the biggest bear hug of thanks you ever saw.

Once I flew several hours looking for a twelve year old boy thought to be wandering lost somewhere on Big Red River only to learn later that he was in Austin, Texas with relatives all the time. His daddy and I flew for about four hours up and down, cross and across, with no results. Even though the kid had driven himself to Texas and our efforts were in vain that morning, I felt I had helped a little bit. The many "Thank Yous" I got from the worried parents helped confirm that.

Most pilots are more than happy to share their skills, abilities, and aircraft to help anyone who has a need. They work cheap too. A hug, a cup of coffee, or a simple thank you is plenty enough.

The saddest of all my searches began early one April morning when the telephone rang just before sun up. My friend Joe Grubbs was very solemn and to the point when he said, "Butch, Bill Walker is missing on Lake Tom Steed. The weather is so cloudy and foggy the Highway Patrol won't launch a boat or an airplane to go look for him. Would you fly your 170 while I look?" Joe went on to say that Bill and his fishing friend Russell Bates had gone fishing the afternoon before and something had happened to cause the boat to sink. They had already found Russell dead, but there was no sign of Bill.

I told Joe I would meet him at the airport in about twenty minutes. When I got out of bed, I looked out the window and saw fog, low hanging clouds, and the wind was blowing hard out of the west. It was not a good day to fly anywhere and I wondered if I could do it, but there was no hesitation to try.

As Joe and I taxied out in the Cessna 170 I could tell it was going to be a challenging ride. We leveled off at 500 feet above the ground and flew the twenty miles to the lake. Very little was said. Both of the men were good friends and our hearts were heavy as we feared what we might see. We were afraid we would find Bill and afraid we wouldn't. As we flew over the boat dock area we could see the empty boat trailer and a dozen or so people standing on the ramp. I told Joe that we probably should just fly around the lake and check the shore line first.

The winds remained high, the water was white-capping, and the ride was very bumpy. I struggled to keep the 170 level and straight and as we circled the lake the fog began moving in closer and the clouds got lower. I noticed when I made my turn on the west side of the lake I couldn't see the other side of the lake only a couple of miles away. I then decided to start flying across the lake at spaced intervals and then dropped down to 200 feet. We scanned every bush, tree, and shrub, hoping to see Bill clinging to one of them.

The third pass I spotted an orange dot about 300 yards off my left wing. As I turned the Cessna, I pointed the object out to Joe and we flew toward the dot. It was a safety vest. As we got closer our worst fears were confirmed and tears swelled up in our eyes as we saw the lifeless body of our friend Bill floating on his back about 75 feet from the shore line, his vest snagged on a bush.

I flew a tight circle around his body and called Altus Air Force Base on the aircraft radio and asked them to contact the Lake Patrol to send a boat over to our location. I continued to circle and watched as the patrol reluctantly crossed the white-capping lake and retrieved Bill. I realized then that the visibility had deteriorated even more and there was no question that it was time to get out of there and get back on the ground. Joe and I flew quietly back to the airport with tears in our eyes unable to really believe what we had just seen.

We never did find out for sure what really happened to Russell and Bill, only that they had been fishing in the channel on the north side of the lake when a squall came up. Apparently as they started back to the boat dock on the opposite side of the lake they hit something in the water which made the boat stop abruptly because Russell's face was bruised and his nose was broken. The back of Bill's head was badly bruised. The boat was never found.

In all my years as a pilot I never was known to take chances in an airplane. I never liked to fly when it was very windy and I didn't like to fly when I couldn't see where I was going, but that morning there seemed to be no question as to whether or not I should fly. Even though there were clouds and fog, even though the wind was howling, even though I sure didn't like what I was doing, I was still able to control the airplane and fly with confidence.

The waiting that Bill's family had to endure that horrible night was over. He was dead, but at least his family knew what had happened to him and did not have to wait several days to find out. There was no doubt in my mind that God had flown with Joe and I that April morning.

AIRPORT CATS

Almost every airport has a cat or dog lying around and since I was in charge, it was my choice to be a cat airport. When I began duties as manager of Frederick Airport in 1984 I was given a yellow teenaged tomcat named "Fred". Fred was a good cat, usually sat on my feet under the desk and kept me company like a cat should, but he liked to explore and wander too much. Fred didn't last very long. He tried to hitch a ride to town one day in the back of a pickup, fell off it, and got run over. Scratch one airport cat.

It wasn't too long after Fred's demise that "Kali" came to interview for the position. She was a little calico kitten, very likable, and pretty, but always wanted to poop and pee in the corner of my office. In those days however, there was not much airplane traffic and a lot fewer people who came out to the airport and Kali's personal hygiene didn't bother anyone much except me. As she grew older she realized the error of her ways, apologized, and began using the cat box I provided for her.

Kali was a constant and loving companion on those long days when the telephone didn't ring and there was no one else to talk to. She at least fixed it so there was someone else to breath air out there besides me. On days when I would be nursing a headache or upset stomach Kali would take notice and come lay in my lap in an obvious attempt to comfort me. I, in turn helped her hurt when the hair balls upset her stomach and she didn't feel good. Most of the time though she took care of herself.

Very few visitors to Frederick Airport were not touched in some way by Kali. Her bright orange, black, and white calico coat drew many comments of how pretty she was. She knew it too and always made sure that some of that coat was deposited on all the folks who dropped by before they left. Governors, business executives, and fancy hi-falootin' women were no exception. They as well as the shorts and blue jean crowd all left with some Kali hairs on them. She inspected the ladie's purses and invited herself to eat lunch with the folks who showed up with a sandwich or donut. And she wasn't particular who she ate with. She liked cake donuts best of all though.

She never left the terminal building area, even rarely went outside. She would sometimes hide just to test me to see if I cared enough to panic if I couldn't find her, but she always knew where she was and yes, I did often panic. At 4:55 each afternoon she would wake up from her nap, stretch, go get a bite or two to eat, get a drink of water, then go to her room (which was the store room) for the night. Daylight savings time confused her and when I would tell her it was quitting time she would fuss and grumble all the way making sure she rubbed some cat hairs on everything as she went.

Kali died August 11, 1991. I was on vacation in Tennessee the day she apparently had a heart attack as Evagean watched helplessly as she drew her last breath. Kali had friends from many states, Kentucky, Florida, New Mexico, Texas, Oklahoma, Arkansas, New York, and Connecticut just to name a few. Everyone helped us grieve when they came by on their next visit and asked, "Where's Kali?" and we had to tell them she was gone.

Some folks thought it was dumb to be so sad over the death of a pet, but others understood the feelings we had at that time. I missed the companionship, friendship, and love that Kali gave to me over the five years she was the official airport cat. Lots of other folks did too.

Fred Barbee was also a cat man. Fred was a good friend to the airport, contributed financially as well as any other way he could to the airport. He liked cats and three or four owned him at home. It was Fred who slipped one over on me after Kali died. I had been catless for several weeks and missed Kali very much. Many of the airport visitors thought that was great, but other folks still thought that an airport was just not an airport without a cat lying around. One morning Fred told me about a cat critter that just happened to show up at the Civil Air Patrol building a half mile down the apron he said it sure did need to be fed, watered, cared for, and hugged.

Evagean called her "Patches". I called her "McSwine", "Patch", "Trash", and "Usonofabitch", but whatever she was called, she took the job of new airport cat compliments of Fred. She looked like she was put together with parts of several other cats, but actually was really kind of cute and nice to have around. About the time we all got used to her though she too disappeared never to be seen again. We think she flew off to the East coast one day in a Beechcraft Twin Baron. As least she had class. Scratch another airport cat.

Chubaca really was also a good airport cat. He hauled in mice and rats by the carton and even an occasional rabbit. He loved to spend his spare time in lofty places such as the large hangar crawling through the channel iron, I-Beams, and steel girders, often 30 feet off the ground trying to grab a bird. He was named after the upright hairy creature on the "Star Wars" series because of a strong family resemblance. He was gun metal gray with very long hair and yellow eyes. When you talked to him he would stare at you with those big yellow eyes and go "RRROOOWWWRRR" like the guy in the movie.

Chubaca was very sloppy in that he never groomed himself, never took a bath, and when you rubbed him his fur was full of hair knots, sand burrs, and weeds. We had to take the scissors to him quite often just so he could turn his head. He was friendly, but when he wasn't hunting in the hangar he spent his time asleep on the couch and grumbled when anyone made him move.

But, Chubaca finally did one day what I figured he would do, but had been hoping he wouldn't. He disappeared one Monday evening and I suspect he too finally hitched a ride with someone in their airplane. Took the evening flight outta there, so to speak, and gone on to bigger and better airports. He had been trying to go somewhere for a long time because I caught him hiding in the baggage compartment of several airplanes and the back seat of the courtesy car several times. He finally got his ride. I thought for a long time he might make his way back home, but never did. He probably cleaned himself up and made a success at some larger airport.

"J. B." was rescued from the animal shelter a couple of months after Chubaca left. The local animal control warden had been looking for me a replacement and he came by one day with the information that he may have found just the right cat for the airport. I went to see, and when I approached the cage, this short haired female cat stuck her arm out, pushed her face up to the bars, and begged me to take her out of there.

She had been spayed, had all her shots, and even came with a cat carrier to boot, so she went across the airport property to become my last airport cat, because I left the airport before she did. J. B. was a cranky ole' cat. If anyone disturbed or perturbed her she would swat you with her claws or bite at you and take a chunk out. She especially didn't like kids. Kids were on her hit list. In fact, she hated kids. She really didn't like anybody very much but me and after the honeymoon was over I don't think she liked me just a whole lot. But, after I left Frederick and would go back to visit, J. B. would hear my voice and come running. She would get in my arms and bury her head in my hand wanting some lovin'. Kathy, the new manager, said she wouldn't let anybody do that to her except me. I liked her despite her disposition. She was a good cat.

J. B. performed her duties as airport cat for several years after I left Frederick, but also disappeared one day and apparently went to the cat heaven in the sky.

Donnie Coleman said, "I dunno where that bitch went, she just didn't show up one day." I think Donnie hit her in the head with a shoe.

AIRPLANE EATS HANGAR

Some pilots have got to have the same suicidal tendencies as armadillos and pheasants. They just seem to do stupid things quite naturally and wander out into the skies disregarding all warning signs and just dare something to happen to them. I have often watched as airplane drivers take off in the worst of weather conditions in an airplane that would not even pass an Oklahoma Motor vehicle inspection. Some I even suspected of having had a drink of something besides water, coffee, or coke, and wondered about their sanity as they climbed in their airplanes. Those I tried to discourage from flying, but most times to no use. Their stupidity began on the ground even before they got in the airplane.

I read in the newspaper one day about an airplane that got away from its owner at an airport up at Enid. It was a cold day and the guy was trying to hand prop the plane, alone, and forgot to make sure it would not go anywhere by itself if it did start. He didn't, it did, and it then traveled about 500 feet down a taxiway into a hangar. It ate the hangar, a Cadillac, then self-destructed itself, creating a total of about $250,000 damage. Ruined that guy's whole day.

A similar incident occurred one really bad cold day at Frederick. A plane load of folks flew a Cessna 210 in from Texas on one of those days you couldn't stand to stay outside even for a minute it was so cold. The folks unloaded and then went downtown to a funeral. I let them put the airplane in the hangar that was attached to the terminal building to keep it out of the 4 degree weather. They came back about eight hours later and while some of the folks were preparing to get in it (it was still in the hangar), the pilot decided to turn the triple bladed prop through to loosen the engine up. The engine suddenly coughed and spit and actually started when he moved the blade about two feet. The pilot jumped out of the way, but his brother had one leg in the right door attempting to get in and the brother's wife who had already got in the airplane was sitting bug-eyed in the back seat. The 210 began moving out the hangar as soon as it started.

The left wing hit the door frame of the hangar, the airplane got outside the hangar, but then spun 180 degrees back into the terminal building. It hit the outside wall, ate a window, and stopped before it came all the way into the terminal building though. The prop chewed big gashes in the metal wall, window, and door of the building before it choked down and died.

The impact literally exploded the window and the wall, blowing glass, wall insulation, and wood chips the entire 60 foot length of the interior terminal lounge area.

Kali, our airport cat, was asleep on the back of a chair when everything broke loose. When the dust settled and we got the folks taken care of, (the pilot was OK, but his brother had a broken collar bone and his wife was still bug eyed and shell-shocked), I started looking for Kali but couldn't find her anywhere. About 45 minutes later she came out of wherever it was she was hiding. Her calico coat had faded somewhat, her eyes were lots bigger, and until the day she died she always jumped when the door on the south end of the building slammed.

Lots of folks have said, "Ah Hah, we knew airplanes were dangerous!" Nuts! Ever count the number of driverless cars that run through parking lots into store windows? Makes no difference what a person is in control or out of control of things still happen, but it would help if they would be a little more careful. It would make for fewer nervous cats too.

ENJJPTP

In 1966 the Air Force made an agreement with the City of Frederick to use Frederick Municipal Airport as an auxiliary field for the Euro-Nato Joint Jet Pilot Training Program (ENJJPT). They agreed to let the general aviation folks continue to use the airport on a joint use deal, but they wanted to send instructors and students to do touch and goes in Cessna T-37 Jet trainers (affectionately called two-ton dog whistles). The instructors and students were NATO folks from 13 different European countries as well as the United States. The idea was to teach them how to fly a jet, then send them back home to fly the bigger, faster, and meaner jet fighters of their own countries. Hopefully they would assist us (the U.S.) someday if we ever needed them.

It sounded like a good deal since the Air Force said they would maintain the primary runway, but their traffic level reached something like 60,000 operations each year and the runway wore out faster. They built a nice modern fire station and kept a couple of green fire trucks out there capable of putting out aircraft and fuel fires. They also maintained a couple of runway surveillance units (RSU's) that communicated with the T-37s and advised civilian pilots of their whereabouts and landing advisories and such stuff.

Some of the local Frederick folks would get all upset when the Tweets (T-37s) disturbed their afternoon naps. That often happened when they used runway 35 and made their departures at full power over town.

Most times things went pretty well but there were a few incidences. The jets would sometimes misjudge their approaches and go "Whump" in the safety area off the end of the runway and dirt would fly as they would bounce and then catapult onto the runway.

One day a Tweet made a good approach, a good flare, but forgot one thing.... to lower the landing gear. The aircraft slid to a stop pretty quick and no one was hurt, but the young IP (Instructor Pilot) was devastated because that Air Force jet and his student were his responsibility. I drove up as the young Captain sunk to the ground with tears in his eyes and hung his head between his legs. Kind of hurt to see that. The last we heard he had been assigned to somewhere in northern Alaska.

Dr. Joe Horton was a long time member of the Frederick Airport Commission who had been on there by his own admission, "So long I can't remember when I wasn't". Doc got into the contract negotiations with the U. S. Government in 1985 because the government's 20 year lease with the City of Frederick was about to expire. Doc was there in 1966 when the first negotiations were made for $1.00 a year and he had been grumbling about that and getting madder each year for 20 years because he felt like the City got shafted, so when the lease came up for renewal he was ready for them.

The U. S. Government representatives showed up one day with contracts already prepared for another 20 years for another dollar and Doc bared his teeth, told them to go to hell and take their Tweety Birds with them. He ran them all off that day but a few weeks later he wound up butting heads with one of the toughest, crankiest, and hard-headedest government revenooers the U. S. of A. could find on their payroll. For eight months they fought, but Doc was successful and got a new contract for $15,000 each year and the Government had to maintain, repair, and overlay if necessary our primary runway in addition to having to pay for everything they set foot on while at the airport.

Doc Horton used to fly a real pretty red and white Bonanza only he never liked to fly alone. He often asked me if I could go with him on trips but I usually couldn't because I was supposed stay there and run the airport, but he always asked and I always said "Maybe someday".

I think he was just enough unsure of himself that flying alone made him nervous.

He bought a Beechcraft Baron one time and sold his Bonanza, but he could never get the hang of two engines going at the same time. Also, the Baron's seat didn't fit Doc's rear, so he sort of quit flying. Probably just as well, because everybody wondered if Doc could find his way back home each time he left anyhow.

One time he was able to fly me, the City Manager, and a City Councilman to Sheppard Air Force Base, and we did make it back, but he had two extra pilots and it was only a 20 minute trip. The Air Force had invited us on a VIP tour of the 80th Flying Training Wing, gave us a free ride in a T-37 jet, a free lunch at the officer's club and a piece of cake. This was about the time the lease negotiations were going on and they were trying to be nice to us. It made him nervous when they told him to taxi the Bonanza right up amongst the jets and park. The Bonanza did look sort of strange sitting in the middle of a whole nest of military T-37s and T-38s.

Doc was a good haggler, but not good enough to make off with the government flight suit, gloves, and boots the Air Force loaned us for the T-37 ride. He sure tried though, but all he got away with were the velcro stick-on patches that told who he was (Horton).

Anyway, back to ENJJPTP. The relationship between the Air Force and civilian pilots got very confusing at times. Since many of the instructor pilots, students, and even controllers were from Europe, language was a problem. Us Southwest Oklahoma Okies just couldn't understand broken German or Norwegian. Tempers would often flare whenever a jet would nearly run over a Cessna 172 or an Ag Truck would cut off a jet on final.

The biggest problem was that the Air Force would forget that Frederick Municipal Airport was not Frederick Air Force Base. I spent much of my time waving my arms and yelling in broken Europeaneze (Okie-pean) driving that point across. It was like driving a ten penny nail up their butt with a twelve pound sledge hammer. The problem remains today.

TURKEYS, DOVES, AND????

Southwest Oklahoma is noted for good hunting, particularly for turkey, dove, quail, and sandhill crane. Twice each year, a very well known group of important folks dressed in all the way from black suits and ties to the more casual attire would descend on Frederick in King Aires, Learjets, Citations, as well as Mooneys, Pipers, and Cessnas for the Oklahoma Lt. Governor's Grand Slam Turkey/Quail/Dove/Anything that would sit still, hunt. It was started by then Lt. Governor Robert Kerr and a couple of local bankers provided the overnight lodging, food, refreshments, and niceties as well as the scoped out hunting areas.

The hunters were rotated by airplane every twenty four hours over a three day period from Poteau, to Woodward, to Frederick, and then to Idabel. Camp was set up on North Fork Red River with local wheels Bill Crawford and Gib Gibson the hosts. Most of the dignitaries that flew in got off the airplanes carrying shotguns that probably had never been pointed at anything, much less a real live turkey, but everyone was treated royally and had a really good time.

Sometimes it would rain and then there weren't too many places for the terrified turkeys or doves to land and sit, much less a place for all those camouflaged hunters with shotguns to be in the dry. The hunters would then head for the "lodge" and begin working on the refreshments. The bug eyed pilots that flew all the dignitaries in would hang out at the airport and wait ... and wait ... and wait, and try to figure out someway to entertain themselves while they waited some more until their passengers returned from the river.

Now, these visitors were not just plain folks. They were somebodies. Folks such as "Stormin' Norman" Schwartzkopf, Ret. General John S. Crosby, Governor David Walters, J. C. Kennedy, Sen. Don Nickles, Mayor Ted Marley of Lawton, Rep. Jim Glover, Rep. Jim Maddox, Sen. Roy Hooper, Speaker of the Oklahoma House Lloyd Benson, and many others including the only woman I ever knew of that came in, Alice Walton, daughter of Sam Walton. (Walmart).

I always felt that had the airport not been there, the hunt could not have taken place because we provided them a landing place and pit stop between airplane and turkey. I had heard of airports like Addison at Dallas that provided miniskirted gas pumpers, but Evagean refused to wear anything like that, so we just tried harder to make everyone feel welcome whether they rode in the back of the airplane or flew the front.

Most of the hunters were inexperienced, so I always advised the local pilots not to fly over the hunting area at the river during this special hunt for in addition to the possibility of frantic, flying turkeys causing a mid-air collision, a dark colored airplane might look like a giant turkey to some of those guys, get shot down, and turn out to be the grand prize of the day.

I always liked to walk around and see the high dollar aircraft that had flown in. Cessna Citations, Gulfstreams, Hawkers, Cheyennes, and even some of those I called rice burners or blowtorches, Mitsubishis would grace our parking ramp.

One morning when I came to work a Bell Jet Ranger was sitting on the ramp, but since stranger things than that had greeted me on occasion, I thought little of it. Later in the day a couple of pickups drove up and lots of camouflaged folks piled out, including Governor David Walters and a whole bunch of shotguns, but no turkeys. Seems as though the gobblers had sense enough to send the hens to the front lines so even the Governor came up empty handed. There wasn't much room for dead turkeys in the helicopter anyhow.

In addition to the many out of towners that participated in the turkey chase some of the local folks who were somebodies were also invited to try their luck at the hunt. They didn't get to fly in though. Had to drive their Cadillacs out to the river.

The day that Alice Walton from Lowell, Arkansas came in was interesting. As far as I know, Alice was the first female woman turkey hunter to ever be invited to the hunt. When her very large airplane landed and she emerged wearing camouflaged hunting britches and jacket and holding a Bud Light beer in one hand and a shotgun in the other she sure caught the attention of the guys hanging around. She actually shot herself a turkey the next day and was grinning from ear to ear when she arrived back at the airport. No one else shot one because all the men were standing around watching Alice. She also won first prize for being champion midget Tootsie Roll eater within a 30 minute time frame. I had a gallon bucket of the little candies out and Alice couldn't resist eating a double handful. She also filled her pockets before she left. She also was the only person to ever get by with drinking a beer at the airport. I wasn't about to tell her it wasn't legal. After all, SHE was Alice Walton!

◆   ◆   ◆

Doesn't have anything to do with the bank hunting bash, but a Beechcraft Baron landed early one cold November morning and four hunters and a couple of dogs piled out. A Chevy Suburban met them, loaded everybody up, and they all disappeared until about four o'clock that afternoon. The Suburban returned, everyone got out, and unloaded a couple sacks of birds. It seems as though they had come to Tillman County from somewhere in Texas to hunt quail and announced it was a good day and they had all shot their limit. They were just simply tickled to death.

When they emptied their sacks out on the floor of the hangar and proceed to dress their kill, I noticed that all the birds had a splash of yellow in the feathers on their breast. They were all Field Meadow Larks. Not a single quail in the bunch. I didn't say a word.

MAAG

In February of 1984, just a couple of months before I took over as manager of Frederick Airport, "Col. Tom Thomas, Retired." arrived in Frederick with a sales pitch to end all sales pitches. He was a very rich man who liked himself, publicity, and airplanes. He had collected some 65 airplanes, all shapes, sizes, and engine numbers. They ranged all the way from a Model A Ford powered Pietenpol to a Douglas C-47 and a B-25 Bomber thrown in for good measure. It really was an impressive bunch of airplanes, especially for one man to own.

Thomas was a retired WWII Army Air Corps pilot and had never been able to get rid of the ego trip of being a Colonel, so he formed his own air force and called it the "Mid-America Air Group", MAAG for short. He found another guy just like himself named Dick Milan to help him gather up troops and the two of them started recruiting members. The pitch was that you joined MAAG, paid $50.00 dues, bought your own uniform which Tom designed, got checked out in one his airplanes, and then you could fly that airplane anytime you wanted to around locally as long as you also flew it when and where HE told you to, such as to air shows, wiener roasts, fly-ins, celebrations, etc.. The catch was that he or Milan could come get your airplane anytime they wanted to, which they did quite often especially after they found out you had repaired it, cleaned it, and got it airworthy. Another catch was that if it broke or needed an engine overhaul while you had it in your possession, you had to fix it at your own expense.

The idea worked pretty good for awhile, but as time went on, Thomas and the City of Frederick and the "MAAG leaders" started getting on each others nerves. After awhile, it became all out war, and "law suit" became a common phrase.

Thomas was always flying into Frederick smelling like a brewery. One afternoon he landed a T-18 Thorp so hard he drove the left landing gear up through the wing, and then went and hid the airplane in a hangar without telling anyone. Often he would fly in and have to have help getting out of the airplane because he was drunk.

He cooked up a big air show at Frederick on June 1, 1985, one to compare with the Confederate Air Force whing-ding in Texas. Lots of folks came out and paid $5.00 to see it. In addition to that though, his birthday was the day before, so to celebrate he started flying about 6:00 a.m. that morning and flew all of his 65 airplanes by 4:30 that afternoon. He called it his "Last Hurrah". It really was quite an accomplishment, however he wasn't in each airplane over 5 minutes.

Thomas' organization really was a great opportunity to get to fly some neat airplanes. There were only three of us at Frederick that could fly taildraggers and I was one of those chosen to fly some of his. I got to fly a Taylorcraft L-2, Aeronca L-3, Piper L-4, a Luscombe T8F and a 1939 Porterfield quite often. We took them to several fly-ins and special events around the area and had a heck of a good time. Most of the time I flew the L-4 because the other guys didn't like to fly from the back seat.

But, one by one, everybody got unhappy or got cussed out by Milan or Thomas and eventually dropped out, told them to go to hell, and quit. A year or so later Thomas struck a deal with the folks at Liberal, Kansas and took all his airplanes to be pickled and entombed in the Liberal Aircraft Museum. When he started moving them, several of them went down along the route and there were airplanes scattered all the way from Frederick to Liberal because of engine failures. One recruited pilot flew a J-3 Cub to Woodward, landed it, and called Thomas to tell him it was a pile of junk fixing to come apart and he was going to leave the airplane there. He caught a ride home.

Thomas died a few years later after getting to command his own air force for awhile all right, but he sure didn't make many friends during the process. His biggest contribution was to help form one of the best aircraft museums in the Midwest up at Liberal. I would certainly recommend spending a day going through it. A bunch of us went up to see it after it was put together, but it was sad to see the airplanes I once flew hanging from the ceiling and pickled, probably never to fly again.

AINT SIS

I just cannot talk about Frederick Airport without remembering Evagean Tucker, or "Moma Maag" as she was affectionately called by those in the Mid America Air Group. I found out several years later a few guys in the group referred to her as the "MAAG Hag", which surprised me because everyone seemed to really like her at the time.

When I began duties as Superintendent of the airport I had no one to help me mind the store. It was just me and me alone. To tell the truth, I didn't really need any help at first because hardly anybody came to the airport and I sold very little fuel. But when Tom Thomas brought the Mid-America Air Group to Frederick within thirty days after I began work as manager, we had that air show and business picked up considerably. Folks began flying in quite often after that. Then, I really needed some help.

My Aunt and Uncle, Evagean and G. W.Tucker, were semi-retired and agreed to help me during the airshow and then on weekends after that until I found someone permanent. G. W. had served in the Pacific in WWII, loved airplanes, especially war birds, so they agreed to work at the airport on Saturdays and Sundays just like I had done when I first started. They visited with folks and pumped a little gas. They didn't even have to sweep the floor. Evagean got hired for money and G. W. came with her and worked for nothing, so I got a "Two-Fer-One", kind of a bonus package.

The day we had the first airshow Evagean got initiated to her job when she drove a jeep up and down the rows of airplanes peddling fuel. She talked pilots into refueling their airplanes with our cheap fuel even though they really didn't need any. After that I knew she could do the job, in fact there was not anything she couldn't do as I soon discovered.

Evagean was my mother's sister. I never called her "Aunt Evagean" because when I was a kid she and G. W. were "Aint Sissy and Unca Tuck". As the years passed and I grew up a special relationship developed and I then called her "Sissy", then eventually "Evagean" like all the other grownups did.

Those were only a few of the titles that landed on her shoulders. She was called Eeeeva-geeen, AvaJane, and many variations thereof. When Tom Thomas came to Frederick with all his airplanes and mini-airforce she sort of became the group mascot or den mother and picked up the name "Mama MAAG" and was known by that to all of Tom's troops. She gained Tom's respect when no one else could because she was one of the few people who would argue with him. She would tell him he was crazier than hell and scold him when he needed it. "Mama MAAG" was a high ranking officer in Tom's Air Force, in fact she was the only female to ever get to fly in his B-25 bomber.

Evagean loved to fly. She rode to a Fly In with me to Pauls Valley one time in a 1939 Porterfield. A Porterfield is long, narrow, and thin, with tandem seats. Every time she would lean forward to talk to me the airplane would take a nose-dive because she would push the stick forward with her chest. When she leaned back we went back up. Sure was glad she didn't talk very long at a time. She kept asking me why the airplane kept going up and down though. On the way back to Frederick my legs went to sleep because the Porterfield was so cramped and I asked her if she would like to push the pedals on the floor when I told her to. She didn't know it at the time but she helped me land it and taxi it in. She didn't real-ize she did it until we got stopped and I asked her to help me out of the airplane because my legs were asleep and I couldn't feel them.

I worked at the airport Monday through Friday working on fuel reports and interesting things like that, but as they say, at an airport, a day can be much like flying itself, hours of shear boredom laced with moments of stark terror.

On weekends, when Evagean and G. W. were there, there was always some-thing for folks to snack on. They were also full of stories. It didn't make any dif-ference who came in, she or G. W. had a story to tell them and always make them feel very welcome. Of course the stories were always about airplanes or flying.

It was not too often that we ever received a request for a chauffeur driven lim-ousine, but one day the phone rang and we got the first one. I was at somewhat of a loss for words because in Southwest Oklahoma folks are happy with a good pickup, but when the lady from New York on the other end of the line insisted on a limousine I had to tell her that I was sorry but the nearest such service was 50 miles away. I then told the nice lady that I had a Dodge courtesy van or a Ford pickup with the combined experience level of 207,000 miles that her party was welcome to use upon their arrival if they wanted either one of them. It was then her turn to be speechless.

She was very nice though and replied that she would talk to her employer to see if he would care for the van and then call me back. She did that in a couple of hours with the answer that they would be happy to use whatever we had upon their arrival in Frederick.

Now, I don't mean to poke fun at anybody, but airplanes do provide a quick mixing of people from different environments, cultures and backgrounds and they don't often mix, especially folks from NooYawk and flatland Western Oklahoma, so we were a bit leery about the arrival of our visitors to be.

The next day a very large blob of airplane appeared on final approach and a Hawker jet (large, very large) landed. As luck would have it, just as the airplane touched down Evagean just happened to drive up on a regular visit to the airport in her new red Cadillac. For some reason she backed up in front of the terminal building where a shady spot was, got out, and walked in without a clue as to what was happening.

When the Hawker taxied up and the folks got out and saw a red Cadillac backed up in front of the building they headed straight for it thinking that these Oklahoma hicks had come through after all. I quickly told Evagean about the telephone calls and she sprang into action. She went outside, introduced herself, volunteered her Cadillac, and drove them to their appointed place. All she needed was a little blue cap. When the folks returned later in the day we all had a nice visit and learned that we were not so different after all.

We laughed and talked and confessed that Evagean was not really a limo driver. They even wrote nice things in our guest book. It turned out that they were originally from Oklahoma and Texas, then later New York, and had to come back on some business. The gentleman lived in a big apartment on Park Avenue, quite a haul from Southwest Oklahoma. He tried to give Evagean a tip, but she turned it down.

Evagean's title was "Assistant Superintendent". She worked weekends, holidays, and most any day I thought I needed to be gone for whatever reason. She was my public relations officer, visitation expert, official greeter, and always showed up at just the right time to take over for me when I would get cabin fever and start to climb the walls.

She was my tour guide, historian, and story teller entertainer, so you can tell she was an essential to our staff of two. When she got sick and couldn't be there, even the folks who flew in just to see her would get grouchy when they would see brother Keith or myself working instead of her and demand to know where she was and what we did with Evagean. They would then grab a quick cup of coffee and leave, but not without telling us to be sure and tell her they came to see her and really missed seeing her.

One day I asked her if she would like to take a ride in Lloyd Oxfords's 250 Comanche, but warned her we would be twisting and turning quite a lot at low altitudes since I was going to be looking for minnow traps on the river. We flew

North Fork Red River all the way from Frederick to the Texas State Line north of Hollis, a distance of about a hundred miles all at about 500 feet off the ground. We took every crook and cranny there was and when she got quiet, which was a little unusual, I asked her if she was alright. She just grinned and said, "Doin' just fine." Anyone else would have already thrown up and turned green.

Evagean never refused to come help me when I called. If she was physically able she came out. I found out later that she came a lot of times when she was sick and should not have done it. I would ask her for a little time off to clear the cobwebs out of my head and here she came. She had a knack for sensing when I was about to go a little crazy from talking to people, drive out, walk in the south door, and say, "Go fly for awhile, I'll take care of things here." She worked eight straight weeks when I got sick and had to have heart surgery, yet she never complained.

There are not enough words to express the gratitude and appreciation I had for her. For eight years she was my assistant, partner, and helper beyond anyone's wildest imagination. She planned our part of the Frederick Army Airfield Reunions, the Fly-Ins, Special Fly Days, and took care of all the handshakin', neckhuggin' and grinnin'. When the King Aires, Hawkers, Learjets, Citations, Cessnas, and Pipers landed she would be right out there on the flight line, sticking out a hand welcoming whoever it was to Frederick. Governors, Lt. Governors, Senators, State Representatives, rich folks, "Hi-falootin' folks, and kids in J-3 Cubs all received the same sincere treatment, a welcome of love and appreciation for anyone who chose to come to Frederick for whatever reason.

The success and progress of Frederick Municipal Airport during those eight years could be attributed to a lot of people, but in reality no one ever did more to establish the friendly atmosphere and promote public relations for the airport than Evagean Tucker. Anyone who ever stopped by there left knowing a new friend. She truly never met a stranger.

She began getting sick more often and got afflicted with the wheezies, the dizzies, the throw-ups, throw-outs, sugar imbalances, and associated bugs. When that happened and she couldn't be there I felt severely handicapped myself. The airport just had a different feel about it without her popping in every day or so.

It was inevitable that the day had to come and it did. Evagean had made several midnight rides to the hospital with breathing difficulties, low blood sugar, and other maladies, and now it was evident she was very seriously ill. We (her family) ganged up on her and made her go home with her daughter Sandra in Kansas City for more tests and treatment. She had to have some plugged up arteries in her neck cleared, but then her kidneys began failing and she had to begin dialyses. It became more and more apparent that she would never return to Frederick Airport in her usual capacity.

She came back to Frederick Airport for one Saturday shortly before she died. We declared it "Evagean Day". It was her special day. We had a cake for her, invited friends from all over North Texas and Southern Oklahoma to come out to visit with her. Many of her friends from over the two States came by and hugged her neck. It was a very good day for her, but it was the last time she ever saw her beloved Frederick Airport.

Many people have been associated with Frederick Municipal Airport since it became that instead of Frederick Army Airfield in 1947. Some have played significant roles in the development of industry that came to be located here. Names such as N. O. Brantly and Emile Marcus come to mind. Ewell Stone, Jim Walker, Stan Burks, and Mike Hynes stand out as persons in the aviation industry who had businesses at the airport or managed it in some way through the years. The past 25 years or so the names of Beverly Akin, Donnie Coleman, and yes, maybe even Lynn Pinson can be included, but I believe of all the people who ever had a part in the history of the airport, no one loved it more or promoted it more than Evagean Tucker.

Evagean died Saturday, June 11, 1994 in Kansas City, only 10 days after her final visit to Frederick. We who loved her so much believe now that she clung tightly to life just so she could come back just one more time. Oh, how she enjoyed those two days. She got to see so many of her favorite people and see the airplanes land and taxi up.

I've often thought about Evagean through the years ... how she was "temporary" help, how she humored me by coming out and taking care of the place just so I could go fly awhile, how she chased down the Governors, Lt. Governors, Senators, Representatives, and all the wannabes as well as they would exit their airplanes to give them a neck hug and welcome them to Frederick. She greeted Alice Walton with open arms. She treated Governor David Walters, Governor Henry Bellmon, Senator Don Nickles, Representative Dave McCurdy, and the two kids on a cross country in a J-3 Cub all as equals. The list could go on and on.

I remember Eveagean and that big fellow from the New York Park Avenue apartment who flew in that big jet and wanted a limousine and she gave him a ride to town in her red Cadillac. I recall Evagean and Tom Thomas when he came to town with his Mini-Air Force and all those loud airplanes. She humbled him just a wee bit by sassing him and telling him many times he was crazier than hell.

I could go on and on, but all the stories I could tell would never completely express my love for her, or her love, devotion, and dedication to Frederick Airport and her enormous contribution to it. I believe that no one ever did more to promote good will, draw customers, and make more friends for the airport than she did.

It was really, really, lonesome the first few weeks after her death. Even though she had not been able to work for almost a year it was very different as it sunk in that she would never walk through the door again. I know her spirit will linger there a long, long time and she still most certainly will create a smile as she is remembered over and over. I cannot help but miss her and wish for the good times that used to be.

But, in our sorrow we are happy that her pain is gone and she has in the words of John Gillispie McGee, "Has slipped the surly bonds of earth, is dancing the skies on laughter silvered wings, and can reach out and touch the face of God." "Happy Flying, Aunt Sissy!"

UNCA TUCK

How he did it no one will ever know, but to finagle a five year old boy and his thirteen year old brother onboard a fully loaded, combat ready, Boeing B-17 Bomber in the middle of World War II at Hobbs, New Mexico Army Air Field was totally impossible. But he did it.

After the big war was over, he and Aint Sissy and baby daughter Sandra returned to his hometown of Frederick. He went to work at the Payne Maytag Store owned by my grandmother, fixing and selling washing machines, refrigerators, and stoves. I thought he was just "It" and I loved to be around him, but why put up with me tagging along behind him at every opportunity just to be near him and asking him dumb questions is a mystery, but he did. Why he bothered to take me with him and make me feel like he needed me to help him as he installed the first television sets and the first automatic washing machines in Tillman County Oklahoma no one will ever know, but he did.

Many years later when our relationship had grown from an uncle/kid nephew relationship into a man/man friendship things changed. The role began to be reversed and it was the man who appeared to be following the boy.

When I received my pilot's license, he was one of my first passengers. He trusted me to fly him to air shows, fly-ins, and for that matter, trips to anywhere as long as it was goin' up and lookin' down. We flew in Cessna 140's, 170's, 7AC Champs, Pacers, Skyhawks, and Skylanes. It didn't make any difference what it was as long as it had wings and would fly. He loved to take the controls and I told him he had a lifetime ticket to go with me anywhere, anytime. But he already knew that anyhow.

Even after the horrors of the War in the Pacific, being stationed on Guam, and toward the end of the war taking pictures from a B-29 Superfortress Bomber over Japan in the summer of 1945 after the bomb was dropped, and even after the many missions in freezing temperatures in a B-17, he still loved the little Cessnas, Pipers, Beeches and Aeroncas. Whenever I would offer him the wheel or stick, he wollared all over the sky because the little ones didn't handle quite like the bombers, but he sure did have a good time.

For over five years he worked and helped me any and every way he could at Frederick Airport, his only pay being the new friends he made, the repeated visits with the old ones, and the occasional flying trip with me to anywhere. He told the stories of his war experiences over and over and they got bigger and bigger and his voice got louder and louder and more colorful every time he told them, but nobody cared. There was never any doubt about his feelings toward the enemy he fought.

He outlasted World War II, one heart surgery and two cancer operations, but one summer day after months of fighting a losing battle, he just got too tired and sick and didn't have the strength to whip the multiple cancerous tumors that invaded his brain.

I know with out a doubt he was looking down from the clouds as many of his flying friends attended his funeral. He was given an aviators highest tribute, the missing man formation, the day we buried him at Frederick cemetery. Four airplanes appeared in the eastern sky as the last prayer was given and the rumble of the engines grew louder. They dropped down and flew low over his grave site that September afternoon. Then the B-25 Bomber peeled off.... and up ... and disappeared into the clouds. I know he smiled. He was my "Unca Tuck".

H. L. AKIN

One March evening in 1975 when Nancy and I arrived at the Frederick Airport for our bi-weekly session of aviation ground school we saw the prettiest red and white "V" tail Beechcraft Bonanza that we had ever seen tied down directly in front of the terminal building. N700X was painted on each side. Of course, all us babies in aviation had to go see it, so we walked out to the ramp, circled the Bonanza several times, oooed and aahed, and wondered who in the world could it belong to and how in the world could anybody fly one of those things.

We were told that a local farmer and rancher, H. L. Akin, had just bought it and had flown it in that very day. I just could not imagine how anyone could learn to fly something as big and pretty and complex as something like that. None of us had even soloed yet so such an accomplishment was almost unbelievable to us.

Twenty two years later on January 2, 1997, I was at Frederick Municipal Airport, not an awe-struck student, but taking care of my duties as manager of the airport. During those 22 years I had seen N700X taxi out and take off many, many, times. I knew it was H. L. because he was the only person that ever flew his airplane. That particular morning though when I saw the red and white Bonanza taxi out as I had so many times over the years it didn't have the same characteristic wobble or sound like it usually did. When it took off the engine sounded different, and it departed the airport and disappeared into the southern sky. Something wasn't right. I was wondering what was happening when the door opened and was shocked when H. L. walked in the terminal building. With a look on his face like I had never seen before, like his heart had been ripped out, he said, "Well, it's gone ... Hot damn it ... Ole 700 X-ray's gone". I could not believe it.... H. L. sold 700X-ray.

I didn't see H. L. for several days after that. I knew it would take a long, long time before the wound would heal though. I thought maybe he would be able to talk about it as time passed, but H. L. Akin had been flying airplanes for a long, long time, over 50 years in fact, and now he didn't have anything to fly. He had flown everything from a J-3 Cub to a Grumman TBM Torpedo bomber and had flown every airplane with a grace and finesse surpassed by no one. He even had instructed during WWII in T-6's and could fly upside down just as easy as he could right side up. He was very, very good, in fact the best, and I just could not see how he could just quit cold turkey, but he never got in an airplane again after 700X left.

I didn't know H. L. Akin very good until I started working at the Frederick Airport. His wife Beverly was airport manager at that time, so H. L. just naturally hung out quite a bit at the terminal building. He had his farm shop in the same hangar where he kept the Bonanza so his farming operations and repairs were centered at the airport. He had installed a "Lazy Susan", a thick, round, steel plate about 12 feet in diameter mounted on a 3 inch bearing in his hangar/shop to put the Bonanza on. He used a garage door opener to open the 40 foot door, would taxi the plane in, get out, push on the tail and turn the airplane around so it faced out the door, ready to go on the next trip.

I had heard stories about H. L. for years and after visiting with him I found out that they were indeed true. He could fly just about anything that had wings on it, especially the stuff with round engines.

When Tom Thomas brought his 65 airplanes and the Mid-America Air Group to Frederick in early 1985, H. L. was selected to head up the local chapter of MAAG. He was also responsible for checking out a small group of us so we could fly some of the airplanes. As it turned out, only three of us could fly a taildragger, so we got to take several of the airplanes to Fly-Ins and Air Shows in the area.

One day I saw H. L. calmly fooling around with a Grumman TBM Torpedo Bomber. "Just tinkerin'" H. L. said, but it wasn't too long before I heard that big round engine burp and growl and then burst off in a cloud of smoke. It then slowly taxied out to the runway. I heard somebody say, "He's gunna fly that thang!" And he did. He sat out there on the end of the runway for about five minutes letting the R-1350 radial warm up, then slowly applied the power to it, took off, flew it around a bit, and then came back and landed it just like it was a big ol' J-3 Cub. Ever so easy, so calmly, so gently.

I saw him do the same thing many times with a T-6, only with it he would go up and would be rolling and twisting like a top up through the clouds as everybody yelled, "Lookit him!"

H. L. and I became good friends over the years. He trusted me and had a lot of confidence in my flying ability. He even said I was one of his best pilots, but I strained that confidence pretty hard one July 4 morning when the tail cone broke on Tom's Luscombe T8F when I landed and it did some silly things with me. He didn't lose his temper or holler at me, just disappeared for awhile and then taxied up in the 1939 Porterfield and told me to get in. He made me go fly and do touch and goes until smiles replaced the lump in my throat. You see, I had put that Luscombe over on its back and torn it up. H. L. kept me from quitting flying forever that summer day.

H. L. Akin, without a doubt, was one of the best danged pilots to ever strap an airplane on his butt. He didn't fly at all during his last years on earth, but he remained my friend until his death in his 80's.

PAULA AND JUDY

Judy Pitts was one of those people who said she could never learn all the stuff necessary to learn to fly. When I first met her I knew she had the want to though and told her so in an effort to encourage her to at least try it. I told her, "Many people really learn to fly for only one obvious reason ... because they want to."

When she told me she had always wanted to fly that was good enough. I hooked her up with a very strong willed and patient CFI Paula Lemons, a frizzy haired young lady from across the river in Vernon, Texas and from then on the sky was the limit. A few screams and a lot of sweat and tears later, Judy had her license to fly. She came close to biting off Paula's pointin' finger several times when Paula would aim that finger in her face and say "NO Judy"! Judy would forget things like descending altitude, decreasing airspeed, and airplane attitude all at the same time.

She spent lots of hours flying around Southwest Oklahoma and North Texas, but never flew solo except when she had too. She would always get Paula to go with her. She and husband Wes moved to Quincy, Illinois where she fell down some icy steps and broke some thing and her flying activity dropped a bit. Even though she didn't fly herself much after she moved from Frederick, if she saw anything with wings on it and a familiar face in it, she would chase it down and climb in.

Judy always reminded me of a 1939 Porterfield I used to fly. The Porterfield was one of those airplanes that could out-fly its horsepower. It could cruise about 90 mph on only 65 horses. It was thin and narrow and the fuselage was about as deep as the wings were wide and you could stand at the rear, site down the thing toward the nose and it didn't look wide enough to even get in. In fact, it looked like a 2 x 6 board it was so narrow. Judy reminded me of that Porterfield because she was a very tall, very skinny woman with unknown horsepower and was in go motion all the time.

After Judy moved to Illinois I saw Paula a little less because she was off teaching another one of the un-teachables. I recommended her to a lady friend from Hollis who by her own admission said it would be a miracle if anyone could teach her to fly. She told Paula she was old, fat, and mean, but she wanted to learn to fly an airplane because her husband Jackie had bought an airplane so they could go see the kids. It wasn't too long after that we heard Janie Amburn was about ready to solo a Cessna 182 Skylane and Paula hadn't even had a finger bitten.

A couple of months after Judy moved to Illinois I thought I was hearing things when I heard a crackly voice come over the unicom radio. There was no mistaking who it was even with the static thrown in because Judy has a very high pitched, crackly, screechy, voice. It wasn't but a few minutes later that I was locked in a bear hug with Judy. She threw a surprise on all of us by flying commercial into Will Rogers that afternoon and another friend Mary Latimer picked her up and delivered her to our front door. After a bit, she and Mary flew on to Vernon, met Paula, and they wound up flying about eight hours that weekend. I really enjoyed the huggin' most of all.

My heart really, really, hurt when I heard that Paula, her husband, and his mother were killed in the crash of a foreign made twin as they departed the airport at Vernon early one morning. The aircraft lost power on one engine right after take off, she turned back to the airport, but the plane went down in the middle of a highway and burned before she could get it back to the runway.

The last I heard from Judy she was in the Houston, Texas area. With Paula gone, I don't think she ever flew again.

JANE SMITH

I met Jane Smith the day she walked in the airport office to finalize a deal she had made with Doug Ade for his 1977 Cessna 172 Skyhawk. Jane had owned a Skyhawk before, even flew that one to Canada with the Flying Farmers group one time, but later sold it in a weak moment. She had missed it long enough and now she wanted back in the airplane business.

Jane and Doug were both tickled to death at the deal they made, which is good. When both buyer and seller are happy it is always good. That makes each one of them think they got the best deal. Jane wanted the airplane and Doug wanted to sell it so he could buy a Piper Lance he had spotted in Arkansas.

But soon after Jane bought N75759 she went back to graduate school to work on her Masters degree in teaching and the Cessna had to take a back seat to her studies. She would come out and fly it occasionally, but not very often. I was checking hangars and airplanes one day and noticed it sitting kind of lonesome like with almost flat tires and a pretty good layer of dust on it. I called Jane and told her I would keep it clean and ready for her to fly if she would let me fly it every so often. She jumped at the offer, even said she would pay me to fly it, but I certainly didn't want to do that. We made the deal that I would keep it cleaned up, aired up, filled up, and ready to fly at a moments notice in return for getting some flying time. As a result, I had an airplane to fly and when Jane had the time all she had to do was come out, open the doors, and take off. I told her if she would call ahead of time I would even open the doors and pull it out for her. Turned out it was a good deal for her and a very good deal for me.

Jane was a fair weather pilot. She didn't like to fly when the wind was blowing at all which in Southwest Oklahoma was most of the time. It wasn't long that I began to notice Jane was just a little bit different about her flying. The problem was she was a little dangerous. The first clue to that was she called me one night about midnight and told me that she had a little "Thingy" happen, but not to worry, she got the airplane off the runway and didn't tear up anything, except the nose wheel pant might be laying somewhere on one of the crosswind runways and I might want to check on that the next morning.

It seems as though Jane had taken a little cross country trip earlier in the day to Paris, Texas, but left there later than she intended to which got her back to Frederick after dark. She had not flown at night since she got her license so she didn't know how to get the runway lights on, so she decided for some reason to land on a cross wind runway that didn't even have lights. She did get the Cessna down on the runway but ran off it on roll out, traveled down the side of the runway in the dirt awhile, then got it back on the runway, but not before ripping off the nose wheel pant. That was one of the first clues that perhaps she should quit flying.

Another flight Jane made got a little more serious. She flew to her graduate study classes at Weatherford, Oklahoma one day and the winds picked up a bit on the way. When she entered downwind there were a couple of other aircraft in the pattern and that bothered her. She forgot to slow down to approach speed, forgot to compensate for the crosswind, forgot her crosswind teaching, and whomped the Skyhawk hard on the runway, hot, fast, and furious. She lost control of the airplane, veered off the left side of the runway, traveled about 100 feet east across the grass, hit a concrete block well house building, and broke the airplane and her nose at the same time. The next time I saw her she had two black eyes, three stitches on her nose, and the airplane was for all intents and purposes totaled.

But rather than let the insurance company have it and go buy another one she wanted to fix 75759'er and wound up spending $28,000 to fix the Hawk, much more than what she could have replaced it for. By the time it got airworthy again the spookies got in her head and she lost the desire, her confidence, and did not want to fly anymore. She was scared to death. She finally sold the airplane for $28,000, what it cost for her to fix it.

A fellow named Tom came to Frederick one day, bought it, and flew it to Massachusetts. I heard later that he disassembled it, crated it, and shipped it to England. Dad-gum, that was a good airplane.

Jane never flew again. She served faithfully many years on the airport board, but never would get in a flying machine after the accident.

JERRY HOSTICK

Evagean asked me one day if I would mind talking to a neighbor of hers who had been a pilot several years ago, but had not been in an airplane in a long time. She wanted to see if I could get him back into flying. Jerry Hostick had flown some back in the 60s, got his priorities reversed and gave it up to run his insurance business and raise kids. He heard about all the neat stuff happening at the airport and thought he might like to start over.

He came to the airport one day, we got acquainted, and then went flying. I used an old 1957 Cessna 172 that I had access to at the time and played like a full fledged flight instructor (which of course I wasn't), put Jerry in the left seat, and we went up for about 45 minutes or so. It got the airplane juices flowing again for Jerry and it wasn't but a couple of weeks that he had a new medical, a new flight review, and not too much later actually bought a piece of a little 1975 Cessna 150. One of his partners quit flying after the engine quit one day on final approach and the other partner gained so much weight he couldn't get in a 150 anymore so Jerry wound up with full use of the airplane.

Jerry ran an insurance business downtown and would take his coffee break at the airport. He would show up almost every morning with a couple of chocolate "Long Johns" from the local bakery. We would eat those things and drink a cup of airport coffee and talk about flying and airplanes. We began to talk about Oshkosh and how much we would like to see it. We talked about it so much we actually made plans to fly there for at least 15 years, and kind of seriously for about 9 years, but always backed out as the time would grow closer to actually do it.

We dreamed and talked about how we would like to take off some pretty morning, he in his 150 and me in my 120, take our time and fly across Oklahoma into Missouri, up the Mississippi River, and hopefully wind up in Wisconsin before we hit the Atlantic ocean.

We ate a lot of chocolate Long Johns and drank a lot of coffee talking about that dream trip. It did eventually become a reality in 1994. That is a story all of its own and comes later.

One pretty Sunday morning a group of flyers from The Greater Oklahoma City Antique Airplane Association stopped by Frederick on their way to McGehee's Restaurant, a place known for the best Catfish in Oklahoma. It was located on Red River at Marietta, Oklahoma about 130 miles due east of Frederick. During the pit stop, the Oklahoma City folks invited anybody who was hungry for catfish to fly along with them. Jerry and his wife Barbara thought that was a real swell idea, got out the 150 and fell in trail with the group. Another couple from Frederick, Bob and Carolyn Maxwell did the same thing, only they flew a Mooney.

There were a few things though that everyone had neglected to tell Jerry and Bob. The runway at McGeHee's was partly dirt, partly grass, had a canyon on one side, a big hill on the other side, and a hump in the middle with a road crossing it. If you landed on the south end you crossed over the parking lot and restaurant and the whole area was surrounded by tall trees.

Jerry, Barbara, Bob, and Carolyn and the other fifteen flying machines all got to Marietta about the same time. When it came time for Jerry to land, to put it mildly, his 150 landed all at once when it got below the tree line out of the wind. Now, by all at once, I mean it quit flying, ka-poot, no wind, no airspeed, no ideas, no nothing. It landed. Solidly. Hard! Jerry said later he thought he had bored three holes in the dirt and grass with the landing gear. Bob said his Mooney did the same thing only he thought he was going in the canyon. Jerry told wife Barbara that was the way it was supposed to be, but Jerry knew better. He told me later he could not enjoy his catfish knowing he was going to have to leave the restaurant in a little while, get back in the airplane, and take off from that same strip.

It's nice when you can have a 5000 foot hard concrete or asphalt runway but sometimes a pilot doesn't get to land on the good stuff cause there sometimes ain't none. Some pilots are really scared to land on grass or dirt because they've never done it. I always thought that was a shame, not only for the lack of gaining the experience, but there always exist the possibility that someday they might just have to land on something soft, or narrow, or squooshie, and if they've never done it before they might not be able to do it when they have to. I understand nowadays an instructor won't even let a student land on anything except concrete or asphalt.

If you go up, you've got to come down sometime … somewhere. Jerry probably made a pretty good landing under the circumstances, but he didn't think so and a good landing in your head has a direct bearing on how happy the rest of your day is. He at least was able to walk away from the airplane after he landed, but best of all, he could fly the airplane again.

AARON HOWELL

Aaron Howell was in his 70's when I first met him. He made his daughter Susan come to the same ground school Nancy and I went to with Junior and Margaret and we met him there. Susan didn't want to learn to fly at all, but Aaron just thought she should because he loved flying so much. She dropped out before the class was completed, but Aaron kept on coming just so he could be around the rest of us.

He loved flying so much he would often wake up in the middle of the night, drive 20 miles to the airport, and take a Piper Tri-Pacer up to four or five thousand feet, throttle it back just above stall speed, and watch the world below until he got sleepy. With that familiar grin and twinkle in his eyes he always remarked how pretty and peaceful it was up there that time of night.

When my friend Cal Hunter bought the Tri-Pacer from Aaron and his partner, I purchased a bunch of block time in it to help raise the money so Cal could pay for it. Aaron then gave me a checkout in the stubby winged little airplane. He told me all about the Tri-Pacer in his slow, methodical voice, never got excited, never grabbed the controls, but when he chopped the throttle and told me to pull back on the yoke as hard as I could and hold it there, I doubted his wisdom. Much to my surprise the airplane did not stall, did not try to drop into a spin and spiral downward, rather it only started descending about a thousand feet a minute with the wings level and the nose up. Aaron grinned his funny little grin at my reaction and told me that we could land the thing in a football field if we wanted to. He did add however, that we might spraddle the gear out in the process but we would survive the "landing".

Aaron told me he joined the Civil Air Patrol when it was first organized in the early 1940's. During the early part of WWII, he flew Cessna Airmasters and Stinson 10's up and down the coast of the Gulf of Mexico looking for enemy submarines. He said he even saw one or two and even dropped a few bombs on them, but was quick to admit he sunk more seagulls than submarines.

Aaron was just a down right delightful man to know and visit with. He had flown almost every conceivable flying machine ever built during his 60 year plus tenure as a pilot. In addition to his experiences as a younger man bombing seagulls he liked to fix and build things. He also worked in the Luscombe factory in Kansas at one time and built the little 8A's and T8F's.

Aaron said he had experienced 30 or 40 engine failures in his 60 year flying career so they really didn't bother him anymore. Back when he first started flying he said that every time he left the ground he more or less figured he would have some kind of trouble so an emergency landing was not that unexpected. He could fix just about anything on an airplane. He might do it with a piece of baling wire, but he would get it fixed. In Aaron's time you had to fix more than you flew, but that didn't bother him a bit.

He actually knew personally some of the great folks of aviation; Amelia Earhart, Wiley Post, Poncho Barnes, Kathryn Stinson, Jackie Cochran, Fred Noonan, Will Rogers, and many, many others. Aaron not only knew those people, but flew with them. It embarrassed him to mention it, but had he not failed his celestial navigation test by two points because he had the flu it might have been him instead of Fred Noonan on that fateful trip in 1937 with Amelia Earhart into the Pacific. Might have been a good day for a fever.

He remembered buying a nickel hamburger for a nice friendly fellow sitting on a tree stump at the Enid airport one day. The man was pounding on an old typewriter waiting for his friend Wiley Post to gas up their airplane.

I came back from lunch one day and found Aaron sitting on the concrete leaning up against the hangar eating a banana and a can of pork n' beans, watching airplanes take off and land. He said "Ain't they pretty?"

He would often come in the terminal building and drink the last cup of airport coffee that was made that morning. It was black and awful looking, but when I would offer to make him a new pot he would say, "Naw, this's jest like I like it!"

Aaron did some work for Tom Thomas while Tom had all his airplanes at Frederick, in fact, he did a lot of the repair work on the T8F Luscombe that I had turned over one time. Aaron flew the T8F to Enid one time to an airshow, but after he filled up with gas and took off, he apparently had bought some water to boot and the airplane quit running about ten miles south of town. Aaron simply made a dead stick landing on highway 81 near Hennesey, drained out the rest of the water, and took off again. No big deal to Aaron.

He also painted the T8F one time in preparation to show off at the Oklahoma City Airshow, "Aerospace America". One not so kind soul walked by, looked at it, and remarked that it looked like it had been painted with the blow end of a Hoover Vacuum Cleaner. "It really kinda did." That comment hurt Aaron's feelings a bit though. He thought it looked nice.

In his later years, Aaron began fooling around with an old gyrocopter that had a 65 horsepower Continental engine on it instead of the original stock gyro engine. He would tinker with it and then go try to fly it. It never would leave the ground. He would then tinker some more and try to fly it some more. His son Richard came up from Texas and they did double-tinker time until they got it where it might fly. Aaron told me he wanted to get it ready to fly to go see that daughter Susan in Alaska who was now working with the Forestry Service as a ranger. Susan was getting her thrills in those days then by rappeling out of helicopters into the Alaskan forests chasing bears.

The day came however, when Richard and Aaron both walked in the airport terminal building with a whole lot of mud and a little bit of blood splattered all over them. The gyrocopter had gone nuts as Richard tried to take it off and it didn't fly nearly as good as they thought it would and it wound up in a cotton field, upside down, badly broken, but not broken nearly as bad as their morale. Disappointed? Yes. Discouraged? No. Give up? Not on your life. They just gathered up the pieces, hauled them back to the hangar, and began to put them all back together again.

Most octogenarians are usually content to just drive a rocking chair or a fishing pole, but not Aaron. He kept on tinkering with flying machines until his health began to fail. His dream to fly the gyrocopter to see Susan in Alaska again became just a dream that would never become a reality, but he kept talking about it until he died at the age of 81. A gentle, quiet man whose love of flying was surpassed by no one.

LLOYD OXFORD

Lloyd Oxford was owner of a 1959 Comanche 250 when I first got acquainted with him. He had flown the Comanche all over the western half of the United States and loved to take fishing trips in it. He often went to Lake Powell, Utah and even up into Oregon and Washington. He would sit in the cockpit for six or seven hours and still be smiling when he returned to Frederick, sore, but happy as a June bug.

Lloyd really loved that Comanche. It was a real nice airplane, retractable gear, constant speed prop, 250 horses, and would cruise about 170 mph at 2100 rpm. I flew with Lloyd occasionally and particularly remember a trip to McKinney, Texas. When we got there one end of the runway was under construction and had a displaced threshold which made the runway about a thousand feet shorter than we were expecting. It was on the approach end so it really wasn't that a bigga deal, but Lloyd had to drag the Comanche in, over fly the closed part and whump it in. That's exactly what he did, only it turned out to be a lot bigger WHUMP than he wanted or expected. Kind of embarrassed him.

Lloyd would come by the airport at least once a week to check on me, visit awhile, drink a cup of coffee, and even though he would spill half of it on the floor walking across the room I was always glad to see him. He always left me with a bit of wisdom, a handshake, and a smile.

One day Lloyd came in the office, tossed a set of keys on the desk, and told me to take the Comanche up anytime I wanted to. Sure made me feel good realizing the confidence he had in me because he was really particular about who flew his airplane.

Lloyd got drafted when WWII began, was sent to boot camp, and was told to get ready to go overseas as soon as boot camp was over. So, after boot camp he got two weeks leave and got to come home. He said all his family cried when he left because he was going to war, but he didn't go that time. Instead the Army sent him to a school to learn about B-17 Bombers. After the school, they said, "OK, go home for a couple of weeks and when you get back, you're going overseas." He came back home and everybody cried again when he left, but again he was sent to another school on airplanes, but not overseas. Same thing happened a couple more times and then it was 1945. Hitler was extinguished, the bomb was dropped on Japan, and the war was over. Lloyd never did go overseas.

On one of his fishing trips to the west coast of Mexico, Lloyd had two other guys in the plane with him. When he got to the Mexican fishing village dirt strip the circuit breaker tripped when he started to lower the gear because he was going too fast when he flipped the gear lever. If you try to lower the gear with speed over 110 mph that often happened. He just lowered the gear manually with the crank, but when he sat down on the dirt strip, the gear collapsed, the Comanche squatted on the Mexican turf and created a small sand storm as it slid to a stop. Kind of ruined Lloyd's fishing trip. His two passengers ran inside to down some Tequilas, but the ordeal sort of ruined Lloyd's fishing and drinking appetite. He was then told he better figure out some way to get that plane fixed before the "Fedder-Allies" arrived because they would cut up his beloved Comanche and haul it away for parts if they found it disabled in the dirt.

Well, Lloyd made a few phone calls and located a guy who lived on the Texas/Mexico border who came, jacked up the plane, locked the gear down and put on a usable prop. He then announced the airplane was ready to go. Lloyd's fishing buddies said "No way" and decided to ride a Mexican bus for four days back to the States. Lloyd said he didn't think he wanted to fly it, so the fixer-up guy said "Well, git in and les' go, I'll fly it!" Lloyd said "Justa minute", went back into the Cantina, downed a couple of Tequilas worms and all, came out and announced that he thought he was ready.

Lloyd sold the Comanche some years later when he found out he couldn't pass the FAA medical anymore. I tried to talk him out of it because I knew he would miss it. He did, but it turned out alright. Lloyd flew one side of a domino table at the golf and country club for many years after that until his death.

There were tears in both our eyes the day N5968P took off from Frederick and flew out of sight headed for Nebraska. Even though an airplane goes away, a pilot will always remember it and the memories of hundreds of hours in the sky will be flown over and over. Lloyd could still feel the controls as he re-flew all those trips in his mind.

Lloyd's wife, Glady's, "Happy Bottom" as he called her, went to Long Beach, California with a friend right after she graduated from High School and wound up helping build B-17 Bombers. Gladys did most of the wiring on the bombers under construction including the intricate stuff in the instrument panels. Glady's said she tried riveting for a few days, but decided that being a "Rosie the Riveter" was not her bag and returned to the wiring business. She did that for about a year, then returned to Tillman County for awhile, then went on to Dallas, Texas and got a job working on the famous Norden bomb site device. That was the top secret instrument that turned out to be so very accurate in precision bombing of Hitler's Germany during the war in Europe.

Gladys and her girlfriends may not have been in the news as much as the guys in uniform, but there was no doubt they played a very active role in the war effort during the 40's. Some of the women joined the WASPS, the unofficial group of women pilots who ferried war planes all over the United States. Other women were actually in the armed services, but in those days they were assigned to desk jobs. All of them contributed as much to bring victory to the United States and an end to World War II as the guys who were over there shooting.

WINGLESS BIRDS

Olvis Jones was the resident helicopter expert at Frederick Airport. He was one of the very first employees of the Brantly Helicopter Company that began building the Brantly B-2 and B2B in the early 1950's. When N. O. Brantly sold the company a few years later, Olvis stayed in Frederick, but remained busy repairing and later rebuilding the little helicopters. His reputation soon became known world wide as knowing more about a Brantly Helicopter than any man alive.

He was always tinkering with one that somebody had brought in for him to fix. He also had two "T" hangars full of them to play with so he never got caught up. It didn't take long to find out that a Brantly Helicopter made more noise than anything else on the airport and there was no mistaking when Olvis was working because of the racket. He would often fire one up, run it up to about 2200 RPM, and hold a piece of cardboard up into the whirling blades to see if it got cut in the same place with both blades. It's a thousand wonders that Olvis still has two hands.

A non-helicopter fellow told me one time he was not about to ride on a flying machine that was doing its best to throw everything off itself that was holding it up. I'm not bad mouthing the things, but they are curious creatures, do command a lot of respect, but I know for sure that Olvis was the only person I knew of who could fix one good enough to keep it from having a mid-air collision with itself.

Another non-helicopter fellow told me one time that a helicopter was just like a prostitute ... no visible means of support.

Olvis converted a B-2 to a B-2B one time. The conversion really only consisted of changing the engine from a normally aspirated one to a fuel injected one, rerouting the air intakes, and a couple of other minor changes. I had done a little drafting work and knew how to make the drawings to submit to the FAA so Olvis traded me some stick time in a Brantly for the drafting work. To a fixed wing taildragger pilot, trying to make that thing go or stay where I wanted it to stay was like trying to stand on a beach ball in the middle of a swimming pool.

Olvis fooled around those Brantlys so much he was almost stone deaf. He wore hearing aids, but they didn't help much except to keep the dirt out of his ears. He later moved away from Frederick and gave up the whirlie birds for good. The last time I saw him he was sitting in his regular spot at the "Hop n' Sack" convenience store in Snyder, Oklahoma drinking coffee with the other retirees.

◆　　　◆　　　◆

This doesn't have anything to do with Olvis but it does have something to do with helicopters. One day a U. S. Army CH-47 helicopter brought a bunch of EURO-NATO military officers, 33 of them in all, into Frederick Airport for a look-see. They were there because Frederick was as mentioned before the NATO jet training auxiliary airport out of the 80th Flying Training Wing at Sheppard Air Force Base in Wichita Falls, Texas.

When the helicopter landed, all the officers were properly greeted by Miss Frederick, the Honorable Mayor, the City Manager, and a bunch of other dignitaries. When they all left for town, me and my Uncle G. W. took the opportunity to visit with the crew of the flying machine. The CH-47 is one of those that has a rotor on each end of itself and is bent in the middle. Naturally, we were curious as to just how the thing could stay in the air once it got off the ground which was a feat in itself because when it took off it looked like a giant alligator rearing up on its hind legs getting ready to bite something.

The crew was very cordial and gave us a real good tour of the machine. They explained that the CH-47 had three engines, five transmissions, and a half mile of rotating shaft all going at the same time. If any of that failed to work, along with a thousand other busy things turning and twisting, they said it was the only item in the Army inventory that could run into itself. They also warned us that if you don't wear ear plugs you would lose your hearing in about three minutes.

About three hours later, all the important folks came back from town, loaded up in the thing, and we all watched as both rotors slowly started moving, then faster, then the "whump, whump, whump" began, the front end lifted up, the rest followed, and away it went. "It really was kinda graceful looking." (Still looked like an alligator.)

CECIL DAVIS

Cecil Davis was a different man and marched to his own drum. He just showed up out of nowhere at a local Civil Air Patrol meeting one night and no one knew who he was or where he came from. As time passed, we found out he had lived in California for forty years in an apartment, had never married, had no kids, worked for Lever Brother's Soap company in the Los Angeles area as an electrician, retired, and moved back to Frederick to help take care of his brother who at that time was terminally ill. His brother died shortly after Cecil moved back, but since Cecil had already moved back, he stayed, and lived in the same house with his sister-in-law Blanche after his brother died.

Cecil was a pilot, had a history of flying, had owned a couple of Piper Tri-Pacers in the past, and was interested in getting in the CAP so he could fly cheap. Even though he was a little different, we all decided he was OK, accepted him into the group, and we became friends.

It wasn't long though that he got the high CAP brass aggravated at him though because he would rent the CAP Cessna 172 for an hour or so each day, do nothing but touch and goes (sometimes as many as 40 or 50 a whack), so they were always having to replace the worn out tires.

He was always talking about how he was going to buy another airplane as soon as he could find one like he wanted. When asked what that was, he said he wanted another Tri-Pacer he thought, but it would have to be just right.

I began looking at airplane for sale ads and each time I would find a good ad on a Tri-Pacer and show it to Cecil. He would always find something wrong with it. If it had a lot of hours on it Cecil would say it was wore out and would need an overhaul. If it was low time he would say something went wrong with the overhaul and they just needed to get rid of it. If they were too high, he of course would say that was too much money. If it was a bargain, something had to be wrong with the airplane because it was so cheap.

One day I asked him, "Cecil, how long have you been looking for an airplane?" He replied, "Since I sold my last Tri-Pacer." I said, "When was that?" He said, "1961". I quit looking.

One day Cecil talked his sister-in-law Blanche into going for an airplane ride. He took her up in a rented Cessna 172. Blanche had not flown in a small plane in forty years so needless to say, she was a little apprehensive and not nearly as enthusiastic as Cecil was to take her.

It was a pretty day and when they came back in an hour Blanche was grinning all over herself and remarked about how nice it was and said "I didn't even get sick!" Cecil said Blanche was ready to go again anytime. I often wondered what they did up there.

LEN MILLER

Len Miller was already an old man when I first met him in 1975, and the older he got he never looked any different. At last count Len was somewhere in his early 90's. I really think Len was around trying to talk Noah into building an airplane instead of a boat but backed off when the clouds started gathering. He really is that old.

He turned out to be a pretty good friend in spite of the fact he cussed me out a few times. He was the only man I ever knew who could give you a good cussin' and five minutes later slap you on the back, call you a good buddy, and invite you to his barbeque party/dance the next week.

Len had been flying all of his life. He was a pilot in World War II, maybe World War I. Heck, he may have even dropped bombs out of a balloon on the British when they burned Washington, but one thing I knew for sure, he was one heckava pilot. He was a CFI and would carry a rolled up newspaper in the back seat of a J-3 Cub or Champ while instructing and whop his students over the head and shoulders when they goofed up. But … when anyone learned how to fly from Len Miller, they knew how to fly! He was probably one of the best old school flight instructors that ever climbed in an airplane. He taught the forgotten maneuvers such as spins and slips so his students wouldn't go out and kill themselves for doing something stupid or for the lack of knowledge of how to do something. Len Millers aren't made anymore.

Len and I were talking one day about the good old days when you could go fly anywhere you wanted to in anything you wanted to do it in and not have to tell anyone about it if you didn't want to. Len hastened to scold me and cuss a bit when I said it would be nice to have some of the old days with cheap airplanes and cheap gas. He told me in so many words that he didn't "give a s—" about the good old days and that there never was a good old day in his opinion. He did not like to take baths in number two washtubs, he did not like to read by coal oil lamps, and he did not like to carry in the wood or coal. He also did not like the idea of keeping milk and eggs in a well pit and sure did not like to run 100 yards in the dark and cold to sit in an out house. He said he only got to go to town once a week when he was a kid and the only entertainment he had was listening to the Atwater Kent radio or visiting with the neighbors.

The only thing about the "good old days" he liked was that it was nice to fly for a couple of bucks an hour.

His wife Melba had to be a very special person for putting up with him all those years. In his early days as a spray pilot, Melba "flagged" for him and would also help him cook barbeque once a year for all his buddies. We would all go eat barbeque in his hangar at the Quanah, Texas airport and sometimes dance the "Two-step" to the music of his brother's string band.

TOM YATES

Junior Jenning called me a one day and asked if I would fly to Norman with he and Margaret and fly a Cessna 182 back to Altus for a friend of his. Seems as though Tom Yates, the John Deere dealer at Altus, Oklahoma had purchased a late model Cessna 182 Skylane, but didn't know how to fly it. In fact, he didn't know how to fly anything, so I was lucky enough to get picked to do it for him. A couple of hours later, Junior, Margaret, Tom, and I were winging it to Norman. We got as far as Chickasha, a town about 35 miles away from Norman when we ran into a wall of fog. We landed, called the place in Norman where Tom had bought the plane, and a nice young lady drove to Chickasha to pick us up. The only problem was that she brought a very compact car and it was very crowded with five people in it.

When we got to Norman, Tom finished the deal on the new airplane and by that time the fog had cleared and we were able to fly back to Chickasha in Tom's new airplane where Jr. and Margaret picked up their airplane. Tom and I flew on to Altus. That trip began a great and lasting friendship with Tom and Ellen Yates, which generated a hundred more stories yet to come.

Tom and Ellen both started taking flying lessons, but it took several months for them to get their licenses. I was called on frequently to fly one or both of them and even Tom's brother Ted, to many places in Texas and Oklahoma for one reason or the other. That gave me lots of hours of experience in that big, beautiful, fully IFR equipped, still smelled new, Cessna 182 Skylane. Not many guys would let his wife fly alone with another guy and furnish the airplane to do it with, but Tom did. That's trust!

One of the best steaks I ever put in my mouth was at the Amarillo Stock Yards Restaurant one day after I flew Tom there for the cattle auction. Still remember the taste of it. The privileges of being able to make an airplane go up and down sure paid off for me for sure.

Tom and Ellen eventually got their licenses and Ellen even got her instrument ticket and that sort of put a stop to my free flying. They continued to fly, but after a couple of years they both got busier and busier, sold that airplane, bought a retractable Skylane, sold that one too, and then quit flying ... for awhile.

Tom and I kind of drifted apart for awhile but then in the summer of 1993, he and his Sheltie dog Kalli drove to Oshkosh, Wisconsin for the EAA Fly-In. He met a guy named "Chuck" from Frankfort, Illinois, and fell in love with a partially built experimental homebuilt called a "Kitfox" that Chuck had for sale. Tom got the fever so bad he bought the thing only 80% complete, trucked it home, and started working on the other 20%. Tom bet Chuck that he would have it finished by the next summer and could fly it to Oshkosh '94. Chuck said he couldn't get it done by then. The bet was that whoever lost would buy the other one and as many of his buddies he could bring to Oshkosh a steak at "Jeff's on Rugby", a popular watering hole, steak house, and pub in Oshkosh. The race was on.

Tom soled the Kitfox on Memorial Day 1994 and flew off the last hour of the required 25 hours the day he left for Oshkosh. That story is related in a later chapter. He won the bet though and I got a free steak at Jeffs since I was there too.

Through the following years Tom and I became really good friends. Quite often we would not see each other for weeks or even months at a time, but then out of the blue a telephone call would come and he would have some scatter-brained idea of something we should do and we would do it. He talked Jerry Hostick and me into going to Oshkosh in 1994, came up with the idea of him, Phil Carson, and me into going to Oshkosh in 1995 and again in 1997 and then in 2000 talked my brother Keith into going as well.

In 1996 Tom, Phil, and myself formed the "Flying Foxes Airplane Company", got an Oklahoma Aircraft dealers license and went into sort of a business. We bought and sold two or three airplanes, lost money on all of them, but had a fun time flying them while we had them. In 2000 we lost our dealer license because we weren't handling enough airplanes and didn't have an office with our name on the door.

Tom bought a little Cessna 140 several years later, flew it for while, but then just sort of lost interest in flying and sold that airplane as well. He still has the Kitfox though, but it was heavily damaged when a hangar fell in on it during a storm and sits in pieces now. He says he's going to put it back together again someday.

Tom, wife Ellen, and their two dogs started traveling all over everywhere in their AirStream camper and he doesn't think about flying very much anymore. I rarely ever know where they are except when I get that phone call every so often when Tom has come up with another scattered brained idea.

There never has been, nor will there ever be, anyone else like Tom Yates.

DONNIE COLEMAN

Didja' ever know anyone who wanted something so badly that they set a goal for themselves, but really thought the odds were so great against them they would never attain that goal, but they kept on working at it anyhow, and studying and plugging, and sweating and practicing, and when some folks would say stuff like "You'll never make it!" they just grinned and didn't say anything, just went back to the working, studying, plugging, practicing, and sweating, and one day lo and behold.... they did it? (Some English teacher probably just had a heart attack reading that fragmented sentence.)

Well, I know such a fellow and was awfully proud of him on Sunday, June 26, 1994 because on that day he put it all together and proved to all the world, his friends, his family, his critics, a flight examiner, and most of all to himself, that he could do it because he did it. He flew a Piper Cherokee 140 to Wichita Falls, Texas and came back three hours later with that coveted private pilot license in his pocket.

Donnie Coleman started working toward that goal many years before that day though. He was a big rig 18 wheeler truck driver for many years then later became a truck mechanic. He would save some money, get enough to take a few flying lessons, work on some more trucks, then take some more flying lessons. When I would ask him when he was going to take the written exam He would say, "Well, I'm just too damn dumb to ever pass that thing, but at least I know how to fly an airplane." Well, he tried it and passed the written exam in January of 1994. Then in June he showed that examiner he could fly an airplane as good as anyone and got his license.

He delights in giving airplane rides to all his friends. Seems as though his skills of flying an airplane far surpass that of driving a car or pickup and people, including me, who absolutely will not get in a car or pickup with him don't mind getting in an airplane with him. He brought three loads of folks out to the airport one day and still had a long waiting line for the next day.

Brandi Scheller was one of Donnie's first passengers. In fact, she brought the whole Scheller family out including cousins, dad, and granddad. Donnie may have started a whole new generation of pilots by his willingness to introduce these folks to the thrill of flying.

When Donnie soled and joined the elite group of people who dared to escape the bonds of earth and all that gravity holding them down by flying an engine powered air machine all alone it was a happening! His red shirt still hangs in the Frederick Airport terminal building.

Soon after Donnie soloed the first time, I needed to take my Cessna 120 to Quanah, Texas for its annual inspection. I asked Donnie if he would fly to Quanah in Len Miller's Cherokee and give me a ride back to Frederick. Since Donnie was only a student pilot at the time I realized that with me in there with him it would make me the PIC (Pilot In Command), which meant that if he messed up and fell out of the sky I would be responsible for the wreck. Not a comforting thought, but I had watched Donnie go up and down without tearing the airplane up so far so I figured I could probably get him out of any mess he might get us into.

I thought about acting like a real live flight instructor and really putting him through all sorts of student testing things so I could yell at him if he wiggled, got off course, didn't maintain altitude, or tried to do something silly, but the mood wasn't with me that day so I just climbed in the right seat of the airplane, put my hands in my lap, and enjoy the ride. I didn't intend to grab anything unless Donnie really got wild.

I would liked to have been able to tell how bad Donnie messed up, but I couldn't. Outside of a stair step take off in fairly gusty winds he did good.... real good. I didn't even have to think about grabbing the controls in panic. He even found his way back to Frederick with no help from me.

Really, one reason I couldn't say much was because just about 30 minutes before Donnie watched me float half the distance of the Quanah runway in the 120 and whoomp it down in those same gusty winds and I'd been flying for 18 years longer than he had then. I made one of those landings anyone would not want to brag about or want anyone to see it, and Donnie saw it

Student pilots are generally some of the safest pilots in the air because they are scared silly they are going to mess up, therefore they are more careful about everything. Then when they get their license they get careless or goofy and get dangerous.

Donnie's wife, Linda, didn't think much of airplanes and even called my Cessna 120 a "teeny little thang" onetime. All the time Donnie was taking flying lessons I encouraged Linda to help him along by agreeing to take that ride that all pilot wives should take with their husbands and that is when a guy gets his license his wife should be their husband's first passenger. When I mentioned that to her she just glared at me and said, "You kiddin? No, heck no, and no way!"

Late one evening a few months later after Donnie got his license, I was out boring holes in the sky with that "teeny little thang" of mine and heard Donnie announce on the radio an intended landing at Frederick, so I followed him in to visit a bit. Lo and behold, would wonders ever cease, who should be the first person to step out of that Cherokee 140 but LINDA! She looked kinda sheepish. "Thought you weren't gunna ever do that!", I said. She replied, "Well, I really didn't like it!. Uh-huh. She's been up with him again since too. I've seen her. Call my little Cessna a teeny little thang, huh!

It wasn't very long that Donnie caught the airplane fever like most other pilots. He got the bad-wants for his very own airplane so he could pat it on its nose, wash it, and wax it, and polish it, tinker with it, and do all sorts of other things that pilots do to their very own airplanes, particularly get to fly it when they want to without having to ask someone.

Funny thing though, he bought an airplane "sight-unseen". It was an airplane that Tom Yates, Phil Carson, and I had thought about buying at one time. We had taken pictures of it, but eventually decided that we didn't want it, but Donnie decided he wanted it, so he just picked up the telephone, called the owner, made a deal, and bought the sucker. That same day the weather turned bad and stayed bad and the guy couldn't deliver it for about five days. Donnie got the dry heaves and figgits after he realized what he had done and walked around for days muttering, "What in the world have I done?"

Well, the day his 1960 Cessna 182 Skylane landed at Frederick and taxied up, and Donnie saw the new paint and how good it looked and sounded, his smile (grin) said it all. "That's MY airplane!"

However, anytime after that when I ask him if he had been flying it he just shrugged his shoulders and said, "Heck no, I gotta work now to make all them payments ... don't have time to fly it!"

Things have a funny way of working out. Many years later Donnie was hired as manager of Frederick Airport, a position he still holds. That was another thing he said he didn't think he could do either ... but he's doing it and doing it real good. One of the best Airport Managers Frederick ever had except me. Still has the 1960 Skylane too.

MARY AND JOE

Mary Kelly and Joe Cunningham were two very special people who were loved by everyone who ever met them. Joe was 20 years older than Mary, but they fell in love, married, and eventually wound up managing the most coveted airport in Oklahoma, Tenkiller Airpark near Cookson in Eastern Oklahoma.

Mary began her career in aviation pumping gas part time at Altus Municipal Airport when she was a teenager. She began taking flying lessons, one thing led to another and it wasn't too many years that she had all her ratings including CFI. Not long after that she was hired as manager of the Altus Municipal Airport.

Joe had a distinguished career in writing, publishing, and teaching. He also was one of the first members of the Oklahoma Aeronautics Commission, which came into being in 1963. When he and Mary crossed paths and eventually married, it surprised everyone to some extent because of the age difference, but everyone who knew them then said, "Well, it only makes sense, they belong to each other!" A wedding reception was held for them at Sundance Airpark near Oklahoma City sometime after the wedding itself. Most all of their flying friends were present.

Each October they would invite the entire membership of the Oklahoma Airport Operators Association (OAOA) to Tenkiller Airpark for a weekend of fun and relaxation. It was so nice to hang out at their airport eating fried chicken, bacon n' eggs, biscuits, gravy, and all that other good vacation food for three days. But, it was especially nice visiting with Mary and Joe and all the local folks who lived in hangar/homes on the airport property up and down each side of the runway. A large gathering of fellow airport operators from all over the state just moved in on them for the weekend.

The atmosphere at Joe and Mary's place was so laid back it just hung all over the place. You could not help but relax. I remember standing on the front porch of our log cabin early one morning watching the gold, red, and brown leaves drift straight down to the ground and the squirrels scampering across the bed of leaves. I could smell the smoke of burning wood from a distant campfire sifting through the trees. I could hear the growl of a chain saw as a new tenant cleared brush to build a hide away cabin near the lake or the airport.

We would visit with old friends, make new ones, and listen to Mary tell stories about Ned Christy, Belle Starr, Pretty Boy Floyd, and other shady folks who made the Cookson Hills their hide outs many years ago during the outlaw days. If that special weekend outing happened to fall on Halloween we would swap ghost stories until late into the night or go visit a haunted mansion near Tahlequah.

We cooked hotdogs over an open fire, covered them with chili, relish, onions, and all that good stuff and then top off the meal with "Smores", things only a few people really knew what they were, or how to make, but still tasted good once someone made them.

During the afternoons we would sit on the picnic bench in front of the airport office and watch the local folks or others from nearby places glide in on the grass runway in their 7AC's, J-3's, 172's, Cherokees, Bonanzas, and even a Great Lakes Biplane.

Joe stayed busy all the time we were there quietly going about his business to make sure we were all comfortable. He was fixing coffee, getting the food, politely listening as we told him flying stories he had heard many times over, or maybe telling a short story himself. We would watch him pump gas for folks and in between all those duties he would work on the next edition of "The Oklahoma Aviator", that is, if there wasn't anything else to do.

Sunday morning we would all meet at the "Smokehouse Restaurant" in Cookson for a mess of scrambled eggs, bacon, bisquits, gravy, pancakes, sausage, and hot coffee. Even though the doctor said all that stuff would make my heart stop beating someday it was good enough to ignore all warnings.

Mary and Joe's place was the envy of every airport manager in the state because of the laid back atmosphere, the beauty of the area, the low maintenance grass runway (complete with lighting and VASI's), and a new terminal building. The other 51 weekends we weren't there Mary taught folks how to fly among other things and Joe worked hard editing and publishing the newspaper in between his duties of chasing deer off the runway and mowing grass.

Mary was involved in everything. She taught, wrote, was President of the Airport Operators Association one year, and was mixed up in the planning of the OAOA annual conference every year. She truly was the Sweetheart of Oklahoma Aviation.

All of us who loved Mary were stunned with disbelief when we heard that she had been killed in the crash of a Cessna 150 at Hatbox Airport in Muskogee. Something went horribly wrong and she and an elderly student were burned to death when the 150 stalled at low altitude and hit the ground just off the runway.

Years later I stood on the spot where Mary lost her life with tears in my eyes. I could not help but ask, "Why, oh why?"

Joe continued to run the airport and publish the paper, but we could tell he was just going through motions. He died one year after Mary's death while mowing grass on the airport at Tenkiller. We all believe he died of a broken heart.

THE LITTLE BITTY ONES

It is hard to believe, but some people just will not accept the idea of actually getting into an airplane and going up into the sky, but yet they do love flying. For that reason, Jimmie Tyler and a bunch of his friends were into aviation in a big, but yet small way. By small, I mean like little, like in model airplanes. "Little bitty boogers!" These fellows had what amounted to a complete store and maintenance shop set up at Frederick Municipal for the specific purpose of planning, designing, building, flying, crashing, and rebuilding flying model airplanes.

They located themselves in an old three room building left over from WWII just off the ramp at Frederick Airport. One room was used for storage of the flyable ones, another room was for the building and rebuilding, and the third one was where they threw the crashed ones (basket cases) to wait until they decided to rebuild them.

These guys spent more time repairing and rebuilding the little planes than flying them though. I often thought they crashed them on purpose just so they could have the fun of putting them back together again.

They picked out the end of a rarely used runway in the northeast corner of the airport to fly. Jimmie took out all the grass and weeds from the cracks and fixed the place up real nice. I would often go watch them, but it seemed like every time I showed up one of the bitty-birds would go berserk and crash. I then decided rather than upset the guys I better not go watch too often. I once watched Jimmie nosedive a seaplane into about nine inches of snow. Tore it all to pieces. Tiny pieces of balsa wood, paper, and stuff were scattered all over a 50 foot area. He was still wiggling his fingers on the radio control box staring at the sky in disbelief after it had disappeared. That one he was not able to fix.

When the National Weather Service installed a NEXRAD weather radar site about a quarter mile north of the bitty bird landing area, the little planes started going nuts like they had a mind of their own. Jimmie and his crew crashed a bunch of them before they realized that the radar beam was zapping out their radio control frequency as the antenna made its circular pass. The bitty plane guys then relocated their runway further south on what used to be runway 08/26 which had been closed for several years.

The old movie, "The Flight of The Phoenix" told the story of a model airplane builder who figured out how to make a flyable flying machine from the wreckage of a crashed cargo plane. It worked and the survivors were able to fly to safety at the end of the movie. I know without a doubt that Jimmy could have done that.

I tried to get him to build a "real" airplane, one that could really be flown, even offered to fly it for them if they would, but Jimmy said he might have to fly it himself if he built it, like get in it and fly it. No way, sed he. I never even got him to go riding with me. He did give the idea some thought though.

"LET'S GO FLYING!"

Oh my, what a beautiful day to fly! It has been so hot and windy but finally a day comes when I can open the hangar doors again and see what color the airplane is. I clean off the wind screen, blow off the dust, look the airplane over inch by inch, drain the fuel sumps, and when I am sure that it is airworthy once again I get in it and strap it on. The smell of the cockpit is so sweet, the engine start sounds so good, and the controls feel so good that all the memories of the last flight are brought back to mind.

I taxi out to the run up area, check the mags, make sure everything still works, take a deep breath, and push the throttle forward. I feel the surge of power as I begin to roll down the runway. Lift off! No longer tied to the ground, the rumble of the tires is gone and the silky smoothness of flight is experienced once again.

I climb to about 800 feet and can now see Red River and the State of Texas off to the South. I turn west and look over the patchwork art of western Oklahoma with the greens and browns, the golds and reds, and the occasional spirals of dust stirred up by farmers working their fields. I follow the jagged scar of North Fork Red River as it works its way from the north, upstream past Tipton and can see Otter Creek invading the river from the east. I then look back to the east as the river wiggles its way north as far as the eye can see.

The middle of the day in the hot days of summer is too hot to enjoy such a pleasure flight at low altitudes, but the early mornings and late evenings are much cooler and the view is so pretty from the air. The trees, the cotton, the alfalfa fields, are all green now, interrupted occasionally by the gold and browns of plowed wheat stubble.

The winds are calm, the air is smooth, and as I fly over the river and a farm pond I can see my reflection in the glassy water. I leave Lake Tom Steed and decide it is time to head back to the airport before it gets too dark. I don't have a landing light on the airplane and the sun is sinking quickly below the horizon now. Dusk is settling in over all of the area and the lights of the surrounding towns and country yard lights are beginning to come on. It's time to put it down.

I point the little Cessna south and see the welcome lights of the airport and the reassuring clear and green lights of the beacon. I pop open the side window, prop my elbow on the ledge of the side window, and fly the rest of the way hands off the controls and my feet on the floor.

I enter the pattern and since no one else is around I have the airport to myself. I enter downwind, pull carb heat, back the power off to 1200 rpm, start the descent and don't even feel the airplane and runway meet until the tires start rolling. Push the yoke forward just a bit, keep the tail in the air and wait until it comes down on its own. Talk about a grease job! Boy, that was a good landing! Just the right way to end a perfect flight.

JUST FLYIN'

I have done my share of the "Hundred dollar breakfasts" over the years. Many times I would get out of bed before sunup, fix my usual healthy heart breakfast of grape jelly covered toast, oatmeal, orange juice, cup of coffee, and then drive to the airport, pre-flight the 120 and fly 85 or 150 miles to a Fly-In just to have another breakfast of pancakes, sausage, syrup, and coffee. Maybe even get a couple of donuts on the side. But it was free since I flew in. Can't beat that!

Sometimes I would get caught out in West Texas when the winds would start whuppin' up over 35 mph and I would nearly lose the breakfast on the way back home, but my goodness, I got a FREE meal!

The meals were always free to anyone who flew in, but it cost the local folks and all those who walked or drove in three or four dollars. Reason is that if you charged a pilot for his pancakes after he flew a hundred miles or so he wouldn't ever come back to that airport ... for any reason.

I'm a little ashamed to admit it but for a period of time I got to the point that I wasn't enjoying flying as much as I used to. After twenty some years of boring holes in the sky in all kinds of flying machines in all kinds of weather the 35 mph winds and 95 degree temperatures started taking some of the fun out of it.

There was a time when it didn't make any difference how hot it was or how hard the wind was blowing, if a flight could be made I did it and grinned with glee with every bump I hit and wiped the sweat with both hands because I was FLYING! The older I got though, the comfort index exceeded the itch to fly.

◆　　　◆　　　◆

One time I flew to Mooreland, Oklahoma on a hot, windy, summer day and landed my Cessna 170 in 35 mph crosswinds and yelled with delight and excitement when I finally fought the airplane down and it weather-cocked into the west wind. I sorta had it under control ... just barely, and when I got it stopped it was pointed west instead of south. Lloyd Howard was with me, he squawled as well, but in fear of his life instead of delight. I was just happy to have done it because then I knew I could do it and I got to add another page to my book of experience.

◆   ◆   ◆

Jerry Bryan went with me one hot summer day in June to Tahlequah, Oklahoma in the far eastern part of the state to an Ercoupe Convention and Fly-In. The "Coupers" felt we were invading their territory in my 170 however, and admittedly, we were very much in the minority, so they made us park on the other side of the airport clear away from the Ercoupes. Later in the day, I took off in a 102 degree temperature with absolutely no wind at all. It was so quiet and still you had to walk fast to make any breeze at all. We ate up all 3500 feet of the runway and staggered into the sky rather sloppily. We flew almost to Shawnee before the airplane was able to climb to a thousand feet. The 170 was running hot, so I would climb awhile, fly level awhile, then climb some more, then level some more to keep the engine from red-lining. Jerry and I just laughed and grinned and sweated and had an awfully good time. It only took four hours to fly the 250 miles home, about twice as long as it usually would have.

◆   ◆   ◆

Brother Keith went with me in a Tripacer one time to fly his daughter Judy and her husband Dan back to Tipton from Tulsa. We took off that morning and things were going good until we hit a wall of fog south of Chickasha. We turned north, landed at Chickasha and waited a couple of hours until we could see the sun. We then took off again, but didn't fly twenty minutes until we were in the fog again and I found myself flying along at 600 feet with nowhere to go but up. I told Keith to stare outside while I stared at the instruments and I began a climb of 300 fpm with wings level until we popped out on top of the clouds into the sunlight.

We flew up there until I we could see "sucker holes" and spots of the ground, so then I spiraled down through one of those back to the 600 foot level, flew to the red light in Tecumseh, turned left, flew on to Shawnee and landed where we waited another couple of hours for the weather to clear.

We did finally get to Tulsa, landed at Harvey Young, loaded up Dan and Judy, and took off again. But on the way home it naturally was another hot day since it was in July and the Tri-Pacer kept trying to go down instead of up. With four bodies in that stubby winged little thang it really didn't even want to fly at all. We climbed and dropped, bumped and grinded, and flopped our way home, but Judy, Dan, and Keith got nervous and after while I did too. All in all it was an awfully good experience because I learned I didn't want to do that anymore. Judy and Dan drove back to Tulsa a couple days later. Didn't even ask if I would fly them back for some reason.

◆   ◆   ◆

Brother Keith decided one time he wanted to learn how to fly a tail dragger and I agreed to show him. We got in my 1948 Cessna 170, him in the left seat and me in the right. I talked him from the parking apron down to the end of the runway, told him what to do and what sorta to expect, and then told him to push the power in ... gently. He did, the 170 veered left, I told him to give it right rudder, he did, and it went right, then left, then right, then he threw his hands straight up in the air and yelled, "YOU GOT IT!!!". Talk about busy feet and hands. That was Keith's last tail dragger lesson with me.

◆   ◆   ◆

A bunch of us were sitting around the airport hangar flying one winter day. It was terribly cold, about 18 degrees, cloudy, but not any wind at all. Just a very bitter cold, cloudy winter day. I had a 1946 Aeronca 7AC Champ sitting out in the big hangar and someone wondered if it would start in that cold weather. I put on my insulated coveralls, went out and sonofagun, after pulling it through several times, priming it, and after a few tugs on the prop, it started and ran, ticking along about 400 rpm. After a while the oil pressure finally came up, so Beverly Akin, myself, and Jerry Hostick decided to fly. Beverly had over 8000 hours, was a certified flight instructor, but it still embarrassed her that she just didn't feel that good in a taildragger.

We put on all the clothes we had and took turns flying that Champ, each one of us flying until the windows fogged up or our hands and feet got so cold we couldn't feel them. Then we would land, leave the airplane running, give the next person the insulated coveralls and let them fly. Boy, we had fun! Beverly regained her confidence and respect that day. It beat the heck of just sitting around hangar flying.

◆   ◆   ◆

I always look forward to October because I can once again feel those cool mornings and evenings and that lovely fall flying air. I can again fly without the bumps and grinds of summer and sometimes even wife Nancy will go with me, not often though.

Flying in the fall of the year can really be a delight. I remember one Saturday evening when it was cool, crisp, very little wind, and just before sundown the colors of the trees, wheat fields, and cotton fields all in contrasting colors was just beautiful. I did some crash and dashes, then flew up near Snyder to give daughter Kari and the grandkids an aeronautical hello, then flew out on the river to look for son-in-law Mike hanging in a tree hiding from a deer. I landed just as the sun was setting, sorry that there wasn't more time to fly. Such a beautiful day to fly!

◆   ◆   ◆

I returned to the airport one day after lunch to find a Cessna 172 Skyhawk sitting on the ramp. It was one of those days when the temperature was already about 118 degrees, winds were hitting about 20 mph out of the southwest and it was not a good day to be anywhere near an airplane.

When I went inside the terminal building I found two young ladies waiting to use the courtesy van. When they came back from having a burger in town, I visited with them a bit and was very impressed by the fact that the pilot, Miranda McGuire and her passenger, Brooke Schrimpscher had flown from the Houston area and were making a four day trip of just flying. Miranda was only 22 years old and had been flying since she was 16. She and Brooke departed Frederick about 6:00 p.m. headed for an overnight stay in Waco, Texas. They were just out flying on a day when most of us wouldn't even think of getting away from the air conditioner.

As hard as it may be to believe, there are days that are just not good days to fly. When the temperature is 30 degrees or below, the winds are blowing 30 mph, light freezing mist is falling, very low clouds, and the forecast is for more freezing rain, sleet, and snow, it is not a good day to fly.

But ... on those days a pilot can still go to the airport and see who can tell the biggest and most hair raising story about adventures of days gone by and hear such things as "W'all that's nuthin', you shoulda been with me the day you couldn't even see the wingtips from the cockpit because of the fog and we never did get down."

DUMB STUFF

Sometimes SMALL airplane pilots are poked fun at by LARGE airplane pilots for doing something that could be considered stupid by those of higher learning. The LARGE guys I am thinking about are those who have logged lots of hundreds of hours, get paid for flying, and supposedly know everything there is to know about flying. But, in my years of fooling around an airport I found that the "Fly for Hire" airplane jocks usually are not quite as smart as they think they were.

One day I looked out the window of my office at the Frederick Airport just in time to see a white blob whiz by the terminal building heading south on runway 17R. It kept on whizzing past the mid-field intersection. The winds however, were 15 mph out the north. Seems as though one of those smart highly paid jet jockey fellows was trying to land a Mitsubishi downwind. He did get it done, but in doing so used up all 6000 feet of the runway and most of his brakes getting the thing stopped. Then he turned around on the active runway and back—taxied the entire 6000 feet back to the north end instead taking one of three exits and using the parallel taxiway.

Was it Forrest Gump who said, "Stupid is as stupid does?"

Even the local guys, Donnie, Rexie, Steve, Bennie, Gary, and Butch know better than to do something like that.

Thank goodness, not all pilots who fly for hire or hold an instrument ticket are like that. Most are very courteous, but those who think they know everything there is to know, especially those who tell you so are the ones who get the "Chicken xxxx of the Year Award."

AN ANGEL?

One of the strangest visitors to Frederick Municipal dropped in on one ordinary day when there wasn't much of anything happening. When he came in the front door, my first impression was that he was just someone who was drifting through the country looking for a job or a handout. He wasn't dressed all that great, was a little smelly at close range, needed a shave, and apparently hadn't had a bath in God knows when. What got my attention though was when he spoke, his speech was in a most friendly manner, very polite, and with a thick foreign accent.

He apologized for taking up my time and said he wasn't an anybody … just a tourist and a "time waster". I asked him his name and where he was from and after a deliberate and thoughtful pause and a glance upward he said, "Jim … just Jim", and he said he wasn't from anywhere particular.

I asked him to sign the guest book and at first he hesitated, then in that foreign brogue he said he would, but first he must look about and think seriously what to write for what he wrote must be special because he could tell this was a special place.

He looked at the pictures and memorabilia hanging on the walls and then with a lot of thought he wrote in the book, "Jim, just a tourist and a time waster. One of the friendliest contacts in a well kept Historic district".

He then thanked me for taking the time to visit with him and left. In fact, he just disappeared. Gone in a poof! Within a few seconds of his leaving I looked out the door and there was no trace of him. It was obvious he didn't fly in because there was no airplane and he sure wasn't a pilot. I hadn't heard a car, so he apparently didn't drive in. When I told wife Nancy about him she said maybe he did indeed fly in. "Maybe he was an angel checking to see how you would treat him", said wife Nancy. Who knows?

A CHRISTMAS STORY

Santa Claus decided to do it different that year. Rudolph and the gang had been slowing down a bit so Santa told them they could take it easy, they could sleep in, and he would make his annual trip in the almost new Cessna 185 he had traded for. Boy, it was nice! Had skis on it, optional belly cargo hopper, and all the seats had been taken out except the two in front. Plenty of room for all the toys and stuff that needed to be delivered Christmas Eve night.

He started packing the 185 several weeks before and had just about stuffed it as full as it could be stuffed. The elves had checked the airplane all over very good for this most important trip. The oil had been drained out and set by the fire in a bucket to warm, the ice and snow had been swept off and all Santa had to do was pour the oil back in, climb in, and bring the big 300 horsepower engine to life and the new era of express Christmas delivery would begin.

After supper on Christmas Eve, Santa got up from his chair, and announced it was time to go. The elves put in one or two more gifts and put the oil back in the engine. Santa finally climbed in himself and fastened the seat belt. Boy, this was going to be a lot warmer than sitting in that open sleigh all night! About that time, wife Bertha Claus walked up to the airplane and said that since this was the beginning of a new era, could she ride along with him this time? Santa grumbled a bit, moved his charts and coffee jug out of the right seat, and told Berty to get in, but just don't mess with his stuff and be sure to not interrupt him and talk to him every time he landed.

Berty got in, slammed her door, and Santa's door popped open. He shut his door again and Berty's door popped open. (I've heard that before). Santa said, "Berty, this ain't gunna work, you just gotta stay home, there just ain't enough room for all this stuff and you too!" Berty puffed up and reluctantly got out muttering something about how much cooking Santa was going to get to do over the next several weeks and something else about some other stuff he was going to get to do without.

Santa hollered "CLEAR", hit the starter and the big Continental started turning over. One blade, two blades, three, four ... then eight blades. The starter got slower and slower and then "oooomph" and "errrrrrrrrrrrbbzzzz". He primed the engine again after waiting a few minutes and hit the starter again. One blade, two blades, three blades, it fired once, fired twice, pock, pock, pockity, pockity, pock, pock, pock, Oooomph. "Phfft!"

Sweat began forming on Santa's brow. He primed it again, this time real good and then pumped the throttle vigorously while hitting the starter switch. One, two, three blades, "FIRE"!! Flames belched out from under the cowling and all the elves ran over each other getting to the fire extinguisher. Berty ran in the house in a hurry when she saw the fire and smoke, but the elves got it all put out pretty quick. Santa was shaking now. Boy, that was close. The whole mess could have burnt up.... airplane, Santa, and most important, all the Christmas toys for every kid in the whole world.

Santa sat there for a minute, his heart beating loudly. That was it. That's enough. He hollered at all the elves, every last one of them, and told them to unload the 185 and put it all in the familiar red sleigh. "Go wake up them reindeers!" Santa yelled, "And jump start Rudolph if you have to!"

Christmas morning arrived and everything had been delivered on time. Berty had gotten over her mad spell and met Santa at the door when he got back with a hot cup of coffee and a plate of biscuits, sausage gravy and grape jam. He was now sitting back in his recliner, boots on the floor, sipping his second cup of coffee. Rudolph and the boys were warming up in their private quarters over a nice bunch of hot oatmeal and prairie hay.

"Progress?" Well, as much as I like airplanes, some things you just can't improve on.

THE NEXT GENERATION

As time passed, I joined that strange group of people who have bragging rights about their grandkids. Daughter Kari and her husband Mike became parents of our first grand daughter, Allie Elizabeth Ayers on December 23, 1993 and I am going to claim "Poppa's rights" and talk about her a bit.

Of course she was pretty, and little, and perfect when she was born, and I was, and still am, awfully proud of her and I'll be sure to tell you so if you will stand still long enough. I do feel a little sorry for Allie in a way however, because as she grows older, folks will most likely begin to tell her about how crazy her old grand daddy, who was, and is, always fooling around with some old airplane. They'll probably tell her about him scaring folks as they would see him land on the grass strip at her equally crazy Uncle Keith's house south of Tipton.

I hope she won't be too embarrassed when folks talk about her "Poppa" and his flying machines, nor the fact that he spent a lot of her inheritance on a dozen or so of them. Maybe she will pass it off as her Poppa just being "colorful" instead of crazy.

No doubt at all though, Allie has some of my blood in her. The problem though, is that mine is mixed with tiny little airplanes and that might just make her stare at the sky someday in wonder with an itch to go up there and see what's there. My dream was to keep the 1947 Cessna 120 and so she could have taken her first flying lesson in it someday. Then as folks zoomed by in their jet cars and saw her flying a 65 year old airplane they could have said, "There goes that Ayers girl flying that rickety old airplane her crazy old granddaddy used to fly and sure as hell, she's gunna kill herself in that thang if she don't watch out". Unfortunately, the 120 did get sold.

I took a picture of her scanning the cockpit of the 120 one time as soon as she could sit up real good just to get things started. She even handled the controls a bit, "Just to get the feel of things".

I did give Allie her first airplane ride on September 25, 1999 in the 120. The juices got started flowing then. "Y'all better watch out." Thar' she goes!

◆   ◆   ◆

Lo and behold, about three years after Allie was born, my first grandson, Jake Pinson Ayers was born. He arrived on December 14, 1996, weighed in at 8 pounds, 15 ounces, and was 21 inches long. He joined big sister Allie and his Moma and Daddy, Kari and Mike Ayers.

I had a dream the other night and I think possibly in the year 2030, the second orbiting space station will be run by Commander J. P. Ayers. He will accomplish this by first soloing the 1947 Cessna 120 that his crazy old Grand Poppa flew to Oshkosh, Wisconsin back in 1994 and that his sister Allie flew back to Oshkosh in 2020.

Jake will also have some yearning for the freedom of flight and will have the same want-to to fly as his Grand Poppa did because of those same tiny little airplanes that are coursing through his blood. Just stands to reason.

When Jake was 9 years old I gave him his first airplane ride. That story was told a little earlier in this book, but what it amounted to was smoke in the cockpit, a lot of smoke in the cockpit, and Jake handled that emergency quite well. In fact, when I told him to get outta the Ercoupe as fast as he could when we stopped rolling, he was already 100 feet behind the airplane before I could look around. I figure now he could get out of a space ship if he had to what with the advanced training I gave him.

◆   ◆   ◆

Just as she was about to decide to be single for the rest of her life, daughter Jo Lynn found a U. S. Army Captain by the name of Rod Boles. She had been looking for the perfect man like her daddy for many years, and when Captain Boles knocked on her door that night and they looked each other square in the eyes, each had been found. Rod was almost perfect and she married him and the U. S. Army when she was 30. I told Captain Boles immediately before the wedding started that he was fixin' to swear before God that he would never mistreat my little girl either mentally or physically and that he better swear to me the same thing or I would "de-captainate" him. He did, and has, and I haven't had to.

It wasn't too long that Jackson Grant Boles, my second grandson was born. He arrived on September 26, 2003, weighed in at 7 lbs. 4 oz., and was 20" long. Jackson, like Allie and Jake, also has the little airplanes coursing through his blood, so I fully expect him to start gazing at the sky with an "I wonder" look in his eyes one day soon.

If Jackson follows in Rod's and his dad Ron's footsteps, he too will wind up in the U. S. Army, but I betcha he will be in aviation, maybeso flying helicopters. (Those flying machines without wings.)

◆   ◆   ◆

Jo and Rod lived in Lawton, Oklahoma, Columbia, South Carolina, Edmond, Oklahoma, and El Paso, Texas after they married. Then Rod lived in Balad, Iraq for awhile and Jo and Jackson lived in Tipton while he was overseas. Then Rod was assigned to Officer's Command School at Fort Leavenworth, KS in 2005 and it was there that my third grandson was born. Rod is now stationed at Ft. Sill, Oklahoma and they live in Snyder, Oklahoma at the present time.

Luke Pinson Boles arrived in Kansas on March 23, 2006. When I first saw that teeny little boy he looked back at me and I was shocked because I could see my own Daddy in that baby's face.

Luke is not quite two years old yet, but according to his mother is practicing for it real good. He hasn't shown any tendency to jump off the house yet, but does run all over the place sometimes holding his arms out and making engine sounds like a P-51. "Here we go again!"

MR. PINSON, YOU HAVE A VERY SERIOUS PROBLEM

The night of February 6, 1990 an event occurred that began a major change in my life. After supper, a shower, and lying back in my Lazy Boy reading the newspaper, I felt a little short of breath. When I tried to take a deep breath, a dull numbness started in the center of my chest and then a severe ache rapidly spread up into my shoulders and down each arm. I tried to get out of the recliner, but couldn't. Nancy saw me and with panic in her eyes, immediately went to the bedroom and got a small bottle of nitroglycerine tablets that my brother Keith had given me a few days earlier. I had told him I had been feeling a little funny and he gave me the pills just in case.

The nitro made the ache go away so I went to bed, but the next day I saw our family doctor who immediately scheduled me for an appointment a couple of hours later with Dr. V. M. Parikh, a cardiologist at Lawton, about 50 miles away. I was put on a treadmill for a stress test and after one and a half minutes of walking, I collapsed. They squirted fowl tasting stuff in my mouth, threw some pills down my throat, and within the hour was admitted to the Comanche County Hospital cardiac care unit. (CCU)

Dr. Parikh said, "Mr. Pinson, you have a very serious problem". After five days in the hospital during which a procedure called a heart catherization (angiogram) and then a balloon angioplasty to expand a 90% arterial blockage on the left side of my heart, I was released with a repaired heart (I thought), but also the fear that I may never be able to fly an airplane again.

Six weeks later I went back for a checkup only to find that the balloon angioplasty had collapsed and I was in serious trouble once again. I was again admitted to the hospital on April 2, 1990 and another angioplasty was attempted that afternoon only it collapsed during the procedure. I was then told that I had to have coronary by-pass surgery and it would be done the next morning. No options.

It was. I woke up many hours later unable to move and felt like I had a football in my throat. I couldn't see them, but tubes and wires were running out of every part of my body. After two days in the intensive care unit I was transferred to a private room and was able to take a look at myself for the first time. I had a foot long gash from my neck to just below the sternum and also about fourteen inches of gash down the inside of each leg from the knee to my ankle. My chest was the color of a massive thunderstorm like is depicted on doppler radar. After another five days in the hospital I went home hoping they didn't drain all the little airplanes out of my blood.

It took almost two years, a pile of paperwork six inches tall, a note or letter from every Doctor, nurse, aide, toilet cleaner, and Candy Striper that ever took a look at me, walked passed me, or wandered down the hall, and a twelve minute stroll on the treadmill, but I did it. Persistence, sweat, aggravation, cussing, a lot of fear, and the aid of many, many good people paid off. I received a special issuance third class medical certificate. I could fly legally again!

About three months after the surgery I drove out to the open hangar where my 1947 Cessna 120 sat. By that time it was covered with dirt, bird poop, and looked like it had been totally abandoned. I was feeling a little better by then so I got a garden hose and hosed it off. Brother Keith saw me and walked out to the hangar and I asked him if he would go with me … I wanted to see if I could still make my Cessna go up and come down.

Keith didn't have to touch anything. I made one of the best take offs and best landings I had ever made. To heck with a medical, I could still fly, and by-damn I was going to! For those two years I fought with the FAA Aeromedical folks, I flew out of Pinson's Cotton patch Airport, went up and looked down, flew the river, and kept my piloting skills intact. When I did receive the special issuance certificate, I was ready. If any FAA person reads this, I just told a big lie.

OSHKOSH '94

Oshkosh, you say! What the heck is an Oshkosh? That's where they make those striped overalls isn't it? Well, yes, they do that there too, but for a fly-person, a pilot, a person who loves airplanes, Oshkosh has an entirely different meaning. It is the largest gathering of the most people in the shortest period of time of air-planes and their lovers in the world. Close to one million people and over 14,000 aircraft all come to Oshkosh, Wisconsin the last week of July to see, to be seen, to look, to gaze in wonder, and participate in the greatest annual aviation event in the world.

Let's put it this way. If you are an avid golfer, imagine being at the Masters or the U. S. Open and actually being a participant in it. If you are a hunter, imagine the hunt, the safari of a lifetime, maybe in Africa. If you are a lover of arts and crafts, imagine participating in and being in something like the "Affair of The Heart Craft Show" only a hundred times as big. If you are a race car driver, imagine being able to participate in the Indy 500. "Get the picture now?"

Most every aircraft type anyone has ever read about or seen pictures of are there. The tiny ultra-lights, the homebuilts, the classics of 30, 40, and 50 years ago, the fighters and bombers of World War II, the jets of Vietnam, the new funny looking high-tech designs, the supersonic British Concorde. They are all there to see and actually touch.

People in aviation you read about for years are there…. Chuck Yeager, Bob Hoover, Bud Anderson, Patti Wagstaff, Julie Clark, Paul Poberezny, the Astro-nauts of the Apollo Space Series. They come from not only the United States, but Africa, Europe, Australia, all over the rest of the world, to Oshkosh.

This is a blow by blow description of a trip made from Frederick, Oklahoma to Oshkosh, Wisconsin for the 1994 Experimental Aircraft Association Conven-tion and Fly-In. I flew my 1947 Cessna 120, Jerry Hostick from Frederick flew a 1977 Cessna 150, and Tom Yates from Altus flew a brand new Kitfox that he built himself. This trip had been talked about and dreamed about for at least nine years by Jerry and me. We had talked about how we wanted to take plenty of time, to be able to fly up the Mississippi River, just flying and seeing. In previous years however, anywhere from a week to three weeks before the Fly-In we would get cold feet or some other excuse would cause one of us to say, "Well, I can't go this year, let's do it next year."

When my friend Tom Yates from Altus heard about all those plans, he said to get ready, there wasn't going to be any backing out this year, we were going to go. Jerry and I didn't take him too seriously because the Kitfox he was building didn't even have the engine and wings on it yet. But, Tom insisted he would be ready to go because he had made a bet with his friend Chuck in Chicago, the same guy Tom bought the airplane from, that it would be flying by the end of May. So with pushing and shoving by Tom, the fact that he did indeed solo his Kitfox on Memorial Day weekend, and in spite of a pinched nerve in my back a week before takeoff, and a fear that we had never felt before, we did it. We actually did it. We went to OSHKOSH 94!

Probably only three people are really interested in this account ... the three that did it. Maybe four counting Dr. John, Tom's brother. But anyway, as the stringy-haired blond waitress in tight-fittin' jeans at the Cajun catfish cafe in Sedalia, Missouri said as she plopped our plates on the table, "ENJOY".

The morning of July 24, 1994 was beautiful. The sun was shining and what wind there was light out of the southwest. It was the kind of day we had expected and wanted, and sure enough, there it was. I arrived at Frederick airport about 7:30 a. m., parked at the hangar, got out and unlocked the door, all the time feeling that this has got to be the craziest thing I've ever done in all my life.

I put all the stuff in the Cessna 120 that I thought I would need, the sleeping bag, the shoe box full of pork n' beans, crackers, and cheese crisps, the canteen, the ICOM handheld radio, the GPS, all the essentials that I thought I might possibly need for the trip. I then rolled the 120 out of the hangar, drove my pickup in the hangar, and closed the doors. I wondered to myself if I would ever see that pickup again.

I started the 120 and taxied to the terminal building where Keith had already made coffee. Jerry and his wife Barbara had arrived and as soon as Jerry got his stuff loaded in his 150, he too taxied up to the terminal area. It was time.

Keith and Barbara took pictures and then Jerry and I looked at each other and said, "Might as well" and then got in the airplanes, and started them. It was at this point that we realized that we were really going to go.... Jerry and I were leaving for Oshkosh, Wisconsin for the 1994 EAA Fly-In and Convention.

If we thought of it that way however, like the whole trip in one lump sum, we got scared, so we would say we were only going to go to see Mary and Joe at Lake Tenkiller and that eased the butterflies a little. Mary and Joe's place was where we were to meet Tom. He had left Altus the day before and spent the night in Tulsa with his daughter.

We lifted off at 8:10 a. m. Jerry was in front but I quickly caught up with him. We headed east, climbed to 3500', and the GPS was indicating that we were really going that way. Jerry wound up in my eight o'clock position, a place where he usually was during the almost 22 hours of the round trip.

Our first stop was Ada, Oklahoma. We had been in the air just about an hour and it was time for a pit stop and we also wanted to keep the tanks full. We landed at 9:20 and just as we touched down an Air Guard C-130 on the ground started its engines and when we stopped at the fueling area, a guy came running out and said "You guys better move them airplanes or that thang'll blow'um away." We started pushing the 120 and the 150 out of what we thought was the way but the C-130 seemed to follow us. Everywhere we pushed them the C-130 was there too.

We moved the airplanes three times and got sweaty way too early in the day. After finally fueling up, we took off at 9:55 a.m. and headed northeast toward Lake Tenkiller Airpark, our destination for the day. A few miles out of Ada I looked over the nose and saw Lloyd Howard's private strip and I saw him taking off in a cloud of dust in the Ag-Cat. I flew over him and waved, but he never knew we were there. He would have been upset if he knew what we did.

I could see Lake Tenkiller over the nose but the only place that looked like an airport was a clearing on top of one of the hills on the east side. I gave them a call on unicom and Joe Cunningham came back with, "That you Lynn?", but by then we had confirmed Tenkiller Airpark by sight. Joe had told us previously they might have a 500 foot displaced threshold because they were moving some dirt around, but we cleared that and made a good landing anyhow. Jerry got worried about only having 2000 feet of runway, particularly for the take-off the next morning. He was afraid his 150 might run in the lake. Anyway, we landed about 11:00 a. m. and our flying for this day was done.

We tied down, Joe welcomed us, gave us their car to put our stuff in and we hurried into the cool of the terminal building to wait for Tom who was coming from Tulsa in his Kitfox. He had flown to Tulsa the day before to visit his daughter and we had arranged to meet at Tenkiller. He got there about 12:30 p. m. and we all shook hands, overjoyed that we were actually there and we were actually on our way to Oshkosh!

Mimi Stauffer and Earl Downs from Cushing landed in a 7AC Champ about 1:00 p. m. and we all went to the Smokehouse Restaurant for dinner. Of course the talk was about Oshkosh. Mimi tried to calm our nerves by telling us that she

flew in a couple of years ago in an Ercoupe with no trouble at all. The big difference was though, she had done it and we hadn't. We were still scared.

Jerry, Tom, and I checked in at the Log Cabin Motel just a couple hundred
yards north of the airpark and then proceeded to laze away the rest of the day. We
talked with folks visiting the airport, pestered Mary & Joe, walked the runway,
and then went back to the Smokehouse for supper. Then we got serious about
the flight we were going to make the next day, spread the charts all over the cabin
and Jerry tried to make some sense of a GPS that he had borrowed. We got it all
figured out though. We would get up early, eat breakfast, and leave for Jefferson
City, Missouri about 8:00 a. m.

Monday, July 25. About 3:30 a. m. we were awakened by claps of thunder,
flashes of lightning, and the sound of rain. At 7:00 a. m. it was still raining. We
did get up early, we did eat some breakfast, but we didn't leave at 8:00 a. m. as
planned. Instead we waited and paced the runway in light rain and overcast skies
until almost noon and then took off at 11:45 in sprinkles and cloudy skies toward
a clear spot in the northeast repeating to ourselves that we could always come
back. Siloam Springs, Arkansas was only about 50 miles away and we could land
there if we had too. Even though we were nervous, the view from the air over that
part of Oklahoma was awfully pretty. As we flew further northeast the weather
didn't get any worse, nor did it get any better. We kept flying and talking to each
other on 122.75 mhz. as Jerry and I started leaving Tom and the Kitfox behind
since we were about 20 mph faster.

Tom said he was going to fly direct non-stop to Jefferson City, but Jerry and I
planned a pit stop at Springfield, Missouri. After we passed by Springdale, Arkansas the weather got a little messier and had it not been for the GPS indicating that
we knew where we were going we might have landed somewhere. Cassville, Missouri was a welcome sight when it became visible, and soon after passing there
visibility improved and we could see further ahead and our breathing became less
labored.

Jerry and I arrived at Springfield at 1:10 p.m., had a little confusion with the
tower, but landed with no problems. They didn't like it because Jerry had
announced us as a flight of two when he called in and then I called in not knowing I wasn't supposed to since my presence had already been announced.

To complicate matters, I forgot the ground control frequency and got lost
taxiing on the ground so the tower folks were very happy to see us get parked and
out of their hair. We gassed up, got a drink of water, and decided to get out town
as quickly as possible, determined not to make anymore mistakes and rile the
tower folks anymore. We tried. There was no problem until I made the mistake

of telling the tower I was ready to depart before Jerry and he was in front of me. They got unhappy all over again and canceled my clearance when I told them to let Jerry go first and they then made me wait and take off after a 727 jet landed. I sure was glad to leave that bunch of Missourians behind.

We pointed slightly northeast and soon began to see the beauty of the Lake of the Ozarks. It looked kind of like several fingers of a hand. We flew up the eastern side of the many "pockets" of the lake, saw the lakeside homes, and watched the folks sailing and motor boating. Sure was pretty.

Jefferson City appeared over the nose and we flew directly over town, saw the airport on the other side of the Missouri River, gave them a call, and landed without incident at 3:05 p. m. Those folks were a lot nicer than those down south. As we landed we noticed that there was a lot of sand on some of the runways. We found out later that it was because the entire airport was completely underwater the previous year during the flood of '93. Jerry and I tied down the airplanes and then saw Tom's brother John looking at us like he thought he ought to know us from across the ramp. We introduced ourselves to each other, shook hands, and he gave us a cold coke from the trunk of the red convertible he was driving. We visited and looked while waiting for Tom to arrive which was about 45 minutes later. Tom landed with a sore butt and almost empty tanks, but we had made our second leg, and were now deep in Missouri, a long way from home, but the sun was shining, we were grinning, and it was a great day. We were impressed by the high water mark on the terminal building which was about 10 foot up on the building.

John and Eileen Yates were so nice to open their home to us. Eileen fixed a dinner of roast, potatoes, gravy, the whole works, plus two deserts including chocolate covered strawberries. We were really hungry since we had skipped lunch, having munched only on a package of cheese crisps north of Springfield. After dinner, Tom, Jerry, and I drove to a mall to get some flashlight batteries, came back, showered, and went to bed. Tom and I shared a room upstairs and Jerry stayed downstairs with Gunther, the family Doberman. Tom snored. Jerry was afraid to.

Tuesday, July 26. We woke up again to the sound of rain. We looked out and it was overcast, raining, and sure not a good morning for flying. Eileen had again outdone herself by fixing a breakfast casserole and we ate good once again. When she left for work we got out the charts and tried to plan the day's route hoping the rain would stop soon. This was supposed to be the long day since we wanted and needed to get to Madison, Wisconsin if we could, a long way off from where we were. And it was still raining. We optimistically spread the charts and planned anyhow.

It looked like the weather might clear so we called a taxi and went to the airport even though it was still raining lightly, and by the time we got there the skies were looking a bit better, particularly to the east. We met a couple of corporate pilots who had a lap top computer and they tapped in on a new thing called the Internet and showed us a radar picture of the area we were wanting to go. There was a corridor of clear in the direction we wanted to go so we decided to do it. One of the pilots grinned when he found out I was flying a Cessna 120 because he had learned to fly in one in the early 60s and seeing mine brought back some nice memories for him.

Jerry and I divided Tom's luggage, camera, and other stuff between us so John would have a place to ride in the Kitfox. He was going to fly with Tom to Muscatine, Iowa then switch over and ride with Jerry on to Madison. Tom had to replace a faulty ignition switch while we waited for the skies to clear, then we took off from Jefferson City at 11:35 a. m., headed up the four lane highway northeast pointed toward Hannibal, Missouri, again in light rain and clouds but the visibility was not too bad and we could at least see where we were going.

We discovered that we were supposed to talk to each other on 122.75 mhz. instead of 122.8 mhz. or 122.9 mhz., so we kept in touch with each other on that frequency. Jerry and I again outran Tom and John and it wasn't long before we could see that we were going to break out into the sunshine a few miles southwest of Hannibal, Missouri. When I saw Hannibal, I could see the Mississippi River for the first time. I called Jerry and said, "Jerry! There it is! The Mississippi!" He could see it too as it wound northward. We altered course just a bit at Hannibal, and headed northward up the river toward Quincy, Illinois, flying sometimes on the west side, then crossing over to the east side so we could see better from the left window. We flew past the bridge at Quincy that was on television news last year that had been closed due to the flood, then on to Keokuk, Iowa. We were finally doing what we had talked about for nine years … we were flying up the Mississippi River, at 800 feet above the ground, taking in the beauty of what we had talked about for so long. It was unbelievable. We were actually doing it!

As we flew and talked, we saw strange looking crops below and wondered what was growing down there that was so pretty and green. A pilot from somewhere heard us talking and asked where we were and when we told him, he said it was corn and soybeans and that all that land was under water last year. It was unbelievable. As we flew we listened to other pilots on the plane to plane frequency and we realized all of a sudden they were all going to Oshkosh, just like us. We heard pilots coming from California, some were crossing Illinois, some were flying over Lake Michigan, and some were already in Wisconsin.

When we flew over Keokuk, Iowa we left the Mississippi River for a while and headed to Muscatine, Iowa where we landed at 1:50 p. m., a flight of a little over two hours from Jefferson City. We were hungry and tired and it was definitely time to get out of the 120 for awhile. We had been told that there was a truck stop across the highway from the airport, but after landing was told it had closed. Tom and John were about 45 minutes behind us, so Jerry and I got the planes gassed up, borrowed the airport car and went into town to a Hardee's and got some lunch. We brought back a snack for Tom and John to save some time because we still had a long way to go before the day was over and it was getting late.

Tom and John landed just as Jerry and I finished eating our sandwich and they ate what was left. We were going to rest a little while but noticed that the clouds were moving in again so we loaded up and departed Muscatine at 3:55 p. m. headed for Madison, Wisconsin. Before we left however, we had to rearrange the luggage so John could ride with Jerry because they were to land at Dane County airport, a Class C airport, John would get the rental car, and then Jerry would fly back and meet Tom and I at Morey Airport, a small airport just inside the Class C ring on the west of town. I could fly low and get into Morey with no trouble without a transponder.

The clouds were getting lower and light rain began falling every so often, but conditions got no worse so we kept flying. The Magellan GPS that I borrowed from Keith was having difficulty locking in on the satellites and I got a little worried because nothing was recognizable there. The GPS finally settled down and gave me a reading and I got more comfortable. As we neared Dubuque, Iowa I saw the river again, but the GPS zapped out again so I resorted back to pilotage and started looking for landmarks leading into Madison.

The chart showed Morey Airport to be on the west side of a small lake which was on the west side of Madison. I saw Madison, the lake, but no airport. I dropped down to pattern altitude and continued to look for Morey. The beauty of the Wisconsin landscape was spectacular as the sun peeked under the cloud layer in the western sky. Finally, as I neared the lake, I saw a row of airplanes parked on the other side of some trees, identified it as Morey, gave them a call on the unicom, but there was no response. I was ready to land so I called in the blind, entered left downwind, couldn't see any traffic, and landed at Morey Airport, which turned out was actually at Middleton, Wisconsin, at 5:30 p. m., breathing a sigh of relief as I taxied to the gas pump.

When I climbed out of the 120, the first thing I noticed was that it was cool.... jacket weather. The next thing I noticed was that I felt like I had taken a step back in time to the 1940s or 50s, a most funny feeling. It was so quiet, the buildings were just like they were 50 years ago, including the "Morey Airplane Company" sign painted on one of the hangars. I walked over to a small group of people and asked if I could get some gas and a young man said I would have to check in at the office, but yes, he was going to be there for awhile and he would even wait for Tom and Jerry. I walked inside the old hangar office and a short, plump, white-haired Wisconsin looking woman stared at me and said rather abruptly, "Ve closs ut fife o'clock!"

Explaining my need for fuel and the hopeful arrival of Tom and Jerry, she warmed up a bit and said we could get gas if the boy would stay and do it for us and I told her he already said he would. Jerry arrived about 20 minutes later, Tom entered the pattern another 15 minutes or so, John showed up with the car a few minutes later and we were all on the ground in the State of Wisconsin.

We called the local Holiday Inn, got reservations and looking all the world like seasoned pilots, checked in and were treated to some very nice, but expensive, hotel rooms, but we decided we deserved them after the day we had been through.

Jerry and I were roommates for the night and after much discussion and indecision, we wound up at a "Chili's" for supper, were lucky to get a pleasant and friendly waitress, and nervously enjoyed our last meal. Tomorrow was the day. Our next stop was the biggy, ORSHKORSH!

Jerry snored too, but I got a good nights rest thanks to a set of foam ear plugs.

Wednesday, July 27. We woke up, ate what breakfast we could considering our nervousness, checked out of the hotel, and drove to the airport. It was downright cold, sure-nuff jacket weather. We had worried for days about how we were going to carry all our stuff from the airplanes at Oshkosh to the car after we got on the ground at Wittman field, but finally one of the brighter members of our group suggested we leave everything in the car at Morey and carry only the necessary navigation stuff in the airplanes, that way we wouldn't have to carry much of anything to the car at Oshkosh. Everyone said that was the smartest thing anyone had suggested the past three days. I agreed since I was the one who made the suggestion.

After Jerry made several trips to the bathroom the airplane engines were started and we departed Morey at 8:40 a. m., turned out toward Ripon, the rendezvous point of every airplane in the United States, Canada, and parts of Europe going to Oshkosh. We felt like we were flying over the English Channel to do war with the Germans. We were scared spitless. We were certain we were going to meet sudden death by colliding with all those other airplanes at Ripon, especially those like we saw in the videos and had heard about for eight years. Curses, Tom Yates, why did we let you talk us into this? The GPS was clicking off the miles and finally I saw I was 12.1 miles away from Ripon. I flew on further, saw a lake that had to be Green Lake, looked at the GPS and it still said 12.1 miles. That dirty, sonofagun, it quit again.

All of a sudden I saw a town and the water tower said "RIPON" on it and I were there! Where were all those other 8000 airplanes? Jerry or Tom weren't even in sight. There was Green Lake, and Rush Lake, and there were the abandoned railroad tracks, and there were also three or four airplanes in front of me heading northeast. I got in line and flew over the railroad tracks looking for the strobe that was supposed to be in front of me and finally there it was. As I got closer and was listening closely on 120.7 mhz. the voice of Fisk identified the other airplanes. Finally, a voice said, "Blue high-wing taildragger, rock your wings." I did, and the voice said, "Good rock blue taildragger, clear Fisk and proceed 070 degrees for landing on 36L, listen 126.6." I had no idea where Jerry or Tom were and at that point I really didn't care.

I could see Lake Winnebago ahead of me and also could see the hundreds, no, literally thousands of airplanes in front of me. Oshkosh tower cleared me to land on 36L and as I turned final the whole thing lay before me. I was going to land at Oshkosh! I set up to land on the numbers, but the tower told me to extend and land long because there was another airplane landing behind me. It then occurred to me that there was probably another airplane coming over the top of me and going to land in front of me.

Touchdown! 9:40 a. m. Not even a bounce! The eagle had landed! Tears tried to come in my eyes, but I couldn't allow that because I needed to see where I was going. The emotion of the moment, the elation I felt because my dream had finally come true. I had finally, really and truly, flown to Oshkosh.

With a grin from ear to ear, I held up a cardboard sign requesting "Classic" parking. I turned off at the second taxiway and a guy on a little motor scooter led me about 100 yards to the middle of row 83 next to a 7AC Champ. In less than a minute a Kitfox taxied up on my left side. Another fellow on a John Deere Gator drove up, welcomed me to Oshkosh, and gave me a registration paper to fill out and sort of told me where everything was.

I got out of the 120 and looked around at the gorgeous day. The sun was shining, the airplanes were still landing, there were rows and rows of planes in front of me and the rows were rapidly filling behind me. I stared in disbelief at everything before me.

Tom, Jerry and I had all agreed to meet at the Kitfox display area wherever it was, so I walked north to the building to register myself and the 120 and then walked north until I finally got to the tent where the Kitfox exhibit was, at least a one mile walk. They told me that the Kitfox airplanes were back where I had just come from so I headed back south looking at everything as I went. Walking along looking, I heard someone yell "BUTCH", and there was Tom walking out from between two tents with a hammer in his hand. He had to pay a $20.00 deposit on the hammer to borrow it and he was still fussing. It was almost noon, but at least Tom and I had found each other. Jerry and John were still missing.

Tom and I got some lunch and it wasn't too long until we found Jerry and John. The rest of the day was spent looking, walking, and looking some more. Finally about 6:30 p.m. we decided to go find Dan and Debbie Gibson's home where we had made arrangements to stay.

Dan and Debbie Gibson, their two sons Ben and Jacob were delightful people. We finally found their farm home which was about halfway between Oshkosh and Ripon at Pickett, Wisconsin. After meeting and visiting with them and deciding which bed each of us was to get, we went into Ripon to a nice restaurant, had a good dinner, which was much more relaxed than the one we had the night before at Madison. We toasted our success at being where we were and agreed that we had done an outstanding job of getting ourselves there.

Thursday, July 28. We woke up early, Debbie had left coffee and rolls for breakfast, then we piled in our rental car and drove back to Wittman Field. We checked the airplanes and then started walking and looking. It was overwhelming. There were airplanes as far as you could see, warbirds of every description, P-51's, T-6's, B-26's, B-17's, and Corsair's. There were the Kitfoxes, Cessnas and Pipers, the newest Lancair's, the Glasair's, and of course the classics and antiques. No way to describe it. It was like three State fairs rolled into one, but at Oshkosh everything that could be seen was related to aviation. There was the Fly-market, where you could buy everything from a nut and bolt to an airplane wing and engine. There were the exhibit buildings where you could buy a GPS, Loran, Nav-Com, or anything related to avionics. We walked until our legs turned to rubber. We would rest awhile, then walk some more. If we got separated we would meet at the Antique/Classic headquarters "Red Barn", rest some more and then start all over again. We visited the EAA wearhouses were where you could buy jackets, tapes, T-shirts, books, and all kinds of clothing and trinkets.

All day long every day there were fly-by's of different kinds of aircraft including the Tri-motor Stinson that was giving rides over the area, then in the afternoon was the airshow. We saw the Gee-Bee, Rare Bear, an aerobatic Kitfox, Julie Clark in her T-34, Delmar Benjamin, The French Connection, the Harrier Jet, Gene Littlefield, Sean Tucker, Patti Wagstaff, Chuck Yeager, and Bobby Jounkin. The list goes on and on.

That evening after the airshow, we went to "Jeff's on Rugby Street" a local restaurant Tom had been to before for dinner, then went back to the Gibson home to rest our weary bodies.

Friday, July 29. We got up early again but didn't get in any hurry that morning. We had coffee and cereal, then headed back to Wittman field, but on the way decided to see if we could find Fisk, Wisconsin, a place we had heard of for so many years because that is the place the incoming aircraft are recognized on their approach to Oshkosh. We turned off the highway, headed north and found Fisk or what there was of it. It consisted of one elevator. No Chamber of Commerce to greet us. We saw the strobe light blinking on a hill a little further north and drove up to the site of the voice of Oshkosh which consisted of three guys sitting on the porch of a trailer house with a set of binoculars and a radio. That was it. We visited with them a while, watched a few airplanes come in then after thanking them for letting us look, drove into Wittman field where we had to park about two miles away from the main gate and walk some more.

We split up that morning because Tom wanted to see Kitfox stuff, John wanted to read his gun book, Jerry wanted to go to some of the EAA seminars, and I wanted to see the Fly-market. We agreed to meet at 1:30 for lunch, after which we wanted to go to the EAA museum that afternoon.

I walked through the Fly-Market, up through the rows of war birds, through the show planes, through the exhibit buildings, and then walked to row 83 to check on the 120. It was such a pretty morning, I spread a towel on the ground, leaned back on a tire, and watched the airplanes taxi by for the Parade of Flight for that day. Chuck Yeager and Paul Poberezny taxied by in a couple of P-51's, giving two "Young Eagles" a ride of their lifetime.

John, Jerry, and I caught a bus over to the museum, but Tom had already seen it so he tried to see all the Kitfox stuff. The museum was outstanding. John said that it was even better than the Smithsonian and we spent most of the afternoon there, leaving about 4:30 p.m.

When we walked out it was raining! We found Tom and ducked into the EAA Wearhouse (a place to spend lots and lots of money) for some more trinket buying but mainly to get out of the rain. It rained and rained. I spent $2.00 for a yellow trash bag called a raincoat and we gave up our plans to stay for the Bob Hoover event at the Theater in the Woods and walked the two miles back to the car in the rain. We found a place to eat, nothing special, but it was good and dry. Again, legs rubbery, we went back to the Gibson home and Jerry and I started planning for our departure the next morning. We had to go home.

Saturday, July 30. We woke up early because John had to catch a commercial flight at 6:30 a.m. We drove him to the airport, thanked him for all his professional psychiatric help for our heads and the free Ibuprofen for our bodies and then went to a Hardee's for breakfast. John was a Doctor of Psychiatry, but he offered his services, both physically (800 mg. Ibuprofen for sore, achy muscles) and mentally (you will get home without crashing) to us throughout the week. The weather was cloudy and somewhat foggy, but by the time we took Jerry to his airplane it was looking a little better.

We had been listening to departure control all morning on Tom's handheld radio and pretty well knew which runway we would be using so that was no surprise. Jerry and I agreed to meet at Portage, Wisconsin because according to the departure information and the fact we would be departing different runways there was no way we could stay together or even know where the other one was. Tom was going to stay until Tuesday because Ellen was to fly into Chicago and drive up with Chuck. They would arrive sometime later that morning so Tom didn't have to think about leaving now.

Tom let me out at the main gate and I went by Flight Service to check weather. They told me it was six miles and fog, but should be no problem after take off. I caught a tram to the 120, loaded up, and my nerves and adrenalin were going high speed. I heard the loudspeakers start sputtering like a big round engine with the 7:00 a. m. wake up call and watched as several other aircraft taxied by and noticed that each one was escorted by a guy on one of those little red scooters, so I stopped one, told him I wanted to leave, and he said he would be right back and take me to the departure area.

With his help, I pushed the 120 into the taxi lane and started the engine at 7:20 a.m., taxied onto the taxiway and then got in line to depart. There were 5 other planes in front of me and I was listening on 118.9 for departure on runway 18R. As I did my runup, Oshkosh tower asked me if 1605V was ready to go. I acknowledged I was, got cleared for take off, and I departed Oshkosh at 7:30 a. m. heading south with instructions to climb to 3000 feet, maintain heading for 5 miles and then proceed on course. As I was climbing out I glanced back through the right window of the 120 at that giant, sleepy, airport that was just beginning to stir for the day. I was still amazed that I had even been there.

I couldn't see good at all because of the fog if I climbed past 2000 feet, so I followed the airplane in front until I cleared the 5 mile area, then turned west toward Portage, Wisconsin with the GPS telling me I was going the right direction.

Visibility got a little worse and I was afraid I was going to wander into the incoming traffic around the Ripon area, but soon decided that I was indeed on course to Portage. I arrived at Portage at 8:20 a. m., gassed up with car gas, got a cup of coffee, and waited for Jerry. We had agreed if we totally lost each other, we would call Keith in Frederick and tell him where we were. Keith had not heard from Jerry and Jerry had not arrived at Portage either. I told the lady there that I was going to go on to Muscatine, Iowa and to please tell Jerry I would wait there regardless of how long it took to make contact. I departed Portage at 8:55 a. m., climbed out into some low clouds yet visibility was pretty good and the view of Wisconsin was beautiful.

About 50 miles out of Portage, I called Jerry again on 122.75 and heard a "Bzzzpt". I called again and again heard a "bzzzpt." I said, "Jerry, is that you?" "Bzzzpt." "Jerry, if that is you, key your mike twice because you have no audio." "Bzzzpt, Bzzzpt." Sonofagun! We did this for a few minutes and determined by one Bzzzpt and two Bzzzpt's that Jerry was south of Portage, and then his audio came back and the radio began working again. We had found each other for sure and we were both on our way to Muscatine. He had been delayed because when he started to leave Oshkosh the visibility had dropped to less than 3 miles, the tower closed, and they wouldn't let him leave.

I landed at Muscatine at 10:55 a. m. and Jerry arrived about 25 minutes later. We gassed up and again borrowed their courtesy car to go into town for some lunch. Back to the same Hardee's we had eaten at before and then back to the airport. We left Muscatine at 1:05 p. m. and headed slightly southwest for our next stop at Kirksville, Missouri.

We leveled off again at 3500 feet and flew over central Missouri well west of the Lake of the Ozarks, yet picked up the Missouri River and noticed where the flood of '93 had cut across a lot of the land. We landed at Kirksville at 2:30 p. m., gassed up, drank a coke, spread our charts all over the floor of the terminal building, and planned the next leg. We left Kirksville at 3:15 p.m. and headed for Sedalia, our planned stop for the day.

As we neared Sedalia, we discussed the possibility of going further, but our butts were getting numb, our legs were asleep, and there was the possibility that if we flew further we might encounter closed airports, so we landed at 4:30 p.m.

after finding out on the radio that there was a Best Western Motel located there, and yes, they would come get us.

The fellow at the airport suggested we eat at a Cajun catfish place only a block south of the motel called "LeMaire's", so when we got checked in we took his advice and went there. The atmosphere suggested early confusion, the stringy-haired blond waitress with tight fittin' jeans threw the plates on the table with a friendly "Enjoy", and the meal was excellent what with the catfish filets and dirty rice. Really good eating. After supper, we walked a couple of blocks to loosen up the muscles, then went back to the room. Jerry took a nap before it was time to go to bed and I watched the weather channel, planned the next days trip, and then we quit for the day.

Sunday, July 31. In spite of our intention to sleep in, we woke up early and could not resist the Sunday morning breakfast buffet at the motel. Got that done, checked out, and waited for the motel maintenance man to take the "Pilots" as we were referred to by the motel people back to the airport. It was a beautiful morning, sunny, and no weather worries except the expected head wind. We departed Sedalia at 8:30 a. m., bound for a fuel stop at Coffeville, Kansas. The scenery was prettier up north, but we were now in more familiar looking country.

We arrived at Coffeville at 10:50 a.m., gassed up, and after visiting with a couple on their way back home to Florida, took off at 11:25 headed for Stillwater, Oklahoma where we intended to get my friend Kevin Reeder to take us to lunch. We crossed back into Oklahoma about 11:45, flew over Bartlesville, and arrived at Stillwater at 12:45 a. m. We got gas and called Kevin, but he wasn't home. We talked to his answering machine instead. Since we couldn't get to town, Jerry and I broke out the emergency shoe box full of chips, pork n' beans, and crackers and had lunch at a back table in the Stillwater terminal building. It tasted pretty good.

We left Stillwater at 1:40 p. m. and started encountering rough and warmer air, so for the first time we decided to climb to 4500 feet to see if it would be a little more pleasant. It was cooler, but still bouncy, so we stayed there. I opened the window of the 120 and hung my elbow out until it got cold, then shut the window again. This is our last leg home. Our trip was almost over.

In the area of Fort Cobb Lake we were able to contact Frederick Unicom and I asked Keith to call Nancy and Barbara and tell them that we were going to be there shortly. In just a few minutes, Jerry and I lost each other for the first time on the whole trip and in spite of the fact we would tell each other our position, neither of us could locate the other and we imagined for many miles that we were only 10 feet apart or less. I could just imagine the embarrassment if we were to collide less that 50 miles from home. At least looking for each other gave us something to do while we flew those last few miles.

Finally we had Frederick Municipal in sight, and Jerry said he would enter a base leg for 17R, so I decided to make a straight-in. The 120 and I landed at Frederick at 3:45 p. m., and Jerry landed about two minutes later. We taxied up to the terminal building and Nancy, Barbara, and Keith walked out to greet us.

It was over. We had done it. Our dream had come true. We had actually flown to Oshkosh and got back alive. Now we could now talk about it over and over for many years to come.

We had been in the air 21.6 hours for the whole trip.... 10.1 hours going and 11.5 coming back. A little over 1800 miles. We were tired, very tired, but not too tired to smile and grin as we remembered the past 8 days and already began to re-live them.

Tom left Oshkosh on Tuesday, August 2 and wandered down to the south edge of Chicago. The next day he made it to Peoria, Illinois, got into bad weather and had to spend the night there. The next day he made it into Hannibal, Missouri, left there in a thunderstorm, and got back to Jefferson City to see John and Eileen again.

He flew to Shawnee, Oklahoma the next day, spent the night there, then flew into Altus on Saturday, August 6. We had all made it home. What an adventure!

It only took a couple of weeks before there was talk about the next year. Oshkosh '95? Nothing serious, just talk. "Well, maybe."

A DREAM FULFILLED: BY KEITH PINSON

Well, he did it. After several years of just talk, and eight more years of serious talk, Butch finally went to Oshkosh.

After several weeks of planning, charting routes, checking and cleaning their airplanes, packing, and all sorts of details, Butch and Jerry Hostick never would admit they were really going to go, but they did.

Actually, I don't know who was more surprised when they took off last Sunday morning, me or him. But it really happened. Butch in his 1947 Cessna 120 and Jerry in his Cessna 150 left Frederick airport at 8:15 that morning. Barbara and I watched them till they were out of sight, then looked at each other and Barbara said, "I guess they are really going to go".

They met Tom Yates from Altus in his newly finished Kitfox homebuilt at Lake Tenkiller later that day, and off they went on an adventure the three of them will talk about for a long time.

Many of you may not know what Oshkosh is. Oshkosh, Wisconsin is the site of the world's largest Fly-In and Air Show and is sponsored by the Experimental Aircraft Association. There are several hundred acres of airplanes parked wingtip to wingtip ranging from a one-person ultralight to the Supersonic Concorde. There are homebuilts, antiques, classics, all kinds of restorations, modern aircraft, and warbirds from the old Jennies to the most modern jets. I've never been there, but have read many magazine articles and seen many pictures and have heard stories from those who have been there, and it is probably the ultimate in a fly-person's dreams. I am very pleased and very excited that they finally got to go.

Butch called me the other morning about an hour after they landed at Oshkosh. I say landed; the 120 was parked there, but Butch was so excited, he was still several feet in the air. It really felt good to talk with someone who was so thrilled. He has called a couple of time since; his feet and legs were sore from so much walking, and his eyes were bloodshot from so much looking; but he was still taking it all in and having a wonderful time. I am sure this won't be the last time; he knows he can get there now.

Butch and Jerry will be landing here in Frederick sometime next Sunday afternoon. They will be full of stories, tales of adventures about the trip, and I'm sure they will have a new enthusiastic outlook on life. Ask them about their trip—I'm sure they will tell you all about it.

OSHKOSH '95

Oshkosh '95 is calling. Like a seductive lady with eyes the color of piano benches and the sweet smell of pleasures experienced in the past, Oshkosh is beckoning me back to be with her once again for a few fleeting days of ecstasy.

Of course, good buddy Tom Yates, instigator, troublemaker, Kitfox pilot, general agitator, but awfully good friend had nothing to do with stirring the juices of temptation when he called me the other evening and said, "We can get a round trip ticket to Chicago for a fraction of what it would cost to fly ourselves there in the 120 and the Kitfox like last year. We can rent a car in Chicago, drive through the beautiful countryside of eastern Wisconsin and see Oshkosh without the frettin' and worryin' of engine and weather problems, and be back home by the next Sunday!

I had said after our adventure of a lifetime last year I could die happy after making the trip to Oshkosh '94 in the Cessna 120, but as I read about the '95 Fly-In in SPORT AVIATION and thought of all the stuff I missed seeing last year and all the stuff I would like to see again, I sure did battle with myself not to go again.

Wife Nancy, bless her heart, just shook her head when she heard me talking to Tom. Little did she know when she married me years ago that I was infected with the airplane virus, meaning that my blood had tiny little airplanes in it that made me want to be in the sky or be near the things that would put me there.

Oh, Tom, Phil, and I left Oklahoma City Will Rogers Tuesday, July 25 on a Boeing 737. They wouldn't let us fly it though.

Oshkosh '95 was, for lack of a better word, terrific. I thought Oshkosh '94 could in no way be improved upon, but it was. Another 1500 or so airplanes flew in, probably another 2000 people came in, and the convention area was expanded to accommodate another 300 exhibitors making a total of over 600 companies showing off their good stuff and tempting all us pilots to buy their stuff.

The biggest difference about this year however, was the fact that Tom, Phil, and I flew the Boeing 737 to Chicago and drove the rest of the way to Oshkosh instead of flying our little airplanes like we did last year. But, by doing so, we missed the thrill of scaring ourselves to death, so next year we'll probably fly the little Cessna's again and wander our way from Oklahoma to Wisconsin looking and seeing and having the experience once again of getting ourselves there, landing ourselves at Oshkosh, and getting ourselves back home, all the while feeling the thrills and elation of doing it ourselves. I also missed having Jerry Hostick with us this year. Didn't seem right without him.

I found out that even the lightest of carry on bags can get very heavy when standing in line for boarding passes and walking half mile concourses, especially in a place like Kansas City and Chicago Midway. They wouldn't let us fly the airplane either. Damn! Didn't like that! It sure is a lot easier to just throw your stuff in the back of your own airplane and fly it the way you want to.

Phil Carson is a mighty nice guy, but a rather serious fellow, but I guess he has to be since he's a banker. Much more so than Tom or myself, but had it not been for Phil, Tom and I would probably be in jail. When asked on the way home what his impression of Oshkosh was, he said, "I have never in all my life seen anything like that!" That was said with a big grin too and bankers usually don't grin much either.

Phil didn't yield to temptation even once and buy something he didn't need. While Tom and I went bananas trying to figure out how to bring home everything we saw including several airplanes, Phil remained calm, cool, collected, and un-temptable. Tom even took an empty duffle bag with him to bring back all the new stuff. That's anticipating temptation.

In addition to all the kitplanes, homebuilt planes built from scratch, antique, and classic aircraft that came to Oshkosh, warbirds were there as well. The theme of the '95 Fly-In was a tribute to all those men and women who fought in World War II. There was a lot of talk about 1995 being the 50th anniversary of the end of the "Big One" and Oshkosh followed that idea.

"Tribute To Valor" was the theme and it was emphasized everywhere on the airport, but to really appreciate it you had to walk through the warbird section and see the over 200 airplanes that were built in such a short time to serve such a serious purpose, that of winning the war in the Pacific and Europe. Many of them I didn't know what they were, but I did stare in awe at the only flying B-29 Superfortress, the B-17's, B-25's, A-26's, B-26's, P-38's, P-51's, T-6's, T-34's, Wildcats, Hellcats, L-Birds, and even the British airplanes such as the Spitfires and Hurricanes.

If you looked closely, you might see a fellow or two in their 70's or 80's standing beside one of those airplanes trying to remember where the ladder was to climb into the cockpit. You might also hear them tell with tears in their eyes some of the hair raising stories about what they had done in one just like it and lived to tell about it 50 years later.

There was a virtual "Aluminum Overcast" when all those airplanes were put into the air during the Sunday afternoon air show. Fellows like Chuck Yeager and Bud Anderson, top aces of World War II spoke of those times and then each climbed into the cockpit of their respective P-51 Mustangs and flew over Oshkosh to prove that they still had the "Right stuff".

General Yeager skipped the Mustang a couple of times when he landed and the airshow announcer said, "General Yeager is adjusting his landing." Yeager adjusts, but does not bounce.

Overall, Tom, Phil, and I had an awfully good time, got to visit again with Dan, Debbie, Ben, and Jacob again, but had to tell them goodbye Saturday morning. We went to the airport and stayed until after the airshow, then got in our rental car and drove back to Chicago. We had reservations at a Marriot Residence style motel which actually was an apartment located in one of the suburbs of Chicago.

After checking into the motel, we found a Greek restaurant just down the street, walked in and the waiter with a white napkin draped over his sleeve greeted us at the door. After looking us over pretty good, he reluctantly led us to a table and let us sit down. Tom was the only one who knew what the menu said so Phil and I let him order for us. I still don't know what I ate.

When it came time for desert, Tom ordered one "Baklava", a very sweet Greek pastry. But when he asked for three spoons as was his custom, the waiter flipped off his napkin, and emphatically said "NO". He finally brought Tom our desert with one spoon and Tom took his knife and cut it into three pieces and we ate it with our fingers.

The next day was rather uneventful as we caught our plane at Chicago Midway and flew back to Oklahoma City, then drove home in Phil's car.

It was a good trip, after all we went to Oshkosh again, but we all agreed not to travel that way again. It was much more fun to fly our own airplanes. After all, flying ourselves there and back is most of the adventure.

OSHKOSH '96 ... THE MISSING YEAR

I'm suffering withdrawal pains even before it happens. Oshkosh '96 is coming up in three weeks and I can't go.

Good buddy Tom has called repeatedly over the past several weeks saying, "Well, whadda we gunna do about Orshkorsh?", and I keep telling him that I just can't go this year. But, when I step outside early in the morning and smell the cool summer air I am immediately mentally transported to Dan and Debbie Gibson's front yard only eight miles away from Wittman Field and can almost hear the inbound airplanes flying overhead as they prepare for landing at the mecca of all general aviation.

I just can't go this year. I won't get to see Dan and Debbie and Ben and Jacob, and Fannie Mae (the dog) and I will miss the excitement as Tom and Phil prepare for each day's drive to the airport, but I just can't go this year. I won't get to eat the Wednesday night special of prime rib at "Jeff's on Rugby Street" nor get to talk about the great and wondrous things that we all saw and did that day, but I can't go.

I just can't go this year. Brother Keith is going to Colorado and there is no one to take care of my responsibilities at Frederick Airport.... However, come to think of it, good ole Robbie at Altus said he would work for me if I really wanted to go.... Naw, I better not go this year.

Tom called again yesterday and said Phil wanted to fly his Cessna 140 and have the lifetime experience of flying into "Orshkorsh" too. Phil had never been before in his own airplane. Sure would like to see his first reaction as he encounters all those airplanes. Said he wants Tom to go with him in the same airplane so he won't get confused or lost. They don't realize just how small a 140 cabin can get after two or three hours flying, especially with two bodies in it, but that's what they plan to do if I don't go.

I can't go this year.

Oshkosh! My, my, what a place! Now if by chance AVEMCO (Insurance Company) called me and told me that I won the J-3 Cub Grand prize or maybe get a call from EAA telling me I won the Cessna 150, I would have to go then.

Tom and Phil are leaving tomorrow and I'm still waiting for the telephone call.

I'm going to go back for sure someday. I want to take brother Keith up there in his Ercoupe and fly along with Tom and Phil and show Keith the Mississippi River and how pretty Wisconsin is this time of year.

I didn't get to go this year....

I was visiting with Mary Kelly, Manager of the Tenkiller Airpark a couple of months after Oshkosh '96 and she told me that a whole gaggle of folks from Eastern Oklahoma flew up there. Mary and Joe Cunningham have flown to Ireland in a single engine airplane, have flown to Alaska and back, have flown half way to creation and back including around the world with Tom Quinn and Sen. Jim Infofe, but had never been to "OSHKOSH" before. Amazing! Mary could not believe what she saw when she got there.

Hearing her talk about it got my juices going again for next year.

When you get to Oshkosh, the biggest adventure is simply landing, which I've been told is something like approaching a tipped-over beehive without getting stung. I take great pride in bragging to anyone who will listen that I did it in 1994.

In order to get a parking place at Oshkosh you need to get there a couple days before it starts. The trend lately has been to get there earlier and earlier and now some folks are getting there as much as a week early. Paul and Tom (Poberezny) just keep moving the opening day up a day and folks just keep coming a day earlier. Pretty soon it will begin in April.

I read somewhere that if you don't get everything you want, just think of the things you don't get that you don't want. Makes sense.

Tom and Phil flew up there together in Phil's 1950 Cessna 140A but wound up having to battle bad weather, a broken generator, and stay two extra days on the way up and back because of the crappy weather. They each bought a new GPS but couldn't understand the book, so they called me one night just to get me to explain how to work the thing good enough so they could find their way home.

OSHKOSH '97

Well, early in the spring of 1997, Tom, Phil, and I were already scheming another flying trip to Oshkosh, all the time telling our wives, Ellen, Ruth, and Nancy that we were just thinking about it, but knowing in our hearts we had to go ... the pull of aviation Mecca was too great to ignore, especially since I didn't get to go in 1996.

Sunday Morning, 9:00 a.m., July 27, 1997, the engines were started on N5353C, Phil's 1950 Cessna 140 and on N111L, Flying Foxes Airplane Company's 1952 Cessna 170B with Tom at the controls and me in right seat. The airplanes were packed with the customary water jugs, pork and beans, crackers, sleeping bags, and Tom's camera pack loaded with three cameras and half a dozen lenses. We had our duffle bags loaded with stuff such as extra shirts, pants, charts, and GPS's. We even took stuff that we didn't know we took until we got back with it. The excitement was at its peak as we took off from Altus Municipal Airport headed for our first stop, Coffeville, Kansas.

We had originally planned a stop at Stillwater, Oklahoma, but with a ground speed of 135 mph Stillwater showed up pretty quick so we continued on to Coffeville, Kansas. It was already beginning to get hot. The summer sun was pushing the temperature up in the 90's when we landed at Coffeville at 11:22 a. m. We made arrangements for the planes to be refueled and we borrowed the worn out airport Oldsmobile to go into town to have some lunch.

At 1:05 p. m., with me at the controls of the 170 this time, we departed Coffeville headed for Hannibal, Missouri, some 250 miles away. It was a hot, bumpy ride even at 5500 feet, but now the gravitational pull of home was lessening and the lure of Oshkosh was beckoning and we seemed not to notice the heat and bumps as much. The fact that the oil temp on the 170 was nearing redline as we were climbing out didn't even seem to bother us very much. Our excitement increased as we began hearing the other pilots headed for Oshkosh. talking on the plane to plane frequency of 122.75 mhz.

A cold front was predicted to pass through Missouri sometime that afternoon and we could actually see the cloud layer approaching as we passed over Nevada, Clinton, and Sedalia, Missouri, but we managed to stay in front of it.

My first landing in the 170 since February was at Hannibal, Missouri at 3:40 p. m.. It was as Tom put it, "A carrier landing". It wasn't too bad except for a small skip and a slight wiggle, but at least I got it down without embarrassing myself too much.

We had planned to stay all night in Hannibal, but when we taxied up to the "terminal building?" which had two small rooms attached to an open hangar, doors wide open with no air conditioning, and not a breath of cool air even at a fast walk, Tom said, "Whaddaya think"? Phil and I said "Let's get the heck outta here before that cold front traps us here".

We could see the clouds approaching from the northwest as we departed Hannibal at 4:05 p. m. We headed up the Mississippi River north toward Muscatine, Iowa, eyeballing the lowering clouds and heavy rain shafts off our left wing. They were still in Missouri on the west side of the Mississippi River, but I could see that Tom was oooching ever so slightly away from them as we continued north toward Muscatine, Iowa. We had the extra GPS programed in on Keokuk, Iowa just in case we had to stop there in a hurry.

The poor visibility made sight seeing and picture taking out of the question, so Tom concentrated on flying on the Illinois side of the Mississippi as the thunderstorms and lightning stayed on the Missouri side of the river. We were constantly aware that we might have to divert from our route at any time.

When we passed over Keokuk we could see there was a dark cloud wall of something in front of us. A few miles due west of Burlington, Iowa, Phil tuned in Muscatine AWOS and found out that Muscatine was reporting thunderstorms with north winds at 17 with gusts to 35 miles per hour. He didn't even get the five in thirty five out of his mouth when Tom had banked the 170 to the right to Burlington, Iowa, a large, inviting airport in the clear only a few miles to the east.

Our first day of flying was finished when we landed at Burlington at 5:05 p. m.. As we were taxiing in, we heard five other airplanes calling Burlington unicom announcing their intentions to land as well. Two Aeronca Champs from the Dallas area, an Ercoupe from Prescott, Arizona, an RV-6 from California, and a souped up Cessna 150 from the Amarillo area all landed right after we did.

Burlington was a nice airport, only when we walked into the terminal building we found that in spite of the fact they only used Unicom, the airport had an air carrier service and was busy as heck. After we got inside, we discovered that the door went only one way and we couldn't figure out how to get back out to the airplanes on the ramp. After wandering around the building very obviously lost, we were given the code to the electric gate on the other end of the building and we finished getting our stuff out of the airplanes. We were ready for a cool room, shower, and a good dinner. "By the way, the gate code is 245."

The three of us and the six other pilots crammed into a Dodge Caravan, compliments of the local BEST WESTERN motel, and we headed for the PIZAZZ Motor Inn, a ten minute drive away.

After checking in with a corporate discount since all three officers of the Flying Foxes Airplane Company were there, Tom, Phil, and I headed to the motel restaurant and enjoyed a good dinner of crunchy catfish, prime rib, and Chinese Stir Fry. We then each went to our rooms to get some sleep.

Monday morning we awoke to overcast skies and light rain. We ate a complementary breakfast courtesy of the hotel, packed our stuff, and caught the airport van back to the airport about 9:00 a. m. After checking weather and packing the airplanes again, we started the engines and departed Burlington at 10:05 a. m. I was again in the left seat of N111L and immediately after liftoff Tom and I were looking at a wall of clouds with blue on top. I climbed to 3500 feet, looked down and saw patches of ground so I chose to stay on top. Phil decided to fly low as we flew toward Davenport, Iowa, where we would turn a corner more to the northeast, a course that would take us on to Madison, Wisconsin.

The broken clouds soon filled in below us and Tom and I found ourselves VFR on top over solid clouds. It was then I realized that I probably had not made a wise choice and should have stayed below with Phil. Thank goodness for those little handheld GPS's. We relied on them to keep us on our course and tried not to think about the engine quitting, but the further north we flew we could see a big area of blue sky and green landscape. Near Davenport we broke out over the beautiful Wisconsin countryside with the Mississippi River winding around below us. A breathtaking view!

Phil was still flying under the cloud layer and had cut a corner and flown over the Quad Cities area and by doing so had actually moved ahead of us. We realized on this trip that it wouldn't take much at all for the Cessna 140 to not only keep up with the 170, but maybe even outrun it.

As we approached Madison, Wisconsin, we could see Lake Mendota, a big lake that literally is a part of the city. After contacting Madison approach control, we flew over the lake, over downtown Madison, the State capital building, the University of Wisconsin campus, dodged a few antenna towers, and was cleared to land on runway 18 and I repeated my "carrier landing", one so short that I turned off on the first taxiway, which turned out to be the wrong one and ground control quickly let me know about it. They were nice about it however, and directed us to the general aviation parking area and the Wisconsin Aviation FBO. At 12:24 p. m. we once again climbed out of N111L, ready for a rest.

We refueled again, ate lunch at the airport cafe, and Tom caught a ride across the airport to the commercial side to get our rental car. I volunteered to drive the 85 miles from Madison to Oshkosh so Tom could fly N111L and make the infamous Oshkosh arrival by air.

Tom and Phil departed Madison at 2:35 p. m. and I left the parking lot about the same time in a little green Ford Contour, a small four door sedan with only 1700 miles on it. It smelled funny as I pulled out on the highway, but I thought little of it at the time.

Tom and Phil each landed at Oshkosh about one hour later at 3:35 p. m. with no problems and were parked side by side in row 56 near the Antique and Classic Little Red Barn Headquarters when I found them. They couldn't have been parked in a more convenient place.

The Ford Contour ran good when I left Madison and I began driving up Highway 151. The car still smelled funny though. It felt funny too since I was used to sitting in the 170, but the air conditioning was nice for a change. I then realized I didn't know how to get to Oshkosh on the ground so I stopped at Beaver Dam, Wisconsin to get a road map since Tom had kept the sectional chart. The car still smelled funny, so I looked under it, saw nothing unusual, so kept going.

When I drove into one of the airport parking areas at Wittman Field Oshkosh one of the EAA traffic directors stopped me and said, "Are you aware that your car is smoking badly?" I immediately parked and discovered there was oil all over the front of the car. I raised the hood and there was oil all over the engine. In fact, the whole front end was a drippy mess. Just what we needed, to be afoot in Oshkosh with "Jeff's on Rugby" within eating distance.

I found Phil and Tom pretty quick and after an unsuccessful attempt for them to register the airplanes before closing time at 5:00 p.m. we walked to the oil-coated Ford, dreading what we might discover. We raised the hood again and then saw the hole where the oil cap was supposed to be and saw the oil cap just laying on the battery. Whoever did the pre-flight on the Ford at the rental place had goofed. We checked the oil level and it was only half a quart low so we put the cap back on, drove to a car wash, cleaned the thing up, bought a quart of oil and were on our way to "Jeff's". Our car crisis was over.

We enjoyed our meal just as we expected to, then drove to the Gibson home, about eight miles away near Pickett, Wisconsin. Ben and Jacob were waiting for us in the front yard and when Dan and Debbie heard the noise they also came out to greet us. It was great to see them again after two years and we enjoyed a good time of handshakin' and neck huggin'. Even Fannie Mae, Katy Mae, and Duago were happy to see us. (The Gibson dogs).

Tom volunteered to sleep in the basement, Phil chose Jacob's bedroom and I got Ben's bedroom. After visiting awhile, we took our showers and went to bed. It had been another long day full of excitement and anticipation of arriving at Oshkosh, but at last we were there again.

Tuesday morning we were anxious to get to the airport. When I woke up I could hear the inbound airplanes flying overhead since the Gibson home was directly under the flight path from Ripon to Fisk. We couldn't wait to get there so we could watch the arrivals as they touched down.

The actual opening day of the convention was not until Wednesday so none of the exhibits were open yet. Most of the people were busy setting up, so today we would be busy watching airplanes, people, and just enjoying being where we were. We found a good place in the shade, sat down, and spent the entire day watching airplanes land and walking past the ones that were already parked. At one point that morning, we watched over 50 AT-6's fly in at one time. We walked at least five miles that day and by 5:30 p. m. we were ready for the return trip to Jeff's.

Wednesday, the crowds were getting bigger and all the exhibits, food booths, the fly market, and forums were in business. I had walked so much on Tuesday my back and right leg were hurting really bad. I had slipped a disc in my back a couple of weeks before so I spent most of the morning sitting down at the forums full of Motrins.

Wednesday noon we met Len Miller from Quanah, Texas at the control tower. He and a gang of four had flown his Piper Aztec up the day before. Before we left home we had arranged to meet and see if we all got there in one piece. We told him about "Jeff's" and he told us about "Roxie's," a good place they had found to eat at in downtown Oshkosh.

Wednesday afternoon I spent flat on my back on my sleeping bag under the wing of N111L, watching the first days airshow. Bob Hoover, Sean Tucker, Patti Wagstaff, the French Connection, The Northern Lights, Delmar Benjamin, were all unbelievable in their airshow performances.

At 7:00 p. m. we were eating prime rib, baked potatoes, and salad at Jeff's. Life don't get much better than that!

Thursday, Tom, Phil, and I split up and we went different directions. I went to the fly-market, bought some gifts at the EAA Wearhouse, sat under the wing of the Cessna 170 for awhile, then caught the shuttle bus to the EAA Museum. I ate a hotdog, went to the Pioneer Airport, walked up to Compass Hill, toured the museum, then caught the shuttle back across the airport where the center of activities was, toured two of the four giant exhibit buildings and watched the last part of the afternoon's airshow.

Tom, Phil, and I met at 5:00 p. m. and decided to go to "The Roxie" in downtown Oshkosh for dinner, where I ate one of the best filet migons (they call them tenderloins in Wisconsin) I have ever eaten. As we were being seated at our table, we heard a loud voice tell the waitress, "Feed those guys real good, they've been going to Jeff's to eat and don't know any better." Len Miller and his crew were at the table next to us.

We took Ben and Jacob, the Gibson boys, to the airport with us on Friday. I went to some of the forums on appraising and evaluating aircraft, stress management, and listened to Linda Finch, the lady who flew Amelia Earhart's route around the world about three months previously. Tom, Jacob, and Ben went to see the Warbirds, while Phil went another direction. We met about 4:30 in the afternoon, watched some of the airshow, then left at 5:00 p.m. to pick up Dan and Debbie. We took them to Michael's Restaurant in Ripon for dinner since this was our last night in Wisconsin and had to head back to Oklahoma the next morning.

Since Tom flew N111L into Oshkosh, I got to fly it out. Phil and I wanted to leave as early as possible so we had Tom take us to the airport at 6:30 a. m. Saturday to try for at least a 7:30 a. m. departure. That didn't happen because the Wittman field was closed due to low lying fog and scud. Flight Service told us that it should burn off within the hour however, and we should have good weather all the way to Oklahoma if we wanted to go that far.

After the weather briefing we were required to get a departure briefing which amounted to an EAA official advising us which runway we would depart and how to exit the Oshkosh traffic area. We then walked to the airplanes, untied them, did the pre-flights, pushed them out into the lane, and then found a red-vested EAA official on one of the little red motor scooters to assist us. He was a very friendly fellow from Canada and followed us back to the airplanes and visited with us until the scud burned off and the airport was opened.

Finally at 8:15 a. m. I started the engine of the 170 and Phil was right behind me. The fellow on the scooter then directed us into the line of airplanes awaiting departure. There were at least 35 airplanes in front of us waiting for takeoff and the tower was directing them to depart side by side on the same runway. I was directed to taxi into position on the right side of runway 18R, an RV6 was on the left side, then they told me, "High winged Cessna cleared for takeoff", then immediately the RV was cleared, and away I went, trying desperately to make a good takeoff and not wander off my side of the runway into the path of the RV.

I was instructed not to climb over 500 feet AGL for at least five miles away from Oshkosh so I wouldn't interfere with any incoming traffic landing on 36R, only a few hundred feet to the east. My heart began slowing down and I realized I could breathe again when I passed Fond du Lac, some 20 miles south. Little did I know what was waiting for me at Madison, where I was to meet Tom and Phil.

As I neared Madison, I dialed in the correct frequency for Madison approach control and gave them a call. No answer. I called them again, and again, and again, and again. Still no answer. During the breaks in my transmissions, I could hear numerous (numerous meaning bunches) other airplanes calling Madison approach as well and Phil in N5353C was one of them. Finally, Madison Approach came back and said "Cessna 111L, stand by." That's all, just stand by, and here I am with the airport in sight.

I neared the Class C airspace and gave approach another call. This time they did acknowledge me and told me to turn to 090 degrees, then 360 degrees, then contact Dane County tower and expect to land on runway 22. I did that, the tower did that, I did that again, and I plunked the big Cessna down on the end of runway 22 with a pretty good wheel landing and turned off at the exit for Madison Aviation, the local FBO at 9:15 a.m.

As I was taxiing in, Madison ground control called me and informed me quite politely, but firmly, that I had flown too close to the Class C airspace. I thanked them for that information, but was puzzled why they wouldn't answer me back when I so desperately wanted them to. At least they didn't know my name and didn't ask for it. They just knew that the pilot of a Cessna 170, N111L, had made a blunder.

When I got out of the airplane, Phil taxied up in the 140, got out, and said "Did you ever hear anything like that traffic?" He had busted the Class C circle also, but they were too busy talking to me to fuss at him. Both of us were just very happy to be on the ground.

We saw Tom walking out trailing his suitcase on wheels and we then transferred all our stuff from the little green Ford to the airplanes and got the car turned back in to the rental agency.

Scrambled eggs, hash browns, bacon, toast, orange juice, coffee, and grape jelly never tasted better than it did at the airport cafe that morning. I decided that my arteries needed some reinforcement to keep them from collapsing, so the healthy heart diet went out the window that day and it tasted great.

At 11:20 a. m. with Tom flying left seat and me taking pictures we departed Madison, Wisconsin, we headed for Muscatine, Iowa, about 133 miles away. Visibility was pretty good, it was cool, and this leg of the trip was nice. We were chatting with Phil on 122.75 and just before we crossed the Mississippi River we heard someone ask "Phil, is that you?" Sonofagun it was Greg Camp from Altus and he was about 50 miles to the north of us working his way home from Oshkosh as well.

When we landed at Muscatine at 12:45 p. m., Tom apparently wanted to see what the far end of the runway looked like because when he landed he touched down at mid-field and had to turn off at the last taxiway. We took the scenic route back to the terminal building.

We fueled up, spread the charts out and tried to figure out where to go next. At 1:35 p. m. with me again at the controls of N111L we headed for Harrisonville, Missouri, a place we thought would be a good place to stay overnight. It was just outside the Class B airspace of Kansas City which made me a little nervous, but we figured we could do some sneaking if we had to.

I didn't get an answer from Harrisonville unicom when we neared the airport, but we entered downwind and then noticed that there were "X's" on the runway and nothing but dirt all over the airport. The runway was under construction and closed. Phil and I talked on unicom and we decided to head due south to Butler, Missouri, only about 20 miles to the south. We landed at 4:20 p. m., finishing up the longest leg of the whole trip.

Butler had much to be desired. Not as bad as Hannibal, but it was hot, the little-bitty airport building was not air-conditioned, and the guy pumping gas didn't know how to figure the fuel tickets. Tom tagged him "The Rocket Scientist". After about 30 minutes of putting up with him, we figured out it was only 211 miles to Stillwater, Oklahoma where there was a cool Fairfield Inn and the famous Mexico Joe's restaurant was within walking distance of the Fairfield. Tom lifted the 170 off the ground at Butler at 5:00 p.m. headed southwest to Stillwater, Oklahoma.

Even though it was only a two hour flight the pressures of the day's activities began catching up with us. We were dog-ass tired, having flown so many hours and having not slept good the night before. The stress of leaving Oshkosh, getting in and out of Madison, and the poor visibility the whole trip was just about enough for one day. When we landed at Stillwater at 7:10 p. m., we were definitely ready to quit for the day. Even Phil, who never gets enough flying, said he had just about enjoyed all he could stand for one day.

We tied down the airplanes, got them refueled, and then tried to figure out a way to get to the Fairfield Inn. They wouldn't let us keep the airport courtesy car overnight, my friend Kevin Reeder wasn't home to answer his telephone, Gary Johnson, the airport manager was on vacation, Stillwater taxi service closed at 6:00 p. m., and the Fairfield didn't have a shuttle. We had rooms, but no way to get to them.

Finally, I remembered that my daughter Jo's best girl friend, Suzanne Rossen Barth, lived in Stillwater. I called her, reminded her who I was, and begged for help. She and her brand new husband of one month, David graciously came got us and took us to the hotel. I think David thought these three old airplane driver geezers were trying to hit on his new wife because he didn't smile very much. I'm sure he did when I called Suzanne again the next morning to bum a ride back to the airport because we couldn't get from the Fairfield back to the airport.

After checking in at the motel, we walked a block down the street for a Mexican dinner. It was good at the time, but it turned out to be one that would return to haunt me about 3:00 a. m. the next morning with enough gas to blow up the whole city of Stillwater.

Sunday morning greeted us with cloudy skies and light rain. After David and Suzanne delivered us back to Stillwater Airport about 10:00 a. m. we checked weather, watched the skies, and visited with the local airport gas jockey until the rain lessened and Flight Service said it was OK to go. We departed Stillwater at 11:40 a. m., headed for Altus, Oklahoma, the last stop of the trip.

We flew in light rain until we passed Guthrie, then the skies were back to the severe hazy again. The Oklahoma heat became more noticeable the further southwest we flew.

We landed at Altus Municipal at 1:25 p. m. with N5353C landing first and N111L right behind. One week, four hours, and twenty five minutes after we began our trip, we were back where we started from. Another trip, another adventure, one that lasted almost eight days, spanned almost 1800 miles, and took 18 hours flying time, had come to an end. Three very happy, crazy, middle-aged adventurers had achieved one more goal we could brag to our grandgoobers about. We flew to "ORSHKORSH" and survived the trip once again!

Only twenty four hours after our arrival in Altus the most amazing thing happened. Even though the buzzing of the airplane had not gone away, my butt was still numb, and my legs still had no feeling in them, a fleeting thought crossed my mind as I looked at the mementoes and pictures of the trip … "Wonder what Oshkosh 98' will be like?"

◆   ◆   ◆

ALTUS/OSHKOSH
July 27, 28, 1997

(Times are clock time from engine start to shutdown)

Altus, OK to: Coffeville, KS	233 Miles	Depart 9:00 AM Arrive 11:22 AM	2.3 Hr.
Coffeville, KS to: Hannibal, MO	250 Miles	Depart 1:05 PM Arrive 3:40 PM	2.5 Hr.
Hannibal, MO to: Burlington, IA	65 Miles	Depart 4:05 PM Arrive 5:05 PM	1.0 Hr.
Burlington, IA to: Madison, WI	162 Miles	Depart 10:05 AM Arrive 12:24 PM	2.3 Hr.
Madison, WI to: Oshkosh, WI	73 Miles	Depart 2:35 PM Arrive 3:35 PM	1.0 Hr.
Total Distance	783 Miles		9.1 Hr.

OSHKOSH/ALTUS
August 2, 3, 1997

Oshkosh, WI to: Madison, WI	61 Miles	Depart 8:15 AM Arrive 9:15 AM	1.0 Hr.
Madison, WI to: Muscatine, IA	133 Miles	Depart 11:20 AM Arrive 12:45 PM	1.4 Hr.
Muscatine, IA to: Butler, MO	249 Miles	Depart 1:35 PM Arrive 4:20 PM	2.7 Hr.
Butler, MO to: Stillwater, OK	177 Miles	Depart 5:00 PM Arrive 7:10 PM	2.2 Hr.
Stillwater, OK to: Altus, OK	141 Miles	Depart 11:40 AM Arrive 1:25 PM	1.7 Hr.
Total Distance	761 Miles		9.0 Hr.

TOP TEN REASONS TO HAVE GONE TO OSHKOSH '97

10.   Learn how to make an illegal penetration of Class C airspace at Madison, Wisconsin.

9.   Learn how to land and take off at the same time 100 other airplanes do.

8.   To find out that Butch turns green and chokes at the mention of congested airspace, Phil can go to Oshkosh and not buy anything, and Tom Yates wears a jock strap on his head. (Actually a breathing mask, but Debbie Gibson said it was a jock strap.)

7.   Confirm that a person can still stand up after walking 15 miles in one afternoon.

6.   Determine that a Cessna 140 can fly almost as fast as a Cessna 170 on 1/3 less fuel.

5.   To confirm that you do lose all feeling in your butt and legs after 2 1/2 hours in an airplane.

4.   To learn that most people in Wisconsin have plaques on their walls reading "In Cheese We Trust" along with their GREEN BAY PACKER stuff.

3.   To learn that all that stuff the exhibitors give you that seems so important at the time takes up lots of room when you try to pack it in an airplane.

2.   To continue to be amazed that 24 hours after flying 18 hours to Oshkosh and back, being away from home eight days, and having walked your legs off to the hips, you suddenly have the urge to start thinking and talking about Oshkosh '98.

1.   Just because we wanted to.

NEVER TOO LATE (A FANTASY): BY KEITH PINSON

Butch Pinson started flying in 1975. Keith Pinson started in 1976. Off and on since that time they have talked about flying together, each in his own airplane, to the largest Fly-In and Air Show in the world at Oshkosh, Wisconsin, sponsored by the Experimental Aircraft Association.

Probably every pilot that ever was had wished he could attend this event. It's just one of those ultimate personal things for a fly person when he can say, "I've flown into Oshkosh". Butch managed to go a few times, Keith didn't, but it was always kind of a dream with them to fly up there together, but other things kept happening and the talk always ended in "Maybe some day."

Sometimes, "someday" gets here.

Last Sunday morning at 6:30 a.m., Keith in his 1946 Ercoupe followed in a few seconds by Butch in his 1947 Cessna 120 took off from their own Pinson's Cottonpatch Airport at Tipton, Oklahoma and headed northeast to Oshkosh, the garden of Eden of all kinds and sizes of aircraft, where there are thousands of airplanes and more thousands of people who gather on hundreds of acres wearing themselves out trying to see just part of everything there.

Late the next morning after 895 miles and 9 hours of flying, Butch touched down on the runway at Oshkosh and at the age of 90 and flying an 81 year old airplane, earned the distinction of being the oldest pilot ever to fly into Oshkosh solo in his own airplane. He kept that record for about fifteen minutes when Keith at the age of 98 and flying his 82 years old Ercoupe landed and set a new record, probably never to be broken.

Keep your dreams. Anything can and just might happen.

OSHKOSH '00

2000 was the year that brother Keith finally got to go to Oshkosh. We had tried to get him to go the other times, but the health of his wife Lucy was getting worse and he was never comfortable with the thought of leaving her at home for the time it would take to make the trip. Lucy passed away December 13, 1999. Six months later when Tom, Phil, and I started mulling over the question, "We gunna go to Oshkosh?", we decided Keith just had to go with us this time. We didn't give him a choice, we just told him he was going. He needed the time away after having to deal with Lucy's illness for so many years and then the agony of her death. He finally agreed, but emphasized he was not, repeat, was not, going to fly into Wittman Field at Oshkosh. He would leave the Ercoupe at Portage and ride in with me or Tom or Phil.

2000 was also the year that my daughter Jo Lynn decided to get married. In fact, she got married on Saturday night, July 22, the night before we left for Oshkosh. I walked her down the aisle, gave her away to her new Army Captain husband Rod, went to the reception, spent the night at a hotel in Lawton, Oklahoma, then got up early Sunday morning, kissed my sleeping wife Nancy goodbye at the hotel, and drove home to finish packing for my departure scheduled for noon, July 23.

Tom and Phil took off from Altus about noon Sunday and flew to Keith's Cottonpatch Airport south of Tipton. We divided our stuff among the three airplanes so we could fit all of it and ourselves in them and at 12:49 p.m., Tom flying his 1946 Cessna 140, Phil in his 1948 Cessna 140, and Keith and I in his 1946 Ercoupe, all took off from Cottonpatch and pointed ourselves northeast. Keith couldn't believe it. He had began trying to back out for several weeks and even though he was still protesting and declaring he would not, repeat would not, fly into Oshkosh itself, he was on his way. Little did he know what he would wind up doing.

As we had done in the past, we talked to each other on the plane to plane frequency of 122.75 Mhz. and excitement soon overtook anxiety and we began to relax a bit. We passed over Stillwater and decided to make our first stop at Bartlesville, Oklahoma to check the airplanes and refuel. It took us nearly 3 hours to get there. Bartlesville unicom wouldn't answer us, but the windsock was showing the winds were out of the north a bit. We then saw Phil lining up for runway 35 so we followed. Phil landed and turned off but by the time Keith and I got on short final for 35, we saw another airplane on short final for 17. It was Tom! Landing downwind! I quickly suggested to Keith that he do an immediate go around, so he peeled off to the left and re-entered the pattern for runway 35 again as Tom taxied to the fueling area.

After chastising Tom a bit for landing downwind, we refueled the airplanes, ate some cheese crisps, and took off again, this time headed for somewhere in Missouri. Our destination for the day was undecided, we just agreed to fly as long as we could or until we got tired. Over the radio we discussed stopping at Clinton or Warrensburg, Missouri, but Whiteman Air Force Base was "hot" so we decided to go on to Sedalia since I had stayed there before and remembered LaMiere's Cajun Catfish Restaurant from the 1994 trip. When we got near Sedalia, they wouldn't answer the unicom either, but a fellow who was just flying around answered us, told us the terminal was closed for the day, and asked us if we needed a ride to a motel. We told him we sure did, so he landed when we did, introduced himself, and very graciously drove us to the Best Western Motel. We arrived about 6:30 p.m., thanked him profusely, checked in the motel, and then walked a couple of blocks down the street to LaMiere's where we enjoyed some of the Cajun catfish. That being done, we walked back to the motel, went to our rooms, and the first day was over.

Monday, July 24 we got up, ate breakfast, and the motel folks said they would take us back to the airport in the back of a pickup, but as we were walking out, the same fellow that brought us to the motel the night before showed up grinning and said, "Thought you guys might like a ride back." He drove us back to the airport where we got the airplanes fueled up again. We met another guy and his son pre-flighting a PA-12. They too were headed for Oshkosh.

We took off about 8:30 a.m. and headed for Muscatine, Iowa. It was a two hour flight, but we set the GPS's and headed across Missouri and were doing just fine until the little black wizard boxes flamed out and said they weren't going to work anymore. We started hearing other folks in airplanes saying that their GPS's quit as well. We heard later that solar flares were responsible and after about 30 minutes they started working again. We quit sweating so much, quit pointing at the sectional charts as often, and were again comfortable about the direction we were headed to get to Muscatine.

We landed at Muscatine about 10:30 a.m. After taking some pictures and refueling, I decided to ride with Phil in his 140 to our next stop at Portage, Wisconsin. I wanted Keith to go it alone in the Ercoupe for awhile thinking it would be good for him to fly solo for awhile and get used to flying over strange country alone. We all took off and immediately Phil and I couldn't find Keith or Tom and they couldn't find us. Nobody could find anybody. We talked to each other on the radio, we all said we were "Right here over these white things" and "Right here by that crooked bend in the river next to the town with the funny shaped water tower" and we all said "Well, that's where I am too". We all decided we were all in the same spot and going to collide with each other and kill ourselves over Iowa.

We never found ourselves until we got to Portage at 2:00 p.m.. Remarkably, all of us landed within five minutes of each other. Keith admitted he didn't see the Portage airport until he was on short final and didn't see us until he got stopped on the ground. There were several other airplanes gassing up and getting ready to make the last leg into Oshkosh.

Portage was the jumping off place. That was the place Keith had said "That's as far as I'm going!", but when he started asking questions about the Ripon entry point, the strobe lights, the guys that would tell him to rock his wings, I knew he was going to do it. Other than that he didn't talk much. Tom and Phil, being veterans of going into Oshkosh were a little more relaxed, but not much. Tension was in the air.

We walked down the street a couple of blocks from the airport and got our rental car, the ugliest purple Chrysler something or the other I have ever seen. I had volunteered to drive the car from Portage to Oshkosh instead of flying in so the keys were mine and I drove us back to the airport.

About 3:00 p.m., I sat in the car and watched as Tom, Phil, and finally Keith took off from Portage. When they disappeared, I headed for Oshkosh in the ugly Chrysler. As I drove, I could imagine what was going through Keith's mind and where he might be at that point. At 4:00 p.m., I thought to myself, "Well, he's done it! He's on the ground now and grinning from ear to ear!"

After I arrived and parked the car in the parking lot at Oshkosh about 5:15 p.m., I walked to the antique/classic area around the Red Barn looking for Tom, Phil, and Keith. I found Phil and he told me that they had all got separated soon after takeoff and he had just found Tom, but didn't know where Keith was. We walked down to where Tom was tying down his 140 and he too said he hadn't seen Keith. A bit of concern began to hit me, but I figured Keith was parked further south, so I started walking through the rows of airplanes looking for his Ercoupe. I couldn't find it.

I searched the entire antique/classic parking area and still couldn't find Keith. I was getting scared now, really scared. I checked the registration building to see if he had registered. He had not. I then went to the communications building, explained the situation, and asked if they would page him. He didn't show up even after his name was broadcast over the loud speakers all over the airport. I asked if there were any reports of downed aircraft and they had not heard of any. They called surrounding airports to see if he had landed somewhere else. No one had seen Ercoupe N3539H.

I left the communications building with a sick, desperate, feeling in my stomach. Keith and the Ercoupe were down somewhere. They had to be, or else "Where was he?" I called back to the Portage Airport to see if he had returned there for some reason. He had not. I called his cell phone number repeatedly. He didn't answer.

A feeling of complete desperation crept all over me. I was consumed with the fear that I had killed my brother by egging him on to fly into Oshkosh. I prayed to God that Keith was safe somewhere.

Sitting on a tree stump in front of the "Little Red Barn", I spotted a fellow driving around on one of the John Deere Gators. I walked up to him, explained the situation, and asked if he would drive me over the entire airport, up and down the rows of airplanes, to see if Keith was anywhere on the airport. I didn't know at the time he was a photographer for "FLYING" magazine and not an EAA volunteer, but he graciously quit taking his picture taking and we drove all over the place, back over the antique/classic area as well as the "North 40". Keith was not anywhere.

I shut my eyes and prayed fervently. There was no where else to look so we left the North 40 and headed back to the "Red barn". When I opened my eyes, I heard a distinct airplane noise, looked up, and saw a single, split-tailed airplane on what appeared to be a downwind leg for runway 36. It looked like an Ercoupe, but I couldn't tell if it was for sure.

When the FLYING photographer and I drove up in front of the little red barn, another gator whipped up and the fellow from the communications booth yelled out, "We found your brother! He just landed and is down there!" It had been over three hours since Keith had left Portage and I had been looking for him for almost two of those hours.

When I saw the Ercoupe and saw Keith bending down tying the ropes, I thanked the guys on the gators, and ran up to Keith. With tears in my eyes, I put my arms around him and thanked God that he was OK.

Keith had become confused at Ripon, didn't see the railroad tracks, the arrows, the strobe lights, or any of the things we had told him to watch for. Not wanting to do something he shouldn't, he turned out over Rush Lake and circled around awhile not knowing exactly what to do. He flew until he got low on fuel, went to Appleton, landed and gassed up. He took off again and then flew around the Oshkosh, Fond du Lac area and finally in desperation called Oshkosh tower, explained his plight, and they cleared him to land on runway 36 with hardly any other traffic. It was him I saw, the lone Ercoupe making a most unusual, but not the first I am sure, landings into Oshkosh.

Keith, Tom, Phil, and I walked to the car and headed for "Jeff's on Rugby". We ordered our meal, talked about the scary day, and tried to relax before the prime rib got there. The events of the last few hours then began to fade a bit from my mind.

It was good to see Dan and Debbie and Jacob again. Ben was on a church trip to Florida and would be home later in the week. After visiting with the Gibsons for awhile, we moved into our rooms at the Gibson home and went to bed. Tom got the basement, Phil got a bedroom, and Keith and I shared the other bedroom. It had been a very exhausting day and we were very tired.

Tuesday morning we got up, had the usual laid back breakfast of coffee, juice, cereal, toast, and jelly Debbie had left for us, and then headed to the airport to watch the airplanes start arriving. The entire day we walked and walked and walked. We sat and looked and Keith could not believe what he was seeing. He was in awe.

In the excitement of the day before, Keith had left his master switch on so he wanted to see if the battery was still up. He started the Ercoupe to see if it would and immediately a Gator guard was there waving his arms and yelling even before it got started good. We found out that was a complete "NO-NO". We got chewed out really good, in a nice sort of way, but rest assured, "We know we don't do that anymore.... ever!"

We went back to Jeff's Tuesday evening, but Wednesday we went downtown Oshkosh to "The Roxie" and I had another one of those delicious filets (tenderloin in Wisconsin) ever put on a plate. In addition to the salad and the baked potato, the steak had little onion rings scattered all over the top. The steaks just don't taste like that in Oklahoma. After we waddled out of the Roxie, we had to make a trip to 1009 W. 9th St. to Field's Ice Cream Parlor for desert to top off the evening.

Thursday was spent going through the exhibit buildings, the fly market, watching the Air Show, and watching airplanes come and go. Thursday night, we heard there was a restaurant near downtown that was run by Jeff's brother called "Jansen's Bar & Restaurant". The food was delicious there too. Great big pieces of Haddock fish fried to perfection, country fried potatoes, salad and White Zinfandel to wash it down. Great healthy heart Wisconsin food.

We had heard about the Seaplane base for a several years so we decided to find it and give it a visit. This is an extension of Oshkosh where the folks who fly float planes and amphibians can land on the west shore of Lake Winnebago. Driving south on main street Oshkosh, we soon saw a sign that led us to the place where airplanes with floats instead of wheels landed. It was a quite, secluded place on the shore of the lake with several float planes tied down in the "parking places". We looked around a bit, visited at length with one of the pilots, and watched a Lake Buccaneer do splash and dashes.

When we left the Sea plane base and headed back north on main street, we saw what looked like a scene out of the movie, "American Graffiti". There was a Drive-In and carhops on roller skates were delivering ice cream cones to people standing around classic cars from the 50's and 60's! There were '57 T-Birds, a '56 Ford Crown Victoria, Chevy Sport Coupes, and almost a dozen other cars from that time. We couldn't believe what we were seeing! We pulled in and immediately were transported back in time 35 years, even though we were in the ugly purple 2000 Chrylser. A car hop sailed up on skates, took our orders for ice cream cones, and "zip" she was gone. Just a few minutes later, she had our cones back to us. I looked up on the front of the drive-in. We had found "Ardy & Ed's".

Friday morning we went to the EAA museum. It turned out to be a good day to do it since it was raining and our legs were almost worn off to the knees. Friday afternoon we went slower and slower and really began looking forward to supper time. Our last night in Oshkosh we went to Ripon to Michael's Restaurant. We ate another fine Wisconsin meal on the screened-in dining room tacked on the back of the restaurant.

Saturday morning we got up early because unfortunately it was time to go home. We told the Gibson family goodbye the night before since they would be leaving the house before us. We packed our stuff and I drove Keith, Tom, and Phil to the airport. Tom had decided to stay until Monday, but Phil and Keith were going to meet me back at Portage. Visibility was not good, in fact it was pretty foggy and scuddy, so I figured I would have plenty of time to drive the 80 miles. I really didn't think they would be able to take off from Oshkosh until noon or after. We said "Goodbye" about 8:30 a.m., and I gave a short prayer for Keith so he could find his way without any trouble and drove out of the airport.

I stopped in Ripon at a Hardee's, got a sausage/egg biscuit, stopped again at the local Walmart to kill some time, then drove on to Portage, arriving about 12:30 p.m. As I drove by the airport, lo and behold there was Keith and Phil already there cleaning the windscreens of the airplanes! They had been able to depart Oshkosh within the hour after I let them out and even though the sky was pretty obscured they could see well enough and made good time.

We ate lunch, turned the ugly rental Chrysler back in, and took off from Portage headed southwest for somewhere in Missouri. We didn't know for sure where we might wind up.

We thought about going to Kirksville, Missouri, but changed our minds and headed for Mt. Pleasant, Iowa where we were able to get gas. We took off again, changed our minds a couple of times again about where we wanted to go, but finally headed for Harrisonville, Missouri where we landed about 6:00 p.m. and shut down for the night. Butts were tired. A nice line boy loaned us a four door Ford and we drove into Harrisonville, got some very nice rooms at a Super 8 Motel, and found a barbeque cafe for supper.

Sunday morning it was bad foggy. You could look straight up and see blue sky, but any other direction was scuddy and foggy. We ate the free breakfast at the motel, checked out, and drove back to the airport where it was still foggy. A guy flew in from just south of Harrisonville and said it was not bad, but sure not good. We hurried up and waited some more.

About 10:00 a.m. we decided it was getting better so we took off and headed for Stillwater, Oklahoma. We wound up flying through scud, fog, a little rain shower or two, and lots of haze. Thank goodness those little Garmin GPS's kept working.

We arrived at Stillwater, gassed up again, went to an Arby's for a sandwich, and went back to the airport. We loaded up again and took off on our last leg of the trip. When we got near Cooperton, Keith and I said goodbye to Phil as he continued on to Altus and we turned slightly south headed for Tipton. I took the controls of the Ercoupe for the first time the entire trip as we flew over Snyder and flew over the Ayers home looking for kids and grandkids.

Keith set up for landing at Cottonpatch and we touched down about 1:30 p.m., exactly one week and 30 minutes from the time we left. When we parked and shut the coupe down we looked at each other, grinned, and shook hands. We both said, "We did it"! Keith finally got to go to Oshkosh! We had flown 21.2 hours, and had been gone 8 days. Keith still couldn't believe he had done it and I had just completed my fourth trip to Oshkosh.

OSHKOSH '01

Once again the four over the hill airplane guys got the itch to return to Oshkosh. We didn't know whether it was actually the EAA Fly In that we wanted to go to this time or whether it was the food we had grown so accustomed to eating at Jeff's On Rugby, Janzens Tavern, The Roxie, or Michael's. For Phil and Tom, it was the lure of the 22 ounce Honey White beers that only Wisconsin could provide. We could also remember the need to "fill the cracks" with ice cream cones at Field's Ice Cream parlor or Ardy and Ed's Drive Inn.

Whatever it was, we had to go. Tom Yates, Phil Carson, Brother Keith, and myself couldn't resist doing it again. We were slightly disorganized in this year because Brother Keith decided to drive his Jeep Cherokee and he left one time, Phil and I left another time, and Tom left another time. Keith's car saved us from having to stop and rent a car and that was a big help. He left for Oshkosh at 4:00 a.m. Saturday, July 21.

Tom had some tailwheel problems on his 140 (N2162V) and didn't get to leave Altus until about 2:00 p.m. that same Saturday.

Phil had purchased a 1953 Cessna 180 about three weeks previously and I planned to ride with him because of the extra room. We could easily fly to Oshkosh in one day because it would cruise 150 mph, so we didn't leave until about 7:00 a.m. Sunday morning, July 22.

Keith made it to Springfield, Illinois, Tom made it to Warrensburg, Missouri, and Phil and I were still at home when the sun set Saturday night.

We knew there was some weather problems up north, but Flight Service told us it would not be a factor if we could get to Oshkosh by 3:00 p.m.. Heck, no problem. We had that big, fast airplane and didn't even have to stop for gas the first time until we got to Warrensburg, Missouri.

Since Tom got the late start on Saturday, he called me that night and told me he had stopped at Warrensburg. Phil and I figured he would be long gone by the time we got there, but when we landed at 10:00 a.m. there sat a Cessna 140 that looked an awful like Tom's. We said no, that couldn't be Tom. When we got gassed up and started to leave, we looked at the 140 again and sure enough, there sat Tom in the airplane. He wasn't in any hurry he said. He got to visiting with a

John Deere guy he met that morning at breakfast, and had just been fooling around.

Tom departed just a few minutes before we did and we were able to talk on the common traffic frequency of 122.75 for about 30 minutes, but then the 180 passed him like he was standing still and away we went.

Phil and I were headed for Portage, Wisconsin for our next stop, but when we got about fifteen miles east of Dubuque, Iowa, we hit a wall of thunderstorms, low ceilings, and rain. We turned toward Dubuque, but it was already enveloped in rain. We turned back toward Maquoketa, Iowa and landed there at 12:30 p.m. When we taxied up there sat an early model Cessna 172 and two fellows from Jefferson City, Missouri who had just landed. We talked the situation over and Phil called flight service who said no way could we proceed on to Oshkosh then, maybe later that afternoon because the thunderstorms were popping up all over northern Iowa and all through Wisconsin.

It was unusually hot, sticky, and steamy for that part of Iowa and Maquoketa airport did not have a drinking fountain and the young man running the place didn't even have the air conditioner turned on. We begged him to turn it on, but the one small window unit was trying to cool a very large building and the air just got stickier.

After at least six calls to flight service we gave up at 5:00 p.m., got the courtesy car and the four of us drove into town and got rooms at the Super 8 Motel. I called Keith, who had arrived in Oshkosh about 1:00 p.m., and had been waiting for us at the Vintage Aircraft Headquarters Red Barn. He said Tom had been able to skim around to the west side of Dubuque, waited a storm out there, then took off and followed another storm into Oshkosh. He had just landed. They were going to get to go to Jeff's. Phil and I were marooned 175 miles away.

The Super 8 Motel was nice and it was very refreshing to get a shower and some rest though. I didn't have a change of clothes, but I did have my toothbrush and a few necessary items, even a change of underwear, so it was not too bad.

The next morning we got a little more favorable report from flight service so we hurried to the airport only to have to wait for the guy to come unlock the hangars. Phil made one more call to flight service who told us if we were going to get there we would have to leave then and still it would be "iffy".

We fired up the Cessna and departed Maquoketa at 8:25 a.m. headed the same direction we were the day before. It was fairly good flying until we got near Madison, then began running into rain showers, low clouds, and thunderstorms again. We skimmed Madison, lightening flashed off to our left, and Phil dropped the big Cessna down a few hundred feet to stay out of the clouds. We were just about to turn back to Morey airport on the west side of Madison when the clouds lifted just a bit and we were able to continue on to Oshkosh. I had already decided that if we had to land now, Keith and Tom were just going to have to come get us in the Jeep. We got to Ripon though, fell in line with the other incoming airplanes, and breathed a big, big sigh of relief when we touched down on Runway 36 at Wittman field at 9:40 a.m.

As we taxied to parking on row 75, we saw Tom's 140 parked on the end of row 72. After the engine was shut down, I walked over to Tom's airplane and Keith and Tom were there. The four of us were THERE! We were back in Orshkorsh!

I was supposed to report to work at the NASAO (National Association of State Aviation Officials) tent exhibit to help them set up the display, so I went there and reported in. It was a good thing because about 45 minutes later the thunderstorm that Phil and I had avoided at Madison hit Oshkosh and dumped a load of rain and wind, but I was dry in the tent. At 2:00 p.m. we finished setting up the exhibit, so I walked back to the airplanes and we sat and watched other planes come in. At 5:00 p.m. we walked to Keith's Jeep and headed directly to Jeff's and did not pass GO. It was simply delicious. We enjoyed and savored every bite and gulp.

After dinner we drove out to the Gibson home, visited with Debbie, Dan, and Ben, took our showers and went to bed. The first day at Oshkosh was done. Keith and I got to stay in the basement this time because of more room. Tom and Phil stayed upstairs in the bedrooms.

The next morning we got to see Jacob who had been working the night before when we arrived. We ate breakfast and headed back to Wittman field about 8:30 a.m.

We started trying to see everything we could all at once again and by the end of the morning our legs were already falling off and our hips were aching from all the walking. We settled in under the wings of the airplanes and watched the airplanes fly and then the airshow began at 4:00 p.m.. By 5:00 p.m. though we were getting hungry and headed to the car. We remembered that Junior Rowland, Chris Kliewer, and Tony Scott from Altus were working the West Ramp area and so we stopped by to see them. They were about finished for the day, so we all agreed to meet at "The Roxie" in downtown Oshkosh in about an hour for dinner.

The seven of us had a very good meal, but still had the need to "fill the cracks" so we headed for Ardy and Ed's Drive In on south main for an ice cream cone.

They were especially good since they were delivered to us by pretty car hops on roller skates.

About 8:30 p.m., we again headed for Dan and Debbie's place, the guys from Altus went to their hotel in Fond du' Lac, and another day was done.

Wednesday, I was scheduled to work again, so we got to the airport just in time for me to report to the NASAO tent at 9:00 a.m. I worked until 1:00 p.m., then Keith came by and he and I went to the EAA museum for awhile. After that we wandered through a couple of the exhibit buildings and then again headed for the shade of the airplane wings to watch the airshow again.

That night we decided to eat at Janzen's Tavern on Bowen street.

On Thursday, the long awaited cold front had passed through and the temperature had dropped to 59 degrees by the time we woke up. The shorts were put in the bag and long pants were in order now so everyone except Keith wore the long pants. I was glad to work in the NASAO tent because it was really cool that morning. That afternoon when I finished my duties at work, I wandered through the remaining exhibit buildings, then back to the airplanes. At 5:00 p.m. we again headed back to Jeff's on Rugby for our final meal in Oshkosh.

Friday morning we woke up about 5:00 a.m., ate a quick breakfast, and were at the airport by 6:30. Keith drove Tom, Phil, and myself to the main gate, let us out, and he started the long trip by Jeep back to Oklahoma. Tom went to get his departure briefing and Phil and I headed for the 180 to get ready to leave.

After pre-flighting the airplane we got the attention of one of the guys on a little red scooter, listened to the morning wake up call over the loud speakers of "It's a Long, Long, Way to Tipperarie", a yodel, and then the sound of an engine starting. Then we started our engine and the guy on the scooter directed us to the taxiway for departure on runway 18.

Phil and I taxied past Tom as he was finishing up his final preparations for departure and we were then cleared for take off at 7:10 a.m.. We headed direct to Muscatine, Iowa for our first fuel stop. We had to fly straight south for five miles however before we could assume our course heading.

The weather was beautiful. The Wisconsin countryside was beautiful. The air was smooth. It was the beginning of a good day to fly … for awhile.

We landed at Muscatine about 9:30 a.m., gassed up, and Phil checked with flight service. He came out of the room saying, "It sure doesn't look good the further south we go", but we took off and headed toward Kirksville, Missouri. The further south we flew, the cloudier it got and by the time we were even with Kirksville we were hitting the bottoms of low hanging clouds and mist was hitting the windscreen.

We started to stop at Kirksville, but decided to continue on southwest toward Sedalia, but only a few minutes later we were in very low clouds, light rain, and scud. We diverted to Moberly, Missouri where we landed in light rain. It was crappy, crappy weather and I figured our day was done and we would be spending the rest of the day and all night in Moberly.

Phil however, got an encouraging report from flight service and after going to town for a hamburger, we decided to take off about 1:00 p.m. and head southwest. Immediately after takeoff though, we were back in the scud and low clouds. We flew back north to Waverly, Missouri turned west and followed the highway to a town called Marceline. Phil kept saying, "I don't like the looks of this at all", and I didn't like the looks of that at all either, but I kept the two GPS's programed in to alternate destinations along the route and called out VOR frequencies to him as we flew on.

The flight southwest from Marceline to the Lexington area southeast of Kansas City was to say the least "Intense". We flew in and out of the low hanging clouds, sometimes seeing spotty areas of the ground, sometimes not. We got down to about 800 feet AGL with no relief in sight. Phil is IFR rated and the 180 was IFR certified, but he didn't have any IFR charts or approach plates and had not flown IFR in the 180 before, so we continued on with what we had.

By the grace of God, we started seeing some improvement when we passed Lexington and then much better conditions south of Kansas City. It appeared that we had penetrated the mess we had been in and were now on the back side of all the scuzzy stuff. Phil climbed back up to 2500 feet and we continued on until we eventually reached 4500 feet. We both needed to stop, because our legs ached, our heads hurt, and our bladders were full. In spite of all the misery though, we decided to continue on to Stillwater, Oklahoma.

We landed at Stillwater at 4:15, a leg of just over three hours. I could barely move when I climbed out of the airplane after sitting so long. And Lordy, it was HOT. There was no doubt we were back in summertime Oklahoma!

After refueling and pit stopping, we departed Stillwater about 4:40 p.m. and had a very hot and bumpy ride to Altus where we landed about 5:45 p.m. It was 105 degrees and we immediately sweated down our clothes putting the airplane up. Ruth came and got Phil and I loaded my pickup up and headed home.

Our concern now was Tom. "Where was Tom?" I talked to Keith on the telephone and he had just checked into a motel in Cuba, Missouri and was OK, but buddy Tom was still missing.

We were worried about Tom because of the weather and also that he was flying solo, but about 10:00 p.m. Phil called me and said that Tom had called from

Kirksville, Missouri and was OK, but weathered in. At least he was safe, had not crashed, and we all slept better knowing he was safe.

Tom called me Saturday morning and said he might be able to get out of Kirksville about 11:00 a.m., so he was doing OK. I talked to Keith at 1:30 p.m. and he was just leaving Oklahoma City and would be home about 4:00 p.m. so he too was OK. He arrived in Tipton just fine about 4:15 that afternoon.

Tom called me about 10:00 p.m. Saturday night and said he had flown as far as Coffeville, Kansas where he landed again because of the weather, but in doing so had cracked one side of his rudder horn and his tail wheel was going round and round. He had rented a car and driven to Bartlesville, Oklahoma where he met his daughter Courtney for a birthday dinner. He was going to spend the night there, then would drive back to Coffeville Sunday morning to get the 140.

Sunday afternoon, 2:45 p.m., Tom landed safely at Altus Municipal Airport. We all had made it back home and were all safe. We heard reports that 14 pilots had been killed in plane crashes this year trying to get to Oshkosh '01. Thank goodness none of us were number 15.

Four crazy old men pilots, all over 60 years old, had again had an adventure of a lifetime. We decided that this probably would be our last time to go to Oshkosh for awhile and the four of us may never get to do it again together, but we have so many memories, and laughter, and fun.

If Tom, Phil, Keith, or I don't decide at the last minute to do it again next year or the year after, I hope someday to be able to take all my grand kids, Allie, Jake, Jackson, and Luke to see and experience what I have seen. By that time though I may have to drive one of those little motorized scooters around.

Until then, or even if I never get to go again, the dreams and memories of the last five trips will last a long, long, time. "Thank You Lord, for allowing me to do it!"

OSHKOSHES 05, 06, 07

"Well, whadda ya know!" After a three year hiatus and enduring cold turkey withdrawal pains, I again found myself planning to return to Oshkosh. The name was changed to "AirVenture" a couple of years ago though and I still can't get used to it. Regardless of what it is called though, all those airplanes, all that stuff, and all those people are there.

When I began working for the Oklahoma Aeronautics Commission in 1999, I encouraged the director and other staff members to participate in the event, but didn't have much luck. When Victor Bird became Director, the Commission became more involved with NASAO, The National Association of State Aviation Officials, in fact Vic was elected to the executive board. NASAO had an exhibit tent at Oshkosh every year, and as mentioned before, I volunteered to represent the Commission and work a shift at the exhibit in 2001, so I asked if I could do it again. Lo and behold, Vic allowed me to go, not only go, but I got paid my salary as usual for doing it and all travel expenses paid as well. "I got paid to go to Oshkosh!"

Phil Carson had not missed a year flying to Oshkosh since he first went in 1995, so when I asked him if he had any room in his Cessna 180, he said "Sure". Another friend, Junior Rowland, who had been working as an EAA volunteer on the West Ramp Show area, pulled some strings and I was accepted on the elite crew as a "West Ramp Rat". That was an added perk because the "Rats" had the ability to go anywhere they wanted to, even down the throat of the center taxiway where all the show planes and incoming special exhibit airplanes arrived. We wore orange vests with "West Ramp" professionally scribbled on the backs with magic markers.

So, on at 8:00 a.m. on Sunday July 24, 2005, Phil, Junior, and I took off from Altus bound once again for Wisconsin. The memory of those meals at Jeff's and The Roxie became fresh in my mind as we winged our way northeast. We arrived in Portage, Wisconsin at 2:00 p.m. after a quick stop in Warrensburg, Missouri for gas. No weather problems, just smooth flying.

We rented a car from John Poppy when we got to Portage. John is the Airport manager and ran a little car rental thing on his own. We tied the big Cessna down in Portage because the last time Phil flew into Wittman field he had to park almost to the first stoplight in Fond du Lac, row 230 something, even south of the ultra light area. He said he had enough of that. The car had almost 100,000 miles on it, was a rather ugly blue, and had a big sticker all the way across the back window advertising John's car rental business. It ran good though, and the three of us headed for Oshkosh looking like a traveling billboard for John's Car Rental.

When we arrived, we went to the airport, but didn't check in at the West Ramp headquarters for fear we might get put to work, so we just peeked at the ramp from a distance, and then headed back to the car with "Jeff's on Rugby" on our minds. We were not disappointed.

That week at Oshkosh was one of the most enjoyable I had ever experienced. Of course nothing will ever equal that first year in 1994 when I actually flew there, but working as an EAA volunteer at the ramp allowed me so many extra privileges I not only felt I was doing something special, but being useful as well.

Volunteers (wives of other volunteers) fixed us hot meals every day at noon at the AeroShell Square (as they wanted it called that year) headquarters building. We also had hot coffee, rolls, snacks, fruit, and a shady place to go sit down if we got too hot or hungry. I became better acquainted with Edsel Ford, who I met once when he was head of the Aviation program at Canadian Valley Vo-Tech. Edsel had been co-chairman of the west ramp for many years and was really one of the main bosses of the area.

We parked airplanes, re-parked airplanes, moved them from one spot to the other then back again. We shuffled and re-shuffled airplanes. We wing-walked show planes, exhibit planes, and plane planes all over the exhibit areas, up the aisles and down the aisles. With thumbs in the air indicating "clear" to the tug drivers, we cleared the crowds of people out of the way when "Space Ship One" and other special stuff arrived.

As mentioned earlier, I also worked afternoon shifts at the NASAO tent, became acquainted with Jay Zimmerman from the Minnesota Department of Aeronautics who was in charge of the exhibit tent. The break from the "Ramp" was nice because by noon, I was pretty tired and the NASAO tent gave me a chance to rest up.

After four days of eating, walking, parking airplanes, and enjoying Oshkosh, we drove back to Portage on Friday morning, loaded up the 180, and landed in Altus at 4:00 p.m. that afternoon.

◆   ◆   ◆

It seemed like Oshkosh 2006 arrived just as fast as this paragraph did from the last one, only this year Tyler Brooks, Junior's 11 year old grandson wanted to go. The three of us departed Altus on Sunday, July 23 at 8:00 a.m., only this time our destination was Madison, Wisconsin because we couldn't get a car rented in Portage. We again stopped at Warrensburg, Missouri for gas and had some sandwiches that Marsha Rowland had fixed for us.

When we got to the Madison area, Phil called Madison approach and rather than let us land, the controller headed us north because some little old lady in a Cherokee was in the pattern and we flew almost to Portage before they let us come back. We finally got to land, tied the airplane down, and went inside only to find we would have to get a courtesy car from the FBO, drive across the airport to the commercial side of the airport to get our rental car, then drive both cars back to the general aviation side, return the courtesy car, then we could go to Oshkosh.

We arrived in Oshkosh just in time to pick up our special parking sticker and "West Ramp Rat" credentials at Kermit Weeks hangar. Junior said, "Do we want to go check in this afternoon?" I looked at my watch, it was nearly 6:00 p.m. I quickly said, "Naw, lets go eat", and headed for Jeff's. Not a bad decision.

Oshkosh 2006 very similar to the year before. We did pretty much the same as we did in 05, parked airplanes, re-parked airplanes, and I worked at the NASAO tent.

On Friday, August 28, we got up early at Dan and Debbie's, drove to Madison, and were back in Altus by 6:00 p.m. Weather was good all the way.

◆   ◆   ◆

Oshkosh 2007 was very similar to 06' and 05'. In fact, all three years kind of blended together as one. On Saturday morning July 21, Phil, Junior, Tyler, and I were found ourselves again headed to the North country. It may sound like the thrill was wearing off and to some extent the trips in 2005, 2006, and 2007 were a lot alike, but the thrill, the smell, the taste, and the excitement of Oshkosh never goes away. True, the excitement and awe of that first year in 1994 can never be duplicated, but none the less, when you step foot onto Wittman Field you feel like you "Have arrived."

It was a flawless trip, weather was good, again a pit stop and gas up at Warrensburg, MO, only this year we were able to fly directly back to Portage. Dan and Debbie Gibson had graciously offered a car this year for us to use rather than renting one. Dan even drove to Portage to get us and then took us back when we left on Friday.

We felt a little sorry for Dan and Debbie this year because Jacob, their oldest son had married the summer before and their other son Ben was on a missionary trip to South Carolina. He had also just completed his first year of college at Green Bay. As a result, Dan and Debbie were going through the empty nest syndrome and were really kind of lonesome. So lonesome in fact, they actually looked forward to us old guys making a mess around the house again.

Jr., Phil, and I again worked the Aeroshell Square West Ramp and I also worked the NASAO exhibit again, only this year the Aeronautics Commission had a booth space in the tent and I was joined by three other staff members during the week. Tyler also helped work the ramp even though he was a junior member. He tried his best to drive the scooters and tugs though, but Edsel wouldn' let him.

Dan drove us back to Portage on Friday and we departed at 8:45 a.m. that morning. We heard the Kirksville, MO airport folks were cooking hamburgers, so we landed there for gas and a really good hamburger. Turned out the local chamber members were doing it for good will for all Oshkosh flyers.

The price of gas was more of a problem this year. We paid well over $3.00 a gallon for 100LL the whole trip and even had to fork up $3.78 at Ponca City, OK. Phil's 180 burns about 11 gallons an hour, so the trip is not cheap.

I told Nancy before we left that this would probably be my last year to go because I had been eight years now and always said that if I could go once I could die happy. When we got back though, I couldn't help but think about next year, especially when I found out all the other staff members from OAC told Vic that we definitely should not only have our exhibit there next year, but it should be bigger and better. Oshkosh 2008, here we come!

WHERE DID THEY GO?

I've been telling stories about all the airplanes I've owned, the Cessna 120, the 140, the 170's, the Pacer, the Champ, the Pawnee, the T-Craft, etc. Where are they now? Well, I've owned ten airplanes in all, six all by myself, one with Keith, and three co-owned with Tom and Phil. I have had five forced landings in 35 years and the last one put me out of the airplane business. The Cessna 120 that I had so hoped would fly my grand kids to Oshkosh got sick one day, swallowed a valve, up-chucked, and the engine ground up little pieces of metal and scattered them all through out its insides.

I bought my 1946 Cessna 140, N89092, in 1976. That's the one Ott and I bought together and then I wound up buying his half. Then I decided I needed a 4 seater, so I traded the 140 for N4246V, a 1948 Cessna 170 in 1977.

While I owned the 170 I found that good deal mentioned earlier and Keith and I bought the Piper Pawnee PA-25 spray plane, N6069Z in 1982. We sold it about a year later, but I still had the 170.

Then in 1984 after deciding I no longer needed a 4 seater, I traded N4246V for a 1946 7AC Champ, N83469. I sold it about a year later.

I was then without an airplane, so in September of 1985 I bought a 1955 Piper PA22-150, N2637P, a Tri-Pacer which had been converted to a tail drag-ger. The previous owner let it get away from him on take off and turned it over on its back. I bought it wrecked and Lloyd and I put it back together in about three months, but found out later I could make a good profit and sold it the fol-lowing September.

In January of 1987 I bought my 1947 Cessna 120, N1605V, which I kept longer than any other airplane. Kind of funny too, because when I bought it I really didn't want it because it stunk like cow manure, the paint was faded and chalky, and the whole airplane was really kind of doggy, but the fellow I bought it from had a wife that was going to have a baby in two weeks and he needed money, bad. The day after I bought it, it snowed 9" and I didn't have anything else to do except make it look better, so I started polishing and waxing and de-stinking it.

After I got the stink out and wore my elbows out polishing and waxing it, I began to like the little 120. After 15 years or so I fully intended to keep that little Cessna until I died because it had a strong engine, it had flown me to Oshkosh without killing me, and I knew just about everything there was to know about it. But in March of 2003 the engine dropped that valve and my plans and good intentions changed.

I landed it that day at Frederick, dead stick, and it could go no further. I rented a hangar for about a month, then one day decided to drag it home. I pulled it 22 miles … right down the big middle of State Highway 5…. backwards … tied to the back of my pickup. It worked too. Donnie Coleman cleared traffic in front and Keith kept folks from running over us from the rear and we drug that airplane back home to Cottonpatch Airport early one Sunday morning just after sunup. I pushed it in its hangar home, kissed its nose, and it sat there for about a year. I just didn't have the extra cash to fix it and I knew it would be expensive.

My friend Lloyd Howard's son Paul had been looking for an airplane and I popped off and put a price on N1605V. Paul took me up and bought it. He and Lloyd pulled the engine off, took it home with them, and Lloyd spent over $6000.00 overhauling it. Then they came back, hung the engine back on the airplane, and Lloyd flew it out of Cottonpatch. With tears in my eyes, I watched my little friend disappear into the eastern sky on March 5, 2004. I no longer owned an airplane.

Back in 1995 I bought a 1969 Cessna 150, N60699, just to see if I could make a dollar or two. I kept it and flew it for a few months and then sold it later that year for a pretty good profit.

Tom Yates, Phil Carson, and I bought a few airplanes with the intentions of flying them a bit and then selling them for a profit. We bought a Cessna 150, N50703, kept it for awhile and then sold it for a loss. We tried to justify our loss by saying, "Well, we got to play with it anyhow."

Then Tom and Phil and I bought a 1952 Cessna 170B, N111L. That's the one Tom and I flew to Oshkosh in 1997. We kept it for a year or so and then sold it to a fellow in Kansas. Being an optimist I think we broke even with it, but that's another one we got to play with and fly.

Not having the good sense to float a rubber duck, we again plunged into the airplane business and bought a 1946 Taylorcraft BC12-D, N96452. That one really skinned us. We kept it for three or four years and Phil was about the only one who flew it. I really didn't like to fly it, Tom had about quit flying, so Phil kept the oil warm for us.

It came due for an annual one year and the fabric wouldn't pass the punch test. We were in a mess, so we sold it for enough loss to make up for any profits that were ever made on all the other ones put together. But as Tom said, "Aw, it's only money, look at all the fun we're having!"

After all these years of flying and owning all those airplanes, now I don't have one to go pat on the nose, play with, worry about, or leave to my grand kids to figure out what to do with.

But, I'm looking. "Who knows, maybe so Paul will sell my 120 back to me someday.

"Dang, I sure miss that airplane."

THIRTY FIVE YEARS OF AN
AFFAIR WITH THE SKY

It has been over 32 years since that first solo. Things are a lot different now. I'm older of course, uglier, crankier, my hair is white, the mustache is gone, and my heart and all associated plumbing is clogging up. I've had Coronary By-pass heart surgery, four Coronary stents, and one back surgery. I have accumulated 1400 hours of tasting the love of the sky and the thrill of a takeoff is no less than it was in 1975. The memories are vivid and cherished. Everything is just about over, but the fat lady still has not sung yet, so that means there might still be time for one more airplane.

I was a farmer for thirty years, an airport manager for fifteen years, and on staff of the Oklahoma Aeronautics and Space Commission as a Project Manager for Western Oklahoma for about four years until it dropped the "Space" and reverted back to the Oklahoma Aeronautics Commission. The past four years my primary job for the Commission has been Airports Inspector for all the general aviation airports in Oklahoma. I am responsible for updating the airport master record (5010) for each airport in addition to conducting a safety and standards inspection on each facility. The three score and ten age figure is looming closer and closer, but I am still working and plan to keep on until they declare me incompetent. I drive about 25,000 miles every year to inspect about 50 airports each year and am pretty well known everywhere I go. I know just about every mayor, City Manager, and Airport Manager in the State of Oklahoma. They seem to like me too.

I was honored by my fellow airport managers through the years by being first elected to the Board of Directors for the Oklahoma Airport Operators Association and then rose up through the ranks to serve as President of that organization in 1992.

I've been an AOPA member since 1975, an EAA member since 1979 and have been involved in the EAA Vintage Aircraft Association (Formerly Antique/Classic) since 1984.

I drive my pickup or the State Car more than I fly now and I still take my little Garmin 90 GPS along with me to "play like" while I drive. It still drives wife Nancy nuts when I tell her we are off course or it starts to beep to warn us we are nearing an airport or a controlled airspace.

Almost 50 years of tractor driving and airplane piloting have rendered me somewhat deaf according to wife Nancy. I can't hear the little beeps on the GPS and quite often don't hear her talking to me, but I can still hear water dripping from a faucet two rooms away. "Selective hearing?"

I have flown 16 different types of airplanes and landed and taken off at airports that had a runway just barely wide enough to fit the wheels of the airplane on and other places that didn't have a runway at all. I've flown into some of the biggies like Will Rogers OKC, Amarillo, Texas, Olathe, Kansas, Madison, Wisconsin, and the biggest of all, "OSHKOSH".

I remember holding my breath while riding in the back seat in a Bellanca Scout with Lloyd Howard while we took off out of a cow pasture. We had backed up to a barbed wire fence, held the brakes, pushed full throttle, and started bouncing the airplane as soon as it started rolling so we could clear another fence and turn left in time to miss a mess of power lines.

And of course, I remember those five forced landings.

I have found it interesting that people who love airplanes and flying also have a love for photography, old cars, electronics, and maybe even gun collecting. I have found over the years that airplane people are very generous, trustworthy, and trusting. I would not have been able to fly as many airplanes as I did had it not been for the generosity of many people who owned airplanes and tossed me a set of keys with permission to go fly their plane whenever I wanted to.

I am honored and humbled that so many folks allowed me to take their most treasured possession and all I had to do was replace the gas. As a result, I have been able to fly to Nebraska, Kansas, Texas, Arkansas, Iowa, Missouri, Illinois, Wisconsin and of course, all over the State of Oklahoma.

Some of the folks who contributed to my flying cause with their friendship and trust were Chuck Ball, Cessna 172; Cal Hunter, Tripacer, 7EC Champ, Cessna 172; Joe Grubbs, EAA Biplane, 7ACA Champ, 7AC Champ; Tom Yates, Cessna 182, Cessna 140, Kitfox; Keith Pinson, Ercoupe; Jane Smith, Cessna 172; Jimmy Ripley, Piper Colt; Lloyd Howard, Cessna 172, Cessna 182, Pawnee, Bellanca Scout, Citabria; Ronald Haynie, Cessna 172, Citabria; Lloyd Oxford, Comanche 250; Doyle Higdon, Cessna 172; Kyle Stevens, Cessna 182; Tom Thomas, L2, L3, L4, Luscombe T8F, Porterfield, and a Cessna 120. They are all very special people because you see, they trusted me.

Kids still come out from under trees to watch an airplane fly over just like I did almost sixty years ago. They still hang on fences just to see an airplane take off and land. It was only a few years ago when I had just landed my 1948 Cessna 170 at Pinson's Cottonpatch Airport and couple of kids came buzzing up on three-wheelers, screeched to a stop and said, "We saw you flying and followed you here and kin we look at that airplane?" After a detailed examination of the 170 and many "ooohs, aaawws, and gawlleees", they asked if I would give them a ride.

A couple of days later after getting their parents's permission, I not only gave those two boys their first airplane ride, but a couple of their friends and a big sister got a ride as well. Talk about wide eyed amazement. I sincerely hope they remember that day as well as I remember my first ride with Preacher Cox six decades ago. Who knows, one of those kids may be the pilot of whatever comes after an F-22 Raptor defending our country some day.

One of my young passengers just could not believe it when I told him he was flying an airplane all by himself. It was his first time in the front seat of one and when I gave him the controls his grin from ear to ear was priceless as he held the yoke of the Cessna 150.

Many people have told me stories and experiences, but were not included in this book. Bill and Emmie Braley, Fred Barbee, Cleo Williams, Jim Bricker, Larry Six, Ed Mednansky, Charles Neal, Jimmie Tyler, Henry Owens, and Wayne Hughes to name just a few.

I believe it is an absolute sin for pilots who have the ability to fly and have an airplane sitting in a hangar gathering dust not to offer a kid a ride so their eyes can light up like diamonds. Give them a ride and let them hold the controls and make a sloppy turn and listen to the excitement in their voices as they squeal, "You mean I'm doing this myself?"

It's been said that constant exposure to something will one day lead to some degree of contamination. I've often wondered if anybody ever got contaminated by what I've done over the past 35 years or so and have taken a different look at an airplane than they used to. I sincerely hope that I encouraged some young person or maybe even some old codger to fall in love with flying. I heard it said that it is no sin to try and fail. The sin is to fail to try. "Go for it!"

"Happy landings!"

A TRIBUTE: NANCY

That day I walked into the kitchen and announced that I wanted to go take an aviation ground school, all she said was, "O.K.".

She went to the ground school with me for nine weeks and learned as much or more than I did, but didn't want to take the tests. When I went to Oklahoma City to take the big FAA Private Pilot exam she was there though for moral support. She hugged and kissed me the day I found out I had passed the test and did the same thing when I flew home with that new private pilot license in my pocket.

She said she understood when I bought that first 1946 Cessna 140, and she didn't complain a bit when I traded it off for a 1948 Cessna 170, and traded that one off for the 7AC Champ, and bought the Piper Pawnee Spray Plane, and sold the 7AC Champ, and bought the wrecked Piper Pacer, and sold it, and bought the 1947 Cessna 120, and the 1969 Cessna 150. She still hasn't complained.

And the times I talked about selling the 120 and getting out of the airplane business she scolded me and told me that big toy was good therapy and I better not sell that airplane. She told me it made me feel better when I could fly it and I could just go pat it on the nose when I couldn't. I didn't listen to her and now it's gone.

She never complained about the hundreds of gallons of fuel I burned up boring holes in the sky, the dollars spent on renting different airplanes, or the many hours I have spent away from home playing in the sky or fooling with a flying machine of some sort.

I know she worried about me the times I would barely beat a cold front or a sandstorm home and the times when I didn't get home when I was supposed to, or those times I called and said, "I'm alright, but ... I need a ride home. I had a little problem and had to make an emergency landing."

She has always encouraged me to keep on flying as long as I can. She doesn't like to fly a fraction as much as I do, doesn't like to just "go up and look down," but she has allowed me to have my affair with the sky for over 35 years.

She is my companion, my lover, my encourager, and my wife. I love her very much.

To my dearest wife Nancy, I dedicate this book. Thank you my Love!

EPILOG

Would you believe it? Just before this book was published, negotiations began with the young man who bought my 1947 Cessna 120, N1605V, SN13777, and I'm about to buy it back!!

"GONE FLYING"

ABOUT THE AUTHOR

Lynn R. (Butch) Pinson got his first airplane ride almost 60 years ago. His love of airplanes and flying increased year by year until he earned his private pilots license which opened the door for adventures beyond his imagination.

Battling heart disease much of his life made it necessary for him to obtain a special issuance medical in order to fly many of the years, but the struggle was worth it. This book tells of some of those struggles as well as many humorous stories about learning to fly, tackling a taildragger, his flying friends, acquaintances, and loved ones.

"Butch" has been on staff of the Oklahoma Aeronautics Commission as the Airports Safety and Standards Inspector for almost nine years. Before that he was Airport Manager at the Frederick, Oklahoma Municipal Airport for almost 15 years and prior to that farmed and ranched near his hometown of Tipton, Oklahoma raising cotton, wheat, alfalfa, and Hereford cattle.

Anyone who loves airplanes and flying, or just has a fleeting interest in the subjects will enjoy this book. "Be careful though, you may find yourself trying to fly the chair you're sitting in and tip over."

"Lynn Pinson recalls exciting stories about flying machines and the people who fly them. He writes with a masterful mind and unique style very similar to that of Will Rogers. A great read!" Dr. Cal Hunter, author of _Evidence of Intelligent Design in Human Physiology._

First solo! Cessna 150, N373KV. February 21, 1975

1946 Cessna 140, N89092. This is the airplane Ott and I bought when
wife Nancy was out of town.

My second airplane. 1948 Cessna 170, N4246V, an original ragwing 170.

Piper Pawnee PA-25/150, N6069Z. Nancy said I couldn't afford the divorce if I used it to spray anything.

Piper PA22/20 Pacer. N2637P. Bought it wrecked and Lloyd helped me fix it. (I mostly watched and handed Lloyd things.)

1946 Aeronca 7AC, N83469. This airplane was put together from pieces of several airplanes. I named it "Ugly 1." Look closely and you can see the name on the door.

1947 Cessna 120, N1605V. I bought it in 1987 and kept it 17 years until
the engine swallowed a valve. I made a dead engine, dead stick, landing
with it and didn't tear it up or me either.

N1605V and I on the ground at Wittman Field, Oshkosh, Wisconsin.
Row 46. I couldn't believe I was actually there!

Oshkosh Pilot! Oshkosh 1994. The eagle had landed!

Joe Grubbs' EAA Bi-Plane, N198J. He actually let me fly it!

My Grand daughter Allie Ayers. Her first airplane ride, September 25, 1999. Cessna 120, N1605V.

Four happy geezers at Oshkosh 2000. Tom Yates, Phil Carson, my brother Keith, and me.

Keith getting ready to get on the taxiway and depart Oshkosh 2000. He was really nervous!!

Keith and his second love. 1946 415-C Ercoupe. N3539H. He had just gone up and looked down. On the turf at Pinson's Cottonpatch Airport, 6OK3.

Tom Yates, Phil Carson, and I bought Cessna 150, N50703, to make some money. We didn't. But we had fun flying it.

"Triple One Lima", 1952 Cessna 170B. Tom, Phil, and I ventured into the airplane business again. Tom and I flew this one to Oshkosh 1997. We didn't make any money on this one either. Had lots of fun flying it though.

Jerry Hostick and I getting up our nerve to depart for Oshkosh '94.

A very sad day. Cessna 120, N1605V getting ready to be towed 22 miles back home after it swallowed a valve. I made a dead engine, dead stick, landing.

Tom, Phil, and I bought this 1946 Taylorcraft BC-12D, N96452 as a third try to make money. We didn't. Didn't even like to fly this one.

Flying Triple One Lima, Cessna 170B over Wisconsin in 1997

My Grandson Jake needing some help with a "bitty plane". I gave him his first airplane ride in Keith's 415-C Ercoupe, N3539H on October 8, 2005. We got smoke in the cockpit and had to make an emergency landing. He said, "COOL!"

1969 Cessna 150J, N60699. Bought it and sold it six months later.

Nancy and I at the AOPA EXPO, Long Beach, California. October 2004

978-0-595-47685-
0-595-47685-6

Printed in the United States
132468LV00001B/26/A

9 780595 476855